$35.00

DATE DUE

christine mcfadden
pepper

the spice that changed the world:
over 100 recipes,
over 3,000 years of history

For Ed and Sam

With sincere thanks also to Edward Shaw of Bart Spices
for his encouragement throughout the writing of this book

christine mcfadden

pe*pp*er

the spice that changed the world:
over 100 recipes,
over 3,000 years of history

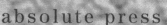

A.

absolute press

First published in Great Britain in 2008 by Absolute Press, an imprint of Bloomsbury Publishing Plc.

Absolute Press
Scarborough House
29 James Street West
Bath BA1 2BT
Phone 44 (0) 1225 316013
Fax 44 (0) 1225 445836
E-mail info@absolutepress.co.uk
Website www.absolutepress.co.uk

Reprinted 2012

Publisher Jon Croft
Commissioning Editor Meg Avent
Designer Matt Inwood
Publishing Assistants Meg Devenish and
Andrea O'Connor
Editor Anne Sheasby
Photographer Jason Lowe
Props Stylist Cynthia Inions
Food Styling Trish Hilferty

ISBN 13: 9781904573609

Printed and bound in Italy by L.E.G.O.

A catalogue record of this book is available from the British Library.

A note about the text
This book was set using Helvetica Neue and Century. Helvetica was designed in 1957 by Max Miedinger of the Swiss-based Haas foundry. In the early 1980s, Linotype redrew the entire Helvetica family. The result was Helvetica Neue. The first Century typeface was cut in 1894. In 1975 an updated family of Century typefaces was designed by Tony Stan for ITC.

Bloomsbury Publishing Plc
50 Bedford Square, London WC1B 3DP
www.bloomsbury.com

6   introduction
11 pepper in history
25 a pepper primer
61 the pepper trade
67 pepper and pungency
75 pepper in the kitchen

89 the recipes
93 salads
103 soups
115 fish
131 poultry
143 meat
157 vegetables
173 pulses, pasta and rice
183 drinks, dips and relishes
197 desserts and sweetmeats
211 cakes and biscuits
225 spice blends, seasonings and sauces

246 information
248 sources
249 bibliography
251 index
256 acknowledgements

introduction

In the western world spices appear to be subject to short-term changes in fashion just like any other must-have of the moment. There was a time when chefs and cookery writers couldn't get enough smoked paprika, then lemon grass and lime leaves were the cook's new best friend, closely followed by cumin and coriander when Middle Eastern cooking came into vogue. Meanwhile, like a genuine friend, pepper has always been there in the

the linen mat, and then guiltily try to stifle my sneezes. What could this grey dust be? I was repelled yet attracted by the curious smell. Once I daringly dipped a licked finger into the dust and tasted the tiniest amount. The flavour was even more off-putting than the smell, but nevertheless intriguing, seeming to come from a mysterious far-away place. I couldn't imagine why grown-ups sprinkled this stuff over their food. Thankfully we children were spared the

' ...pepper has always been there in the background, at the ready when needed.'

background, at the ready when needed.

When I look at cookbooks, even the good ones, I am surprised how rarely pepper is mentioned, even though we can choose from exotic varieties of black or white pepper, fresh, dried or brine-cured green pepper, red pepper, Sichuan pepper, Japanese pepper, pink pepper and more. We can learn to appreciate differences in flavour and aroma, as we do with fine wines, good olive oil or chocolate. We can also make ethical choices about the type of pepper we buy, now that Fairtrade and organic peppercorns are widely available.

My personal fascination with pepper began as a child growing up in the fifties. In those days we ate our meals in a room separate from the kitchen. It wasn't exactly a formal dining room but it did have a large oak sideboard on which sat a pewter cruet on an embroidered linen mat. For some reason the cruet was an object of deep fascination. There was something faintly intimidating about the dimpled dark grey surface of the imperious salt and pepper shakers (mills were not commonplace in those days), the squat little mustard pot and the boat-shaped tray on which they all sat.

But it was the contents of the pepper shaker that really caught my attention. Alone in the room and barely tall enough to reach, I would cautiously sprinkle some of its contents onto

experience, and I don't think my mother ever used pepper in cooking.

Fast-forward to the sixties and my first dinner in an Italian restaurant. The waiter approached, brandishing a massive pepper mill in the way that they do, and asked if I cared for a little pepper on my pasta. Reluctantly I accepted, watching anxiously as what seemed like far too many black specks settled on the pasta. And then I got it... the heady perfume and biting pungency of freshly ground black pepper. I couldn't believe what I had been missing for all these years, or that this was the same spice as the musty dust in the pepper shaker back home.

Fast forward again to my first attempts at cooking once I'd fled the nest. Armed with a pepper mill almost as big as the Italian waiter's and two classic cookbooks – Robert Carrier's *Great Dishes of the World* and Elizabeth David's *Mediterranean Food* – I cooked dish after dish, enthusiastically following the then novel instruction to 'season to taste with freshly ground black pepper'.

Strangely, it did not occur to me in those days to find out more about pepper. Like most people I took it for granted, not questioning where it came from, how it grew, or why some peppercorns were white and some black (green ones were unheard of). As far as I was concerned, pepper was, well, just pepper.

Then, during the late '80s certain American cookery writers began to specify different types of pepper in their recipes – fascinating names like 'Tellichery', 'Malabar' and 'Muntok' kept cropping up. Determined to try these for myself, I began a fruitless search in UK delis and supermarkets, only to find there was little, if any, choice. Pepper was simply a standard commodity.

The breakthrough came a few years later. While rummaging the shelves of a well-stocked London deli, I unearthed an exotic-smelling white cotton bag containing peppercorns from the Parameswaran estate in Kerala, southwest India. The berries were a rich brownish-black and seemed larger and plumper than the average black peppercorn. Back home in the kitchen, the difference was unmistakable. My pepper tasted dull and slightly musty; Parameswaran's had a clean bright flowery flavour with tremendous depth – like a good wine. It tasted not only of pepper but also of complex spices, and it was also much hotter, almost burning the lips.

From then on named varieties of peppercorns gradually began to appear in specialist food stores and delis; samples from spice companies started arriving in the post; and friends would bring me gifts of pepper from their travels. I vividly remember one winter afternoon in Paris when I came across an impressive wooden box of rare peppercorns in L'Epicerie du Monde – a treasure trove of a spice store in the Marais district. I rushed to a nearby café with my trophy and treated myself to a celebratory glass of wine. I couldn't wait to get back to my kitchen in England and start cooking with these beauties.

I began to read avidly about the history and botany of pepper. I was fascinated by descriptions of pepper gardens in India, and longed to visit them. I learned that there were more types of peppercorns than I had ever imagined. Enchanted by their exotic names – long pepper, cubebs and grains of paradise – I yearned even more to visit India and see peppercorns growing.

Food writer Rosemary Moon was keen to share this adventure with me. By the end of 2004 we had booked our flights and with invaluable guidance from Edward Shaw of Bart Spices in Bristol, we began to plot our itinerary. Thanks to Dr Thampi and Mr Ramalingam of the Spices Board in India, we were able to visit remote pepper plantations, meet the growers and their families, and soak up the heady atmosphere of the warehouses and market places of Fort Cochin in Kerala, home of the world's only pepper trading exchange. We were also fortunate enough to enjoy memorable meals in people's homes where we learnt some of the secrets of Keralan cuisine.

I have included recipes from Southern India, but this is not an Indian cookbook. I have chosen a broad spectrum of recipes that demonstrate pepper's versatility and will open your eyes and palate to its many uses. I have developed most of the recipes myself; others were given to me by chefs and fellow food writers who share my passion for this spice. The recipes are mostly geared to busy life styles, but a few of them need more time – earmark these for leisurely weekends when you can enjoy a peaceful session in the kitchen.

I have tried to share my passion for pepper and the joy of cooking with it. We tend to take pepper for granted but I truly believe that the time has come for us to be more adventurous in the way we use it. I hope this book will inspire you to discover the pleasures of this marvellous spice, quite rightly referred to in the Middle Ages as 'black gold – king of spices'.

Christine McFadden, October 2007

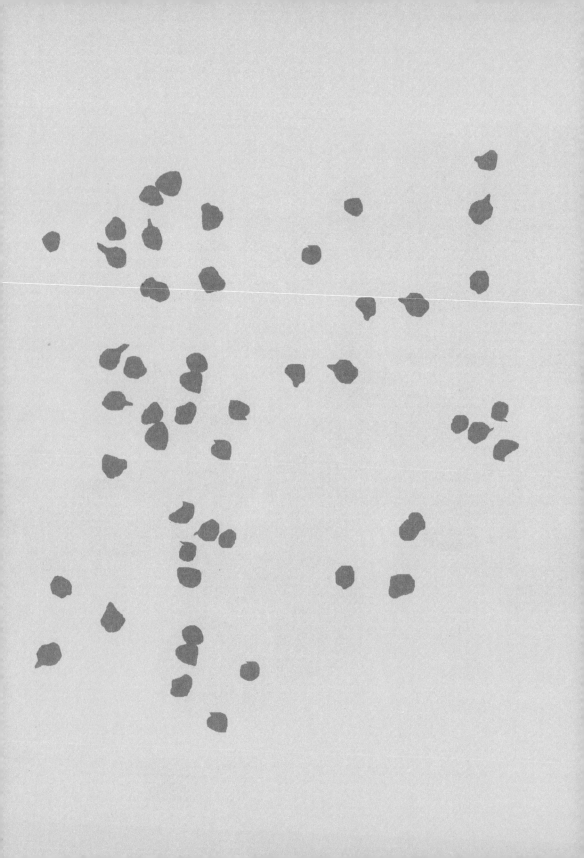

pepper in history

12   *the power of pepper*

18   *pepper in the roman kitchen*

20   *myths and misunderstandings*

22   *pepper and the americans*

23   *death in the pot*

the power of pepper

Few people realise that the peppercorn – that nondescript spice that we use without a second thought – was the catalyst for far-reaching changes in culture, commerce and cuisine. It was also indirectly responsible for the shape of the world that we know today. Such was its value that intrepid explorers set out on awesome voyages in search of it. Merchants risked their lives transporting it across tempestuous seas, parched deserts and vertiginous mountains. Fortunes were built on pepper, bloody battles fought over it, and the New World discovered because of it. Pepper was literally the power behind many a throne.

As several food historians have rightly commented, the history of pepper is the history of the spice trade as a whole, no-one putting it more succinctly than the erudite Waverley Root: 'Certain plants embody so completely the essence of their kind that they stand for the whole category to which they belong', he wrote. That said, it's noticeable from early literature that even though pepper was certainly known as long ago as 1200 BC, it rarely gets a mention until much later. Spices such as frankincense, sandalwood and cinnamon crop up time and again, as are the uses to which they were put – in perfumery and potions, incense and ointments, magical rituals and ceremonies and so on. But where was pepper in all of this?

It might well be, as some writers have speculated, that pepper lacked the heady sensuality of other spices. It is neither resinous nor heavily perfumed nor unguent – in other words, not the type of spice that would immediately spring to mind for anointing a lover or burning as incense.

pepper as medicine

Pepper was certainly widely used in medicine and in embalming procedures. There are records of peppercorns being found in the nose and abdomen of Pharaoh Rameses II. His mummified and more-or-less intact body was unearthed in 1886 at a burial chamber near Thebes, one-time capital of ancient Egypt, where it had lain undisturbed for more than three thousand years. Pepper and other spices would have been used to cleanse the eviscerated body and prevent putrefaction.

Pepper was found in excavations in the Indus valley in northwest India, and is mentioned in ayurvedic medical texts written over three thousand years ago. It crops up in the works of that venerable pair, Hippocrates (ca.460–370 BC) and Theophrastus (370–ca.285 BC), 'fathers' of medicine and botany respectively. The philosopher Plato (ca.428-348 BC) declared pepper 'small in quantity and great in virtue'.

Later on, the Roman philosopher Pliny the Elder (AD 23–79) and the Greek physician and botanist Dioscorides (ca. AD 40–90) both referred to pepper in their works on the natural world.

Though primarily valued as a medicine, there is evidence that pepper was also used in cooking from very early on. Food historian Andrew Dalby cites a latter-day cook's tip dated 3 BC for seasoning scallops with pepper – apparently the oldest positive evidence of its use in the kitchen. The advice came from Diphilus of Siphnos, a Greek dietetic writer, but not everyone shared his enthusiasm. Pliny moaned, 'Why do we like it so much? Some foods attract by sweetness, some by their appearance, but neither the pod nor the berry of pepper has anything to be said for it. We only want it for its bite – and we will go to India to get it!'

ancient trade

Since pepper was native to Kerala in southwest India, these sundry pieces of evidence suggest the existence of a very ancient trade between India, the Middle East and Greece. India was known also to have traded with Malaysia and Indonesia, introducing pepper to the Far East around 100 BC. This region soon became a major producer of pepper itself, perhaps because of the pepper plants brought

by Indian colonists who came in search of *Suyarnadvipa*, a mythical land of gold. Indonesia, in turn, traded with China, and as a result black pepper was introduced into Chinese cuisine; for a while it was the pepper of choice among the very wealthy, who preferred it to Sichuan pepper.

As with any sort-after commodity, prices were maintained by tightly controlled supply; potentates and canny Arab middlemen did not part with pepper lightly. Fortuitous ecology also played a part. A notoriously temperamental plant, the Indian pepper vine is dependent on the heavy rains of the bi-annual monsoons. When the Portuguese explorer Vasco da Gama suggested taking a cutting to transplant in Europe, the Zamorin of Calicut calmly retorted, 'You can take our pepper, but you will never be able to take our rains'.

spice miles

To reach the spice markets of the Middle East and beyond, pepper would have had to make an awesome five thousand mile journey from Calicut, Kerala's trading centre, either by sea or by tortuous overland routes, or a combination of both.

In the words of spice historian Jack Turner, pepper (and other spices) was endlessly shipped and reshipped, from buffalo to barge, from ship to caravan before reaching the Mediterranean ports. Caravans of as many as four thousand camels plodded along well-trodden trade routes known by hauntingly memorable names – the 'Silk Road', the 'Incense Route', the 'Golden Road to Samarkand'.

Once the cargo reached Alexandria, the ancient world's greatest commercial centre, it was loaded onto freighters and shipped across the Mediterranean to the Italian port of Ostia on the mouth of the River Tiber, and from there up-river by barge to Rome itself.

the arab monopoly

For centuries, probably since 1000 BC, traders from Southern Arabia controlled the enormously profitable spice trade. To discourage competition, they artfully concealed the true source of spices by inventing horrifying tales of the huge risks involved (see Myths and Misunderstandings, page 20).

These astute Arab merchants acted as middlemen, controlling all the trade routes and selling pepper at vastly inflated prices each time it changed hands. Gradually, however, intelligence trickled through to Europe that the true source of spices was southwest India. This knowledge and the resulting events instigated the weakening of the Arab stranglehold.

Around 70 AD, an important discovery was made which marked the beginning of the Egyptian, and then the Roman spice trade. By sailing on the back of the prevailing monsoon winds, an unknown Greek sea captain reached India's southwest coast in record time.

It became apparent that the monsoon blew eastwards over the Indian Ocean from April to October, reversing direction for the rest of the year. With the wind blowing from behind, it was possible to set sail in spring from the Egyptian port of Berenice on the Red Sea and make it to India's Malabar coast in time for the autumn pepper harvest.

The merchants were able to load up their cargo and make the return journey in the same year. As a result, Roman trade with India boomed and the Arab monopoly was broken – for a while, at least.

pepper and the romans

As founders of the world's first empire, the Romans had sophisticated cosmopolitan tastes. Their appetite for pepper was insatiable and, with the expansion of the Roman Empire, they were responsible for its migration north through Europe.

Andrew Dalby writes, 'It was for pepper, more than any other single product, that Roman gold and silver coins were exported to India'. The Romans treated it as currency, hoarding vast amounts in the treasury and in the *horrea piperataria* – a spice bazaar and storehouse in Rome's most fashionable quarter. In the words of French historian Maguelonne Toussaint-Samat 'pepper more than any other spice, being stronger and more abundant than the others, came to be seen as a symbol of power and virility, qualities reflected in its powerful and aggressive flavour'.

The Romans were the first to consistently use pepper in cooking, and they did so with boundless enthusiasm, adding it to every imaginable dish and some unimaginable ones (see Pepper in the Roman Kitchen, page 18).

Long pepper (page 34) appeared to be the pepper of choice, perhaps because it was hotter than black pepper, or because it was both pungent and sweet – a flavour combination that appealed to the Roman palate. Dalby points out that it was the most powerful medicine, the best to use in cases of poisoning. We can get an idea of its relative value from Pliny, who reported that long pepper cost 15 denarii a pound – nearly four times as much as black pepper (four denarii), and twice as much as white pepper (seven denarii).

the dark ages

With the collapse of the Roman Empire and the expansion of Islam, the Arabs regained their former grip on the spice trade. In 641 AD the Muslims took control of Alexandria, the key trading centre, and the long-established trade between India and Rome came to an end. Meanwhile, having carefully nurtured relationships with the Arabs, Venice became a key player, controlling the distribution of spices within Europe and levying hefty customs duty on incoming cargo.

Together, the Arab and Venetian merchants formed a double monopoly, a Muslim Wall as it has been called, causing pepper to rocket to luxury status that only the super-rich could afford. The wealthy hoarded it as a cushion against bankruptcy, keeping it securely under lock and key. Vast quantities were wheeled out for banquets, both as an ostentatious display and as a seasoning for the food itself. Pepper was passed round on spice platters before and after the meal, and it showed up in every imaginable dish, usually in amounts that seem bizarre to us but are not so unusual when put in context. The greater the excess, the higher the host's social standing.

German cultural historian Wolfgang Schivelbusch suggests that there was a deep need to emerge from the deprivation of the Dark Ages and indulge in hedonistic epicurean enjoyment. Spices, particularly pepper, were symbolic of power and status for the ruling classes, and their display and subsequent consumption were closely intertwined. Schivelbusch writes: 'Moderation or excess with which they were served attested to the host's social rank. The more sharply pepper seared the guest's palates, the more respect they felt for their hosts'.

He goes on to comment that the medieval hunger for spices was part of a wider picture of cultural development, capable of mobilising forces very much as present day needs for energy have done.

Despite pepper's luxury status, demand was widespread and did not lose momentum, although there was an inevitable drop while prices were sky-high. Pepper maintained its place in the apothecary's shop where it had long been prescribed for numerous and diverse ailments (see Pepper and Health, page 70).

It was also widely accepted as currency and considered a more stable medium of exchange at a time when any sovereign could mint his own coins. Counted out peppercorn by peppercorn, the spice was used to pay taxes and tolls, debts and dowries, rewards and rent.

The phrase 'peppercorn rent' still survives,

meaning a token rent – precisely the opposite to the original meaning. In the Middle Ages, a pound of pepper represented two or three week's wages for a farmhand, and was enough to buy freedom for a French serf. If a man 'lacked pepper' he was in financial trouble.

medieval cuisine

Following the religious wars of the early Crusades, trade gradually opened up between Europe and the Holy Land. Although the Venetians still maintained their iron grip, the Crusaders brought back with them rare spices and other novel ingredients from the East. European cooks took these in their stride and we start to see an enrichment of medieval cookery that went far beyond the needs of basic necessity.

Pepper of all kinds, especially long pepper, cubebs and grains of paradise, is regularly specified in the cookbooks, along with exotic aromatics and seasonings – rose water, honey, almond milk, saffron, ginger, cloves and cinnamon.

The Italians were particularly fond of pepper; it went into spicy cakes and biscuits (see Pan Pepato, page 224, and Taralli, page 223) and the traditional spice cake *Panforte di Siena*. The French, historically conservative with spices and 'foreign' seasonings, preferred ginger and cinnamon, but they developed a taste for grains of paradise (see page 42) – possibly because of the gingery flavour. Religious orders in France and Italy became famous for their gingerbreads, which invariably included a dash of pepper to balance the sweeter spices.

The English seemingly loved any spice going, but pepper was a favourite, appearing in numerous recipes for hearty stews and sauces.

the guild of pepperers

Pepper was so vital to medieval cookery, medicine and commerce that a guild was eventually founded in London. Known as the Guild of Pepperers, and later, in 1345, The Company of Grocers of London, the Guild's remit was to control quality and distribution.

In those days spice imports were often heavily adulterated or bulked out to increase their weight (see Death in the Pot, page 23). This led the Grocers' Company to appoint an official Garbeller (from the Old Italian *garbellare* 'to strain, to sift') whose job was to inspect all spices coming into the country for what were known as 'garbles' – rubbish, dirt and other impurities. This generated considerable revenue from fines and also helped to establish the beginnings of modern quality control systems. The term 'garble' is still in use in the pepper trade today (see Pepper Jargon, page 246).

the spice race

Frustrated by Venice's seemingly unshakable grip on the spice trade, the major western powers eventually took matters into their own hands and set out to find a direct sea route to India and the Spice Islands further on. This proactive stance was fuelled by the writings of Marco Polo, a young Venetian who set out with his father and uncle on a daunting 24-year trek to China. Returning in 1298, his down-to-earth descriptions of pepper plantations on the Malabar Coast and boatloads of pepper arriving at Chinese ports, put paid to the myths and symbolic attachments to pepper (see Myths and Misunderstandings, page 20).

The race was on, spawning an intrepid breed of explorers and entrepreneurs. From 1450 onwards and over the next four centuries the Spanish, then the Portuguese, English and Dutch, and eventually the newly founded United States, embarked on awe-inspiring voyages that took years to complete.

As historians have pointed out, Marco Polo's journals had an extraordinary effect on the future, leading to the toppling of Venice, the destruction of the Arab Empire, the birth of direct trade with the Orient and, ultimately, more-or-less as a bi-product of the search for pepper, the discovery of the New World.

pepper reaches its peak

By the mid-sixteenth century, the world had become a smaller place. Christopher Columbus had 'discovered' the New World by sailing west in an attempt to find a more direct route to the east; Vasco da Gama had reached the Indian Ocean by the southerly route round the Cape of Good Hope, safely crossing the Equator without bursting into flames; Magellan had made it from Portugal to the Philippines via South America; and Sir Francis Drake had completed his three-year circumnavigation of the world by way of the Magellan Straits and the Spice Islands.

With the opening up of both China and the New World, and far-flung voyages now relatively commonplace, we see the beginnings of cross-pollination in world cuisines with pepper adding its unique flavour to the food of countries many thousands of miles from India and the Spice Islands (see A Spice Blend Glossary, page 240).

Pepper became unquestionably the world's most valuable export accounting for seventy per cent of the total spice trade. The heyday lasted well into the eighteenth century but by then the market was saturated and pepper was losing its pulling power.

As Schivelbusch comments, once there was nothing more to be discovered and conquered, and knowledge of the earth became more common, spices apparently lost their tremendous attraction. Consumption tapered off and highly seasoned dishes no longer appealed to the European palate. Pepper retreated from the world stage to the kitchen cupboard, its place taken by exciting New World commodities – coffee, chocolate, tobacco and, later, sugar.

We use pepper today without a second thought, so it is hard to grasp that this mundane brown spice once had a charisma that far exceeded its commercial or gastronomic importance. In native Kerala, however, where the pepper vine is a highly visible part of the landscape, and its fruits vital to livelihood and culture, the charisma lives on.

facts and stats

Pepper history is awash with recycled anecdotes, some of them worth repeating as they illustrate pepper's extraordinary status as an early medium of exchange and as a reward.

- In exchange for sparing Rome during the siege of 408 AD, Visigoth King Alaric demanded 3000 pounds of pepper (or kilos according to some sources) as part of a hefty ransom. The deal turned out to be a short-term expedient; two years later the Goths conquered the city in yet another siege, setting the stage for the collapse of the Roman Empire.
- At the very end of the 10th century, King Ethelred 'the Unready' passed a statute whereby the 'Easterlings' (charmingly named German spice traders) had to pay customs duty in pepper for the privilege of doing deals with merchants in London.
- In 1101 Genoese soldiers were handsomely rewarded with pepper when they conquered the town of Caesarea in the Holy Land.
- In the days of Queen Elizabeth 1, the English stevedores who unloaded the spice ships were forbidden from wearing clothing with cuffs, and also had their pockets sewn up, to discourage pilfering of peppercorns.
- In 1973 Prince Charles took possession of the Duchy of Cornwall and was presented with a pound of peppercorns as part of the feudal rent.
- In the 1980s, when the sunken ship, the Mary Rose, was raised from the ocean floor, a stash of peppercorns was found on nearly every sailor's corpse. The ship sank in 1545.

pepper in the roman kitchen

Although pepper had been known long before their time, the Romans were the first to use it on a day-to-day basis. They also used the more expensive long pepper. Having successfully broken the Arab monopoly on spices, they were able to source pepper direct from India. As a result, the price fell and pepper became the Roman spice of choice, albeit for the ruling classes rather than the masses.

Ancient Roman cuisine is notorious for its exotica and for this we have Marcus Gavius Apicius to thank. An outrageous gourmand who lived in the first century AD, Apicius hobnobbed with the rich and was responsible for orchestrating gargantuan banquets at which rare delicacies were served – roast nightingales' tongues and boiled flamingo, for example.

Apicius is mistakenly said to be the author of a Roman cookbook *De re coquinaria* (On the Subject of Cooking), now confusingly known as *Apicius*, a collection of recipes from various sources compiled some three hundred years after his death. More of a handbook for the slave-cook rather than a cookbook for the intelligentsia, the book nevertheless demonstrates the Romans' continuing love of the flamboyant and cosmopolitan – think of them as early foodies. And despite the received wisdom regarding Roman excess, the book also reveals plenty of down-to-earth dishes and skilful use of seasonings. Roman cooks appreciated complex flavours, particularly sweet-and-sour and sweet-and-peppery, and they knew how to make rich food more digestible. Of the 466 recipes in *Apicius*, pepper shows up in all but fifteen or so. It was the universal seasoning used in preference to salt.

Eyebrows are often raised over the seemingly excessive quantity of pepper used, but this needs to be considered in context. Pepper was certainly used at every opportunity but we can only guess at the amount since the weight or volume of an ingredient, and the number of servings, were rarely specified. The recipes were written by chefs who cooked for the ruling classes, so it was highly likely that many of the dishes were for formal dinners attended by a fair number of guests. The amount of seasoning is therefore not as excessive at it initially seems.

It's worth remembering, too, that Roman cuisine was relatively simple, despite its reputation. The cooks did not have access to many of the ingredients that give modern Italian food its characteristic flavour and colour; tomatoes, peppers and potatoes had yet to be brought from the New World. There were no huge open fires so the massive spit-roasts and cauldrons of long-cooked stews typical of medieval times were not part of Roman cuisine. Instead the cooks relied on spices, herbs and condiments to give their dishes flavour, colour and texture.

What the Romans excelled at was sauces and these were obviously basic to the cuisine. There were sauces for every imaginable situation – hangovers, indigestion, lack of libido – and for every type of dish – fish, fowl, furred and feathered game, vegetables, salads, eggs and fruit. Sauces were served hot or cold, raw or cooked, sometimes integral to the dish, sometimes poured over the food as it was served. Some were used as marinades or vinaigrette-like dressings, others were relishes or salsas.

What is most striking is that with few exceptions sauce recipes begin with 'take pepper and pound with....'. Pepper was absolutely key to the flavour. Most sauces started life in a *mortarium*, a shallow stone dish with a rough interior, in which ingredients were pounded, always in the same order – first the pepper, then the seeds, followed by herbs, liquid and thickeners.

Some sauces contained dozens of ingredients; what the Roman cook was after was a single complex flavour rather than emphasising individual ingredients. A date sauce for boiled ostrich included pepper, mint, roasted cumin, celery seed, long or round dates, honey, vinegar, *passum* (raisin wine), *liquamen* (a type of fermented fish sauce) and oil. Another for flamingo (also to be used for parrot) includes dill, vinegar, leek, coriander, *defrutum* (cooked syrup), pepper, cumin, *laser* root (a rare spice), mint, rue, *caroenum* (wine) and starch.

A pepper mash forms the basis of a thick sauce for forcemeat: 'Soak pepper overnight, grind and immediately pour on *liquamen* so that you make a finely ground pepper mash. Stir in *defrutum* made from quinces that have been left in full sun until it is as thick as honey... and then add a starch emulsion of the liquor from (cooked) rice, and bring to heat over a slow fire'.

There were green sauces for vegetables, thickened with pounded pine nuts – similar to the pesto we serve with pasta. The cooks knew that soda kept vegetables green and used it in various vegetable 'mashes'. A green sauce for boiled mussels included chopped coriander, whole peppercorns, wine, salt and oil – again, not so different to the way we serve mussels today. An 'easily digested relish' included chopped beets and leeks, mixed with pounded pepper and cumin, the ubiquitous *liquamen* and *passum* for 'a certain sweetness', then briefly brought to the boil and cooled. Radishes were served in a simple sauce of pounded pepper and *liquamen*.

Apart from sauces, pepper went into hors-d'oeuvres, salads, vegetables, ham, sausages and cured meats, roasts, stews, even desserts. Custards were sprinkled with pepper in the same way as nutmeg, and deliciously pungent sweetmeats were concocted with pepper, honey, nuts and fruit.

Taking a look at the more unusual uses of pepper, we find it in a stuffing for dormice, an expensive delicacy: 'Stuff the dormice with pork forcemeat and also with the flesh from all parts of the dormouse, pounded with pepper, pine nuts, *laser* root and *liquamen*. Sew them up and arrange them on a tile and put them in the oven or cook them, stuffed, in a *clibanus* (a portable clay oven)'.

Even in those days, cooks obviously knew how to make the most of pepper's pungency and aroma; they added it during cooking, and more before serving to recapture the spicy fragrance of the volatile oils. Pepper was used both ground and whole in the same dish, as in this recipe for *Lucanicae*, a type of smoked sausage similar to the salami we enjoy today: 'Pound pepper, cumin, savory, rue, parsley, bay berry spice and *liquamen*. Add meat which has been thoroughly pounded so that it can then be blended well with the spice-mix. Stir in *liquamen*, whole peppercorns, plenty of fat and pine nuts. Put the meat in the skins, draw them quite thinly and hang them in the smoke'.

In the words of spice historian Jack Turner, take away the exotica and some discordant mixes, Roman cooking was not very different to cooking in the 21st century. It is certainly no more outrageous than some of the fusion food on restaurant menus today. We share the same appetite for spicy flavours, and we travel the world bringing back novel and exotic ingredients, including rare peppercorns, just as the Romans did.

See also
Long Pepper, page 34
Power of Pepper, page 14
Piperine and Essential Oil, page 69

myths and misunderstandings

The spice trade has always been a mysterious world, closed to outsiders and shrouded in legend. Food history abounds with unsubstantiated but seemingly plausible stories, which, through repetition, gain reality. It's hardly surprising, therefore, that an extraordinary collection of myths and misunderstandings have evolved around pepper.

careful cover-up

In medieval Europe, people had only a hazy idea of where pepper came from or who was involved in bringing it to Europe. The spice changed hands time and again on the long journey from the East, everyone profiting at each transaction. The Arabs were particularly adept middlemen, benefiting hugely from Europe's voracious appetite for pepper and other spices.

For the Arabs, mystery meant profitability and they went out of their way to keep the true source of spices a closely guarded secret. To discourage other entrepreneurs, bizarre and spine-chilling tales were invented, inferring the enormous risks involved in being a spice dealer. Cassia apparently grew in lakes guarded by winged animals; cinnamon came from inaccessible valleys infested with poisonous snakes. Spice historian Jack Turner points out that the medieval imagination thrived on such tales, however monstrous, and did not welcome more matter-of-fact accounts from explorer Marco Polo of lands where spices were commonplace, grew on trees and were harvested by real people.

botanical blunders

A number of fallacies about pepper stem from the Roman pharmacologist Dioscorides. He was convinced that long, black and white peppers were the product of one and the same tree, and that black pepper was the mature fruit found in the pods of long pepper. Pliny the Elder, who one would have thought might know better, perpetuates the error in *The Natural History*, adding to the confusion by erroneously describing trees that bear pepper as 'very similar in appearance to our juniper' but with seeds enclosed in pods like a kidney bean. He is careful to point out, however, that the root of the tree was not, as some imagined, the source of ginger.

In his monumental encyclopaedia, *Etymologiae*, Saint Isidore of Seville (ca. 560–636), writes of pepper forests full of writhing snakes that guard the trees. When the fruits are ripe, local people set fire to the forest, the snakes flee, and the thick flames blacken the pepper fruits and make them sharper. He believed that 'pepper is white by nature, although it has several fruits. The immature variety is called long pepper; what is untouched by the fire is white pepper; and the pepper that has a rough and wrinkled skin gets both its colour and its name from the heat of the fire'.

Saint Isidore's canard and others like it, were recycled well into the sixteenth century until the Portuguese pioneer of tropical medicine, García de Orta (ca.1501–1568) put the record straight with his first-hand experience of the pepper plant. As author of *Conversations on the simples, drugs and medicinal substances of India* (published in Goa, 1563), he correctly describes it as a climbing vine, and points out that long pepper is a different species.

pepper and chillies

We have Christopher Columbus and the Spanish to thank for the ongoing confusion over the nomenclature of pepper, chilli pepper and allspice. Landing in Cuba on his epic westward journey in search of pepper, Columbus found allspice, not dissimilar to a large peppercorn, and hot chillies, which he described as the natives' pepper. He brought this exciting new spice to Europe, and called it *pimienta*, the Spanish word for peppercorn.

Allspice was known by the same name, though it was eventually corrupted to *pimento* (see page 55). Columbus also confusingly referred to the indigenous population as 'Indians'.

the taint of rotting meat

There exists an old and seemingly indestructible belief that the so-called gargantuan quantity of pepper and other spices used in medieval times was there to disguise the unsavoury taste of rotting meat and fish. Though repeated by a plethora of authors, almost to the point of modern urban myth status, there is little evidence to substantiate the idea.

My food writer colleague Colin Spencer refutes the theory at some length in his book *British Food: an extraordinary thousand years of history*. He points out the existence of stringent bi-laws, with harsh and humiliating penalties for retailers who sold decaying food. Also to be taken into account is the fact that the huge amount of spices used were to flavour food for large numbers of people, so individual portions were in fact small. Of equal importance is that no amount of spices will disguise the disgusting taste and smell of putrid food. To shower it with expensive spices, which in those days were like gold dust, would have been incredibly wasteful, rather like gulping champagne to quench the thirst. If any disguising was being done, it was more likely an attempt to improve the flavour of highly salted foods – salt being the main preservative in pre-refrigeration days.

Undoubtedly, food poisoning was an issue and hygiene standards lackadaisical – just as they are at times today. However, as Stephen Mennell is at pains to point out: 'That cannot be anything like the whole truth, for the use of spices began to change long before there was any significant improvement in methods of preservation'. The late food historian Alice Arndt puts the view that historians and chefs dreamed up the rotting meat theory because they were at a loss to explain an extravagant use of spices so at odds with their own culinary customs.

See also
Allspice, page 54
Long Pepper, page 34

pepper and the americans

While the fascination with spices ran its course in medieval Europe, North America was inhabited by indigenous tribes and, later, pioneers from other parts of the world. In these early years life for many was a matter of survival, and rare luxuries such as pepper simply did not figure in the culture and cuisine. Needless to say, pepper turned out to be the foundation of future fortunes.

yale and the pepper trade

The roots of the American pepper trade lie with a man called Elihu Yale. Born in Boston, Yale was taken to England aged three and never returned to America. In the 1650s he went to Madras to work as a representative for the British East India Company. Times were good and Yale was able to build a sizeable fortune from trading in pepper.

Several decades later the Collegiate School in New Haven, Connecticut contacted Yale, who by then was living in Wales, and asked him to help finance a new building. Yale's donation was substantial and as a token of gratitude the college changed its name to Yale University – perhaps in anticipation of further donations. At the time news of the name change reached Yale's home in Wales, he was away in India on a trip from which he never returned. Though he ultimately did leave his fortune to the college, the authorities were apparently never able to get their hands on it.

salem and sumatra

In 1795, an intrepid Yankee sea captain, Jonathan Carnes, sailed from Salem, Massachusetts to the Indonesian island of Sumatra. Once there, he managed to circumvent the then Dutch monopoly and make direct contact with native spice growers. With backing from a wealthy Salem family, Carnes returned two years later with a cargo of pepper that made 700 per cent profit and gave America its stake in the world spice trade. Over the next eighty years, fleets of speedy American clipper ships scudded their way across the oceans on the 24,000-mile round trip to Sumatra, returning with lucrative cargoes of pepper.

The connection between Salem and Sumatra is a curious one. It is unique in that one North American port dominated trade in a single foreign commodity from a single part of the world. It wasn't as if there was an inherent domestic demand for pepper; it was not used to any extent in Salem kitchens or indeed elsewhere in America. The reason behind the thriving trade was that money could be made by reshipping the spice to European ports – from Rotterdam to Archangel to Genoa and Naples. Merchants from other American ports came to Salem to get in on the act. Enormous profits were made and by the early 19th century exports alone totalled over seven million pounds in a single year.

The good times did not last, however. Pirates had long dominated the oriental seas, repeatedly raiding and destroying ships from the west. Marco Polo gives one of his typical closely observed accounts: 'These pirates take with them their wives and children, and stay out the whole summer. Their method is to join in fleets of twenty or thirty of these pirate vessels together, and then they form what they call a sea cordon, that is, they drop off till there is an interval of five or six miles between ship and ship, so they cover something like a hundred miles of sea, and no merchant ship can escape them. For when any one corsair sights a vessel a signal is made by fire or smoke, and then the whole of them make for this, and sieze the merchants and plunder them.'

Despite their speed and agility, American clipper ships did not escape. Uncharacteristic though it may seem today, the young Yankee government decided it was not in the country's interests to provide naval support on foreign waters, and the Salem pepper boom eventually came to an end.

death in the pot

Human nature being what it is, adulteration of a valuable and widely used spice such as pepper was inevitable from the moment it reached European shores. Unscrupulous profiteers devised ingenious methods for padding out its bulk; common adulterants included pepper husks, ground fruit stones, linseed, buckwheat hulls and mustard seeds. Isabella Beeton, 19th-century diva of household management, warns of rice flour in white pepper and burnt toast crumbs in black. And there is evidence of worse.

In 1820, Fredrick Accum, a London-based analytical chemist and influential campaigner for uncontaminated food, wrote *A Treatise on Adulterations of Food and Culinary Poisons*, known more sensationally as *Death in the Pot* (from 2 Kings, Ch.IV, v.40). Accum not only describes common methods of adulteration, but actually names and shames the perpetrators. Unsurprisingly, this brought him plenty of enemies and he was forced to retreat to his native Germany.

Accum warns of imitation peppercorns made from compressed linseed, clay and cayenne pepper. To detect these adulterants he advises, 'It is only necessary to throw a sample of the suspected pepper into a bowl of water; the artificial pepper-corns fall to a powder, whilst the true pepper remains whole'. He has no suggestions, however, for detecting contaminated ground pepper, which invariably contained pepper dust, factory floor sweepings and cayenne pepper to provide the necessary pungent bite. This 'vile refuse' was known in the trade as PD (pepper dust). There was even an inferior version, referred to by those in the know as DPD (dirt of pepper dust).

Curiously, Accum dismisses white pepper-corns as an adulterated version of black, and appears mistakenly convinced that true white pepper came from a completely different plant.

Despite various interim Acts, adulteration continued virtually unchecked until the Adulteration Act of 1860. This effectively brought about much needed reform and paved the way for the 1875 Sale of Food and Drugs Act, which forms the basis of current food legislation, although greatly amended.

Writing in the 1940s, John Parry, author of *The Spice Handbook*, stated that apart from 'dust, dirt, stems, chaff or extraneous matter,' whole pepper is not likely to be adulterated, though he acknowledged that the practice had not been entirely eliminated from the spice trade as a whole.

Al Goetze, procurement manager at McCormick spice producers, bears Parry out; Goetze has a legendary collection of stones, rusty nails, giant cockroaches, plastic beach sandals – all found in shipments of spices sold to McCormick. In an article in *The Economist*, he explains that big processing firms and marketers are going straight to the source to clean things up, frightened that such stuff – or, worse, microscopic impurities that come with it – might make it to the dinner plates of litigious customers.

Prompted by increasing consumer awareness of food safety, regulators in the United States and Europe have cracked down heavily on contamination. Meanwhile, in Cochin, India, the Spices Board has established quality improvement training programmes to educate the growers on the procedures and precautions necessary to meet the stringent requirements of major buying countries.

See also
Pepper Organisations, page 247

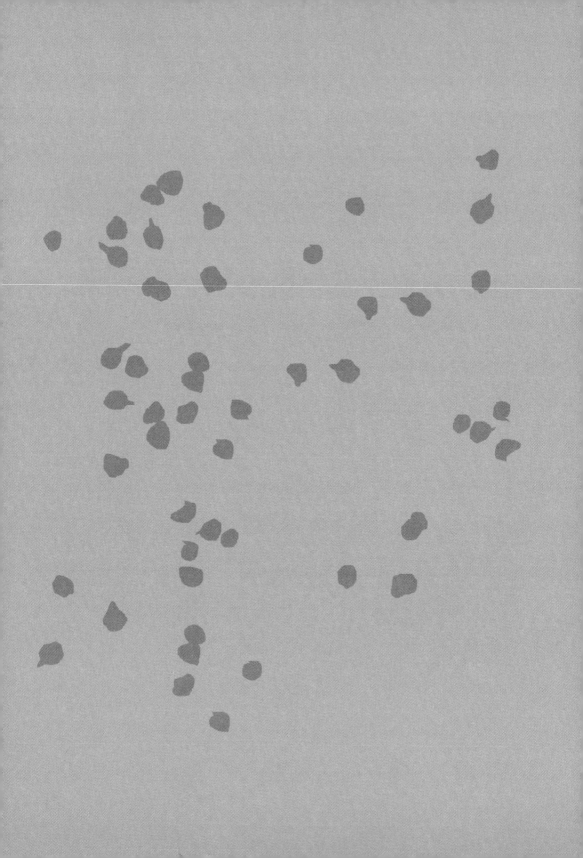

a pepper primer

26   the pepper vine

29   rimbàs black pepper

30   basic botany

34   long pepper

38   cubeb pepper

42   grains of paradise

46   sichuan pepper and sansho

50   pink pepper

54   allspice

58   the greater pepper family

the pepper vine

Before first going to India I had only the haziest idea of what a pepper plant looked like. Though I had seen photographs, I did not know, for example, that peppercorns grow on a vine, sometimes clambering more than ten metres high over a host tree. Nor did I know that there are more than a hundred pepper varieties growing in Kerala alone, let alone those indigenous to Indonesia, Malaysia and Vietnam. All this was soon to change as I set off on a tortuous drive to the Pazhoor plantation in Murikady, high up in Kerala's Western Ghats. I was accompanied by Indian Spices Board field officer for the Kumilly region, the bright-eyed and knowledgeable Mr Ramalingum, or Ram as most people call him.

At first sight, the pepper vine looks just like ivy clinging to a dead tree or telegraph pole. Unlike ivy, though, the pepper vine is not a parasite and does not create that sombre air of neglect and decay that ivy seems to bestow. In fact the vines look positively frivolous as they twirl their way up the supports, their glossy dark green leaves offsetting exquisite waxy white flowers or glowing orange and green peppercorns, depending on season.

The flowers grow in catkin-like clusters about 3–15cm long, developing into densely packed tapering spikes of immature pepper-corns. These round single-seeded berries start life bright green, gradually ripening to yellow-orange and finally to vibrant reddish pink when fully mature.

Pepper is one of India's most ancient crops and is seen as more than a commodity; it is part of the cultural heritage, the spice that put India on the commercial map, and as such it is cultivated with great care and sensitivity. This was immediately apparent on arrival at the Pazhoor plantation where the entire production system is based on impeccable ecological principals. Warmly greeted by owner Biju Paul and his family, we began our tour of the 6.5-acre smallholding.

Ram told me that over 90 per cent of Kerala's pepper is produced on 'homestead' plantations like Biju's where farmers grow pepper interspersed with other crops. Mono-cropping is relatively rare in Kerala but it does exist. Biju's plantation is planted with towering cardamom plants as well as pepper – a belt and braces approach in the event of one crop failing. He grows four or five varieties of pepper including the popular Karimunda and the large-fruited Panniyur, India's first hybrid cultivar developed at the Pepper Research Station in Kerala.

Situated high in the misty hills of the Western Ghats, the plantation is ideally placed for the warm, humid and cloudy conditions in which pepper thrives. Long spells of strong sunlight or dry weather are an anathema to the plant and can reduce all-important yields by as much as 50 per cent. The humus-rich forest soil is ideal, although pepper also does well in other types of soil as long as it is well-drained but also retains water.

In southwest India, the pepper vines start to flower in May or June with the onset of the monsoons. They are ready for harvesting six to seven months later, coinciding with the dry season. In Malaysia and Indonesia the harvest is a few months later.

Weather conditions are absolutely critical especially at the start of the growth cycle. Heavy rainfall in the first few weeks is vital for triggering flower growth. After that, the vine needs continuous showers from flowering until the berries ripen – during this crucial period even a short dry spell can cause setbacks. Once the berries are ripe, however, wet weather is definitely not needed; the berries need dry conditions during harvesting and processing, otherwise there is a risk of mould that can wipe out a crop. Dry weather at this stage also increases the possibility of a second harvest.

With his livelihood in the hands of unpredictable weather, Biju seems remarkably relaxed. As we walk through the plantation he explains that crops this year have been good so far – an improvement on last year. He supplements his income by supplying the local community with milk. 'Without cows agriculture is nothing', he says. To prove his point he shows me his organic fertiliser made from a cocktail of cow's milk, curds, butter algae, urine and manure fermented with rotten bananas, wheat yeast and palm sugar. This incredible mixture works not only as a growth promoter but also keeps pests and rodents under control – understandably they're repelled by the smell.

harvesting

Today the pickers are harvesting the juicy green berries that will be dried until they turn black. Peppercorns destined to be freeze-dried or brine-cured as green pepper are picked two months earlier. Biju's vines are pruned to a vertiginous four to five metres. They twine their way up single-trunked tall trees, known as 'standards' that provide vital shade for the pepper, as well as the pickers. In countries where pepper is cultivated intensively as a mono-crop, the 'standards' are poles pushed into the ground in close-packed rows rather than live trees.

Instead of a ladder, Biju's pickers use the traditional thick bamboo pole with protruding notches for supporting the feet. The picker carefully selects the heaviest fruit spikes and deposits them into a bag tied around his waist. The work is labour-intensive – it takes about two hours to strip a big vine and sometimes a whole day if the yield is particularly good. Harvesting is a continuous process throughout the season since the vine can bear flowers and fruit simultaneously and the berries mature at different rates.

Once harvested, the spikes go into a pepper threshing machine that strips the berries from the stems at a rate of about 300 kilograms per hour – much faster and more hygienic than stripping by hand.

Next, the berries are spread in a single layer in a designated concrete drying area and left for the sun to work its magic. The colour

changes from green to black in one day, and in another three or four days the berries are completely dry. Regular raking ensures they all dry at the same rate. At night they are covered to protect them from damp.

The dried peppercorns are shipped by lorry down winding mountainous roads past tea and rubber plantations, exotic backyard spice gardens and colourful roadside shops. Four hours later they are unloaded in the ancient warehouses of Jewtown, the pepper-trading area of Fort Cochin. After the glare of the sun, the dimness inside the warehouse is a welcome relief but there is no let-up from the heat. Watching sari-clad women swaying to and fro as they sift and grade the berries is curiously soporific, but the pungent dust from the pepper keeps me wide awake and struggling to suppress constant sneezes. After grading and cleaning the peppercorns are packed into sacks ready for selling on the open market and the last stage of their journey.

white pepper processing

Breathe deeply over a bag of white peppercorns and you'll almost certainly get a whiff of something suspiciously like cow manure or socks that are none too clean. Very occasionally you come across clean-smelling white peppercorns. The reason for the smell, or lack of it, lies in the way the peppercorns are processed.

As explained on page 32, white pepper is produced by soaking mature berries in water for a week or more to loosen the outer husk – a process known as 'retting'. In Indonesia the berries are packed in sacks suspended in slow-flowing water, usually a stream, at ambient temperatures. Once dried, the peppercorns end up with the typical musty smell – a result of bacterial action. Though not harmful it can be off-putting.

Elsewhere, in Sarawak for example, top-quality peppercorns are put in barrels rather than sacks and soaked in constantly circulating clean cool spring water for two weeks. Similar care is taken at the Parameswaran estate in the Wynad district of Kerala. Here the berries are soaked in daily changes of spring water for nearly three weeks before the outer skin is removed. In both cases the result is an outstanding clean, white and odour-free peppercorn.

a question of quality

In the words of American food writer Michele Jordan, we look on traditional methods of food production as superior to modern industrialised techniques. We search out the hand-crafted, the sun-dried, the pure and simple, yet many of us also demand that food is produced in ultra-hygienic conditions and are not overly concerned with traditional techniques. In the case of pepper, it almost seems as if there are two distinct markets: the purists who go weak at the knees at the sight of Tellicherry Special Extra Bold, and the rest of the world, including the big spice companies, who simply want bog-standard sanitised pepper regardless of how it tastes.

The paradox for the pepper grower is that the conditions in which he grows and processes his pepper have sufficed for generations. However, if he is to get the best possible price for his crops the stringent standards of the importers, who quite naturally live in dread of litigation from their customers, have to be met.

Pepper is traditionally dried in the open on mats or concrete platforms. As such, it is vulnerable to contamination from bird and rodent droppings, insects, wind-blown dirt and heaven knows what else. Unexpected storms can re-wet an almost dry crop, increasing the risk of mould growth.

Harmful bacteria such as salmonella and *E.coli*, and moulds that produce aflatoxins are the chief risks and the reason why some pepper is irradiated or chemically sterilised. However, such procedures are neither environ-mentally sound nor conducive to flavour quality.

Another option is steam sterilisation, introduced by the Malaysian Pepper Board (MPB) but this is expensive and only a small percentage of pepper is processed in this way.

Many farmers take precautions by plunging freshly harvested pepper into a hot water bath for a few minutes before the drying process begins. This effectively kills off any bacteria without adversely affecting flavour. Outdoor solar drying cabinets can be used to reduce the risk of air-borne contamination. In Sarawak, crops are rapidly dried indoors using hot air systems.

Fortunately, organisations such as the Indian Spices Board and the MPB work with the farmers, teaching them best farming and processing practices, subsidising necessary machinery and helping promote their product. The International Pepper Community and its member countries have drawn up specifications for exported pepper. These cover microbial test procedures and a Code of Hygienic Practice for use by processors, warehouse operators and manufacturers of pepper products.

See also
One Plant, Four Peppercorns, page 31
Pepper as a Commodity, pages 62–63
Pepper Grades, page 246

rimbàs black pepper

Nearly four thousand kilometres east of Kerala is the fertile Rimbàs region of Sarawak on the island of Borneo. Here, in the remote village of Babu Sedebau, twelve families of Ibans, the most numerous of Sarawak's native population, live together in a typical pile-dwelling or longhouse. It is the duty of a good Iban never to leave land uncultivated, so the outlying fields are planted with Kuching black pepper, a local variety named after the state's capital.

The pepper fields are small and pepper is not a primary commodity; the villagers tend it in their spare time. Grown as a relatively short bushy vine supported by wooden posts rather than live trees, this pepper is probably less labour-intensive than its Keralan cousin. However, Rimbàs pepper is excellent quality and if production were to be increased, the crop could bring in more income for the families.

In the interests of preserving native foods, the Italian-based Slow Food Foundation for Biodiversity has given the community its support by creating the Rimbàs Black Pepper Presidium. (Presidia are local projects coordinated and funded by Slow Food to defend and improve artisan food production.)

In 2006 I travelled to Turin to attend the Slow Food Terra Madre event – a bi-annual world meeting of food communities. Here I met Rimbàs Presidium coordinator Mulok Saban, himself an Iban and brought up in a longhouse. Immensely sociable and passionate about pepper, Mulok explained that the aim of the Presidium is to increase production by improving soil quality, and also to improve post-harvest processing and quality control.

Meanwhile, the quality of the pepper has already brought it some success. The Rome Chamber of Commerce has agreed to promote Rimbàs pepper by using it in some of their traditional cured meats, local cheeses and even cakes.

We were able to sample this happy culinary partnership at a promotional lunch at which the menu included *cacio e pepe*, a classic Roman pasta dish with a creamy black pepper and pecorino sauce, followed by spicy *pan pepato* as a dessert. Given the strong historical link between pepper and the Romans, no outcome could be more fitting.

See also
Cacio e Pepe, page 178
Pan Pepato, page 224

basic botany

p e p p e r

Looking through the notes taken on my first trip to the pepper plantations in Kerala, I come across a list of questions for Dr Thampi of the Indian Spices Board: 'Where does white pepper come from?' 'How does black pepper become black?' 'Are red peppercorns the same as pink ones?' 'Why is green pepper usually dried or brine-cured?'

The answers seem obvious now, but at the time I was as confused as the ancient Romans who believed white pepper came from a different plant, and that black pepper was the fruit of long pepper. The fact that I had to ask these questions made me realise how few of us stop to give pepper a second thought, even though it is so much part of our culinary lives.

one plant, four peppercorns

All four peppercorns – green, black, white and red – come from the same plant, or vine. The differences in colour and nuances of flavour are the result of processing methods and harvesting at various stages of ripeness.

The peppercorn consists of an outer shell or pericarp that encloses a single inner seed. The pericarp contains an enzyme that acts as a catalyst in creating the volatile essential oils that give pepper its typical spicy aroma. The seed itself has little aroma since the essential oils are located in the pericarp and not the seed. However, the seed contains piperine, the substance that makes pepper hot. Together, the seed and the shell give us the familiar pungency and spicy aroma of black pepper.

green peppercorns
These are the unripe juicy green berries produced by the vine after the flowers have faded.

The berries, or corns, grow in densely packed spikes and are harvested while still immature but close to reaching full size. At this stage the fragrant oils in the outer shell and the pungency of the seed are not as fully developed as they would be in a mature berry. The flavour is therefore fresh and 'green' and only mildly hot.

If left untreated and exposed to the atmosphere, the berries turn black within a few hours of harvesting – a reaction caused by the enzyme in the outer husk. To prevent blackening, the berries are either soaked and packed in brine, or immersed in boiling water for 15–20 minutes. Nowadays, boiling water is the preferred method since it destroys the enzyme without the problem of a residual briny flavour. After boiling, the berries are laid out to dry in the sun. They remain green but the brightness gradually fades as they dry.

Far superior is freeze-drying, a method which preserves the vibrant green colour and fresh herbal flavour. Smooth, round and plump, freeze-dried berries are closest in appearance and flavour to fresh green peppercorns, and are my green peppercorn of choice. The supplier of these luscious beauties is Poabs Organic Estates, a unique plantation nestling in the fertile Nelliyampathy hills in Kerala. Grown according to biodynamic principles, the peppercorns are freeze-dried on the plantation and are at their peak of freshness. They are marketed by Bart Spices of Bristol in the UK and sold in specialist shops and some of the better supermarkets (see Sources, page 248).

black peppercorns

These are green peppercorns harvested at a later stage. They are usually picked when one or two berries on the spike have changed colour to bright orange or purple – a sign that they are close to maturity. The berries are spread out to dry in the sun, and over a few days change from green to rich brown to the familiar wrinkled black.

white peppercorns

These are fully mature berries harvested once the entire spike has changed colour to orange-red. The berries are packed into sacks and soaked in cool flowing water (preferably a clean stream) for one to two weeks to loosen the husk or pericarp. The softened skin is removed by trampling or rubbing, which reveals a cream or greyish white core. The berries are washed again until completely clean, then left to dry in the sun or in kilns.

Without the husk and its essential oils, the seed alone is responsible for providing the hot pungent flavour. It's important, therefore, that the seeds are fully mature – the stage when piperine content reaches its peak.

red peppercorns

True red peppercorns, as opposed to the pink varieties *Schinus terebinthifolius* and *Schinus molle*, are the fully ripened mature berries of *Piper nigrum*. These are a rarity even in countries where they are grown, since it is a risky business to leave the spikes on the vine for so long. Drought or heavy rain can wipe

p e p p e r

out an entire crop, as can hungry birds.

Ripe red peppercorns are either used immediately while they are fresh and juicy, or they are processed in the same way as green peppercorns. True red peppercorns are easily confused with the pink pepper mentioned earlier. The trick is to inspect the skin carefully; pink peppercorns have a brittle skin which cracks easily and separates from the seed, whereas red peppercorns are smoother and plumper.

Red peppercorns have the rich aroma and pungency of black, combined with a delicious sweetness – a mixture of pineapple, banana and toffee. Unfortunately, the superb flavour is lost in the brining process. Far better are the sought-after freeze-dried biodynamic red peppercorns from Poabs Organic Estates in Kerala (see Green Peppercorns, page 31). These are also marketed by Bart Spices and available in specialist shops and good supermarkets (see Sources, page 248).

See also
Myths and Misunderstandings, page 20
Pink Pepper, page 50
Piperine and Essential Oil, page 69

long pepper

Piper longum and Piper retrofractum

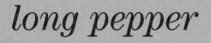

Named after its curious catkin-shaped fruits, long pepper is native to both India and Indonesia. The Indian variety, *Piper longum*, grows mainly in mountainous northern regions but also in the forests of Kerala and Tamil Nadu in the south. The Indonesian relative, *Piper retrofractum*, is a native of Java but grows throughout Indonesia and Malaysia. As is often the case with pepper nomenclature, *Piper retrofractum* is confusingly known as *P.offinicarum* and *P.chabas* too. Interestingly, long pepper is also found in North and East Africa, where it was no doubt introduced by Arab traders.

A member of the *Piperaceae* family, long pepper comes from a tropical climber similar to the ordinary pepper vine (*Piper nigrum*) but with less foliage. The slender greyish-black fruits are between 3cm and 6cm long and are made up of tiny teardrop-shaped seeds fused together in a cartwheel-like arrangement around a central spike. The Javanese variety is larger than the Indian and is generally considered the better quality. It is certainly more pungent.

Long pepper was used in Indian cuisine as far back as 2000BC. It reached Europe earlier than black pepper and was the first pepper to be mentioned in the classical texts of ancient Greece and Rome. Pliny the Elder (24–79AD), author of the monumental *Natural History*, mentioned that long pepper cost nearly four times more than black pepper.

Long pepper shows up time and again in medieval cookery manuscripts and those from the renaissance period. John Gerard (1545–1612) the herbalist, wrote in his *Herball, Generall Historie of Plants* 'It is in taste sharper and hotter than common black pepper, yet sweeter and of a better taste'. By the late 16th and early 17th century long pepper was easy to get hold of and the price had inevitably dropped – by then it was a twelfth of the price for black pepper.

Being both pungent and sweet, long pepper has a different flavour to black pepper, as contemporary cooks appreciated. They often used both types of pepper in the same recipe, as in this 14th-century Italian spice mix: 'take half a quarter of cloves and two onze of pepper, and take the same amount of long pepper and two nutmegs; this will serve for all spices'.

Dishes of meat and fish in aspic jelly were hugely fashionable – the aspic possibly being more important than the food it imprisoned. Cooks would go to great lengths to show off their skills, tinting the jelly with beautiful colours and doctoring it with exotic seasonings, including long pepper.

It is evident from antique cookbooks that the French were keen on long pepper too; it shows up in numerous recipes, both sweet and savoury. A particularly potent mix for seasoning pastry includes generous amounts of long pepper and black pepper, as well as cloves, ginger and other pungent spices. The mix is recommended 'not only for pastry, but also for seasoning all sorts of ground meat mixtures, both lean and fat; larding strips, meat, poultry and all kind of stews'.

the forgotten spice

Despite its early popularity, long pepper gradually fell from use. Food historians Philip and Mary Hyman suggest that this may have had something to do with the discovery of the New World and the arrival of chillies from America. European cooks may not have felt the need for two hot spices, so perhaps gave up on long pepper. Another idea is that long pepper didn't travel well. It contains more moisture than black pepper, so was subject to mould if not properly dried before shipping. Whatever the reason, by the late 19th century long pepper rarely gets a mention and *Law's Grocers Manual* declares it 'unknown to the modern grocery trade'.

long pepper and medicine

Though it lost pride of place in the kitchen, long pepper was nevertheless valued by the medical profession. Nicholas Culpeper, the 17th-century English herbalist, considered it 'more effectual in medicine' than black pepper and prescribed it 'to warm the stomach'.

In Indian ayurvedic medicine long pepper is still prescribed for a medley of ailments including coughs, respiratory infections, hiccups, piles, dyspepsia and anaemia. It is also thought to prolong life, improve intelligence and increase semen. Interestingly, a modern Saudi Arabian study showed that long pepper increased the sperm count and weight of reproductive organs in mice.

long pepper in the kitchen

Long pepper is not as well known in the West as it could be, although there are signs of a renaissance as leading chefs and food writers rediscover its versatility. Long pepper features mainly in the cuisines of India, Southeast Asia and parts of North and East Africa.

According to a medieval
legend, long pepper was
included in a gory recipe for
preparing the Hand of Glory.
The hand of a murderer's
corpse (preferably removed
while the body was still
hanging from the gallows) was
wrapped tightly in a shroud to
drain the blood and then
placed in an earthenware jar
with salt, long pepper and
saltpetre. After two weeks the
pickled hand was dried in the
sun or in an oven. When
sufficiently desiccated, the
stiffened hand was used as a
candle holder which was said
to paralyse the onlooker with
terror and make the holder
invisible.

Indian cooks use it to season delicious raw vegetable pickles
(achar), while Indonesians and Malays simmer it in slow-cooked
fragrant curries. In Ethiopia it's a highly valued spice cupboard
staple, traditionally added to mutton-based stews along with
black pepper, cloves and nutmeg.

Unlike black pepper, long pepper is both pungent and sweet –
similar to a mixture of white pepper and nutmeg or cardamom –
adding a particular quality to a dish. You can use it as well as, or
instead of, black pepper. The strangely sweet aroma has been
likened to 'a cross between incense and orris root powder',
having 'exceptional scents of violet, marshmallow and pine'.
In the mouth, long pepper is bitingly hot with a not unpleasant
numbing tingling aftertaste.

I love to use long pepper in sweet dishes, particularly creamy
puddings and fruit desserts. The broken spikes are superb in
Caramelised Pineapple with Long Pepper and Lime Syrup (page
209). I have also used them to spike a flamboyant cocktail of
Pomegranate and Pepper Juice (page 184). Coarsely ground
long pepper gives a warm spiciness to Chicken Liver Pâté (page
195). It's also good mixed with mashed potato, or sprinkled with
sea salt flakes over crushed roast new potatoes.

grinding

The elongated shape makes long pepper difficult to use in a
conventional spindle-driven mill, but it can be easily ground in mills
fitted with an adjustable Crushgrind® mechanism since there is
no central spindle to get in the way. Alternatively, you can break
each spike into two or three pieces and bash them with a pestle.

buying and storing

Long pepper is becoming easier to get hold of as interest in
pepper grows. The most likely sources are specialist spice
shops and web mail order companies. Kept in a dry, airtight
container away from light, it will keep its delicious aroma and
flavour for up to two years.

See also
Grinding, Crushing, Cracking, page 83
Pepper and Passion, page 72
Sources, page 248

cubeb pepper

Piper cubeba

A member of the *piperaceae* family, cubeb pepper is the fruit of a tropical climbing vine grown mostly in Java and Sumatra. Compared with India's voluptuous Tellicherry peppercorn, the cubeb has a distinctly rough-and-ready demeanour with wizened skin and a thin brittle stalk protruding from one end. Not surprisingly, it is also known as the 'tailed' pepper, which gives rise to some confusion with other tailed peppers: Ashanti pepper or 'false cubeb' (*Piper guineense*) and Benin pepper (*Piper clusii*) from Africa, and also *tsiperifery*, a rare and delicious wild pepper from Madagascar.

Cubebs, as they are usually called, were traded by Arab merchants as early as the seventh century, and by the Middle Ages had found their way to Europe via the Middle Eastern port of Aden and then Venice. At a time when the price of black pepper was sky-high, cubebs were a popular alternative. They were put to good use both in the kitchen and the apothecary's shop, showing up in mysterious remedies and potions, and in fifteenth-century recipes for sauces and meaty stews. They were also candied and eaten whole, probably as a breath freshener. Later, at the end of the seventeenth century, cubebs fell out of favour as black pepper prices dropped and people could afford to buy it.

We can sense the importance of cubebs in *The Land of Cockayne*, an anonymous poem written in the early fourteenth century, when starvation was a grim reality in medieval Europe. An exercise in wishful thinking, the poem describes a utopian world in which rivers flow with wine, houses are built of cake and barley sugar, streets are paved with pastry and cubebs and other spices are there for the asking:

In the meadow there is a tree, very fair to look upon.
Its roots are of ginger and galangal, the shoots of zedoary.
Its flowers are three pieces of mace, and the bark,
sweet-smelling cinnamon.
The fruit is the tasty clove, and of cubebs there is no lack.

shady connections

Derived from the Arabic *kababah*, the very name 'cubeb' conjures up images of faraway places and mysterious goings on. And indeed cubebs do have a somewhat shady history – they were thought to repel demons and were used in incense and spells. According to legend, cubebs were part of a cocktail of spices used to fumigate the cell of a young nun who was plagued by night-time visits from an incubus – a demon intent on having his way with her. The fumigation was a partial success in that the unwelcome visits stopped, but the incubus continued to stalk the nun once she left her cell, so stronger measures apparently had to be used.

As well as curbing demonic ardour, cubebs were used for the opposite effect in certain circumstances – they were believed to promote fertility and stir flagging libidos. Nowadays, cubebs are still popular with practitioners of hoodoo, an African-American form of traditional folk magic. A Californian occult store advertises them 'to control a lover and to increase sexual heat; will also help you meet a new mate'.

cubebs and medicine

Mumbo-jumbo apart, cubebs were valued by the medical profession and were used by Arab physicians as early as the ninth century and in Europe throughout the Middle Ages. However, they gradually disappeared from use, though there was a comeback in the 19th and early 20th centuries. Being strongly antiseptic, cubebs were an important treatment for gonorrhoea in pre-antibiotic days. They were considered less disagreeable than other remedies on offer, especially during prolonged treatment.

Cubebs were also valued as a remedy for flatulence and dyspepsia, and for catarrh and other respiratory afflictions. Curiously, until the 1940s there was even a cubeb cigarette for treating asthma and hay-fever – a remedy seemingly at odds with the affliction. Edgar Rice Burroughs, famous creator of Tarzan, apparently liked to smoke these as a student, although obviously not for the medicinal properties.

cubebs in the kitchen

Though not much used in the West today, cubebs are an everyday spice in Indonesian cuisine. Maintaining their Arab connection, they also feature in North African dishes such as lamb stews and tagines, and in the complex Moroccan spice mixture *Ras el Hanout*.

Compared with black pepper, cubebs are not as bitingly hot. They have a distinctive aroma – slightly sweet and camphorous with a hint of nutmeg. The flavour of a raw berry is fresh and piny – a bit like mouthwash – with a bitter taste that lingers in the mouth. This doesn't sound too promising, but once cooked, the berry develops a much fuller flavour with a pleasant rounded spiciness.

Because of their assertive flavour, I find cubebs are best in meat dishes, particularly slow-cooked stews, although Gérard Vives, chef and pepper aficionado from France, recommends them with game birds, *foie gras* and even in apricot or citrus sorbets. You can use them instead of Jamaica pepper (allspice) in spicy cakes and biscuits when you want a little extra hit of heat. Or replace the white pepper in Quatre Épices (page 230) with cubeb pepper and use the mixture to flavour a terrine or pâté.

buying and storing

Cubebs, along with other exotics such as long pepper and grains of paradise, are becoming easier to get hold of as interest in pepper grows. Specialist spice shops and web mail order companies are the best hunting grounds. Buy a small amount at a time and grind the berries as needed.

Cubebs hold their flavour and aroma for a year or two as long as you store them away from light and in an airtight container.

See also
Exotics Tasting Notes, page 79
Sources, page 248

grains of paradise

Aframomum melegueta
Aframomum granum-paradisi

p e p p e r

With such a hauntingly beautiful name, this magnificent African spice instantly conjures up thoughts of exotic faraway places; in medieval times people really did think it had come from an earthly paradise. As inspiring as the name is the flavour – a complex and heady mix of ginger, black pepper, nutmeg and cardamom, albeit without the camphoric notes of the latter. The grains are pungent like pepper, with aromatic essential oils similar to those found in allspice and cloves.

Also known as 'melegueta pepper' and 'alligator pepper', the grains are in fact unrelated to true pepper. They belong to the *Zingiberaceae* (ginger) family and, unlike pepper, are the fruits of a rhizome rather than a climbing vine. Native to the tropical west coast of Africa and parts of the Caribbean, the plant thrives in the wild but is also cultivated commercially in Ghana, the chief country of export.

The rhizomes sprout long reed-like stems with flamboyant pink flower trumpets growing from the base. Once the flowers die back, the plant produces large oval capsules inside which are the grains – tiny fig-shaped seeds with a reddish brown skin and white interior.

Grains of paradise were hugely popular in medieval times when the demand for spices was high but the sea route to India and the eastern Spice Islands had not yet been discovered. The spice made an epic journey by camel along ancient routes leading from Africa's Guinea coast across the Sahara to the Mediterranean ports in the north. From there, it found its way to Europe where it was highly prized as a medicine and a seasoning, showing up in numerous medieval recipes.

Grains of paradise went into the standard spice mix for *hippocras* – a sweetened wine which was popular as a pick-me-up and a postprandial drink. Chaucer mentions the grains, and the spice mix, in his translation of *Romance of the Rose*, an epic 13th-century French poem that was a best-seller at the time:

> There was eke waxing many a spice,
> As clowe gilofre and Licorice,
> Ginger and grein de Paradis,
> Canell and setewale of pris,
> And many a spice delitable
> To eaten when men rise from table.

Though highly coveted in medieval kitchens, grains of paradise were later abandoned during the Renaissance as the price of pepper dropped. The spice remained popular with the herbalists and apothecaries, however, and was still used to flavour wine and beer.

Herbalist John Gerard (1597) wrote: 'The grains chewed in the mouth draw forth from the head and stomacke waterish pituitous humours.... They also comfort and warme the weake, cold and feeble stomacke, helpe the ague, and rid the shaking fits, being drunk with Sacke'.

Back in Africa, grains of paradise were a staple seasoning and a folk medicine, so important that the Grain Coast was named after them. The story goes that slave traders, showing uncustomary benignancy, always made sure there were adequate supplies of the grain for the slaves packed on the ships heading for the New World.

grains in the kitchen

In Ghana and neighbouring countries, African cooks use generous amounts of the grains as an everyday seasoning. It goes into an incendiary blend of black and white peppercorns, cubeb pepper, chillies, allspice and ginger (page 234), used as a dry rub for grilled meats, as a table condiment, or as an all-purpose seasoning for soups and stews. Outside the region of production, the grains are one of many spices used in the complex Moroccan seasoning *Ras el Hanout*. They also feature in the sweetly pungent Tunisian five-spice seasoning *Qalat Daqqa* (page 230).

In the west, grains of paradise are deservedly coming back into use, thanks to food writers and chefs who are at last rediscovering the remarkable flavour. Enormously versatile, the spice is equally at home in savoury dishes as in cakes and desserts. Though pungent, it has more subtlety than pepper, and goes well with vegetables and lighter foods such as fish and chicken. Try it in a creamy parsnip gratin (page 170) or use to replace black pepper in Stir-Fried Butternut Squash and Shiitake Mushrooms (page 166). The grains are especially good sprinkled over pan-fried halibut with a dribble of oil and lemon.

Finely ground, the grains perk up mild dishes such as tabouleh and couscous, and make an excellent seasoning for pasta and risotto. They also add a bit of zest to a traditional

syrup of grains of paradise and rosemary

In a small saucepan, dissolve 150g/5^{1}/$_{2}$oz sugar in 125ml/4 fl oz of water and 175ml/6 fl oz of dry white wine. Add 3 tbsp rosemary leaves, 1 tbsp chopped fresh ginger, 2 tsp crushed grains of paradise and about 2 tbsp good quality balsamic vinegar. Bring to the boil then reduce the heat and simmer partly covered for 10 minutes. Allow to cool, then taste, adjusting sweetness and acidity as necessary. Leave to steep for longer if you want a stronger flavour. Strain through a fine-meshed sieve, then store in the fridge. Serve over ice cream or fruit.
Recipe: John Ash

Bolognese sauce. I particularly like to see them crushed and displaying their snowy white centres in a deep garnet Bloody Mary cocktail (page 187).

Moving on to desserts, John Ash, Culinary Director of Fetzer Vineyards in California, combines the grains with rosemary in an exotic syrup for spooning over ice cream or strawberries (see left). They are superb in a filling for pumpkin pie or in a moist spicy pumpkin cake (page 215). Best of all, though, are dark and peppery chocolate truffles coated in a sparkling frost of caster sugar and finely ground grains of paradise (page 205).

buying and storing

Grains of paradise are becoming easier to find but are still not as widely available as they might be. The best hunting grounds are West Indian or African stores (look for the whole dried pods), or specialist spice shops and mail order companies such as Seasoned Pioneers.

It's interesting to mix grains of paradise with peppercorns, or with cardamom and fragments of nutmeg, in the same mill; or even have a dedicated mill if you like the flavour.

Grind the grains as you need them, and add an extra sprinkling just before serving; that way you get another whiff of the blissful aroma.

Stored in an airtight container away from heat and light, the grains will keep for two or three years.

See also
Spice Blends, Seasonings and Sauces, page 225
Sources, page 248

sichuan pepper and sansho

Zanthoxylum simulans and *Zanthoxylum piperitum*

These closely related species come from two types of prickly ash tree native to the mountainous regions of south and central China, Japan, Southeast Asia and India. Sichuan or Szechwan pepper (*Zanthoxylum simulans* image, far-left) takes its name from the cuisine of the Sichuan province of southwest China – a damp and rainy part of the world known for its spicy food. Sansho (*Zanthoxylum piperitum* image, near-left) comes from Japan and is one of the few spices used in the cuisine.

The spice is completely unrelated to the pepper family (*Piperaceae*), though like a number of 'non-peppers' it has adopted the archetypal name. It is also called flower pepper, Indonesian lemon pepper, Japanese pepper, and sometimes, mistakenly, 'fagara', a different species of prickly ash native to parts of the United States.

The tree produces berries, or fruits, which split open when ripe, rather like a beech bud. The dried fruits are an attractive pinkish-brown with short thin stems and a hard shiny black seed inside. Surprisingly, all the flavour is in the outer husks; the seeds don't taste of much and are usually discarded. In Japan, where nothing goes to waste, the leaves and flowers are used in preference to the husks, which are considered too rough-and-ready for the delicate simple food. The young leaves are used fresh (kinome), or dried and ground (sansho).

Sichuan pepper has a wonderfully addictive buzz. The heady aroma from a freshly opened jar and the sensation that comes from nibbling one of the tiny husks are enough to induce mild euphoria. At first the spice delivers an intense citrus woodsy flavour, sweetish to begin with, then resinous, and then slightly acidic like lemon sherbet. It is not hot, containing neither piperine nor any of the essential oils that give true pepper (*Piper nigrum*) its characteristic aroma and flavour. However, as the late American food guru Waverley Root wrote: '(Sichuan pepper) lets itself be swallowed innocently and then smites you with a heat wave when you are off your guard'.

What Root was talking about is the delayed action – a curious numbing tingle rather than a burn – that spreads over the tongue and lips. Chewed once or twice, the effect is mild and you may wonder at first why nothing is happening; chewed for longer, the effect is much stronger and takes some getting used to. The numbing sensation is known as *ma* in Chinese which means 'anaesthetic' and 'pins-and-needles'. It is caused by chemical compounds known as sanshools which are thought to react with taste receptors on the tongue and around the lips.

For many years American
lovers of Sichuan food had to
risk cloak and dagger tactics
to get hold of Sichuan pepper,
thanks to a long-standing ban
on imports enforced by the
United States Department of
Agriculture. The pepper was
thought to host an insect
capable of carrying a
bacterium, which, while not
harmful to humans, causes
citrus canker which could
potentially devastate US citrus
crops. The ban has now been
lifted provided Sichuan
peppercorns are heated to
70°C before importation.

Fuchsia Dunlop is the only non-Chinese and female student to
graduate from the cooking school in Sichuan's capital Chengdu,
and as such, is the acknowledged western diva of Sichuan cooking.
In her authoritative book *Sichuan Cookery* Fuchsia explains that
the numbing effect comes only from good quality Sichuan pepper.
The finest grows in the mountains of Hanyuan county where
local people say its fragrance is so strong that you can rub the
raw spice on to your palm and still smell it on the back of your
hand, through skin and bone. Pepper from Hanyuan was used
as a scent before it became a cooking spice, and it was so highly
prized that it was offered in tribute to the emperors of China.

sichuan and sansho in the kitchen

Sichuan pepper is usually roasted or dry-fried to release the
aromatic oils (see opposite) before using in other dishes.
This really does make a difference – it tames the tingling and
produces a noticeably more mellow flavour. Roasted and ground,
the spice is an essential ingredient in Chinese Five-Spice Blend
(page 231) and in the memorable Sichuan classic, Pock-Marked
Mother Chen's Beancurd (page 176). It is also traditionally mixed
with rock salt and sometimes other spices for use as a spicy
condiment or dip (page 194).

Whole husks fried in oil add their delectable spiciness to wok-
cooked dishes – the fresh lemony zing is perfect for fatty meats
like duck and pork. You can also use the cooled flavoured oil to
dribble over Asian-style noodle salads. For a fantastically fragrant
and numbing sauce for cold meat or poultry, pound whole uncooked
husks (minus stems and seeds) with spring onions and sea salt,
then stir in a dash of soy sauce and sesame oil. As Fuchsia advises,
this is only worth making if you have top quality pepper bursting
with fragrance.

Sichuan pepper is one of the very few spices that grow in
Tibet where it is known as *yerma*. Cooks there use it to give
zest to soups, sausages and tasty raw vegetable pickle. It also
goes into sheep's head stew (*luggo*), an important national dish
served on New Year's Day.

In Japan, ground sansho adds mild heat to noodles and soups.
It is one of the seven spices in the Japanese seasoning *shichimi
togarashi*, a blend which typically includes sansho, chilli flakes,
black and white sesame seeds, powdered tangerine peel, ginger
and dried seaweed. I like to use a smidgen of this in a dressing

dry-frying sichuan pepper
Heat a wok or heavy pan over medium heat. Add the husks in a single layer then stir for about 3 minutes until fragrant and on the point of smoking. Take care not to let the husks burn. Remove from pan and leave to cool before grinding.

for noodle-based salads or sprinkle it over plainly boiled rice. Tasting faintly of seaweed it also makes an excellent seasoning for grilled fish and seafood.

My Japanese food-writer friend, Emi Kazuko, tells me that in early spring small tender sansho leaves are used as a fragrant garnish for clear soups. The leaves also add vibrant colour to pale vegetables such as bamboo shoots, which emerge at the same time of year, or daikon slowly simmered in clear stock. Later in spring, the flavour becomes stronger and tiny greenish yellow flowers come into bloom. These are floated in soups or used as an exquisite garnish for grilled fish or poultry. The split husks develop in September and these occasionally appear in ready-made dishes, such as long-simmered kelp in soy sauce, to be eaten with rice.

buying and storing

According to Fuchsia Dunlop, most Sichuan pepper sold in UK Chinese supermarkets is not worth considering. Instead she recommends Bart Spices Sichuan pepper, widely available, or ordering it from the Cool Chile Company. Pepper from Seasoned Pioneers is also good quality, available by mail order or from specialist shops and supermarkets.

Top-notch Sichuan pepper should consist of husks only, so check the packet for stemmy detritus. There will inevitably be a few black seeds which can be removed by sieving. Don't allow any seeds to infiltrate husks that you intend to grind; they become unpleasantly gritty and stick in your teeth.

Stored in an airtight container away from light, the husks should last a year or two. However, sansho powder loses its flavour more quickly and will last only a few months. Believe me, there are few things more unpleasant than stale sansho.

It's rare to find fresh sansho leaves outside Japan, and even there the season is short. However, if you happen to come across some in an Asian store, keep them tightly sealed in a plastic bag in the fridge and they should last for several days.

See also
Spice Blends, Seasonings and Sauces, page 225
Sources, page 248

pink pepper

Schinus terebinthifolius
Schinus molle

Hailed as 'the food fancy of the 1980s' at the French Fancy Food Show, pink peppercorns were the seasoning of choice during the heady days of nouvelle cuisine. Valued more for appearance than flavour, the vibrant rosy-pink berries found their way into every dish imaginable. Nowadays they are most often seen in the company of black, white and green peppercorns in clear perspex pepper mills, again added for glamour rather than flavour.

Despite the name, pink peppercorns are not a member of the pepper family and do not taste in the least peppery. They are often confused with true red peppercorns, the fully ripe berries of *Piper nigrum*, although the differences in size, texture and flavour are fairly apparent. The pink variety are smaller with a brittle outer husk that dents easily and is separate from the small seed inside, whereas true red peppercorns have a large seed tightly packed in the husk.

Pink peppercorns are pungent, yes, but they contain neither piperine nor the essential oils that give true pepper its unmistakable aroma and flavour. They have no noticeable aroma until crushed – then they reveal complex layers of unique flavours, intensely fruity and sweet to begin with, then spicy and pungent with resinous notes of juniper, pine and aniseed. The botanical name *terebinthifolius* is derived from the Latin *terebinth* meaning 'turpentine' and there is certainly a hint of that too.

Unlike true pepper, pink pepper grows on a tree rather than a vine and the berries grow in clusters rather than spikes. The better-known species, *Schinus terebinthifolius*, is native to the Indian Ocean islands of Réunion and Mauritius where it is grown commercially. It is also indigenous to Brazil, and was later introduced to Florida where it was initially valued as an ornamental and shade tree but now grows so rampantly is considered something of a pest.

The leaves are glossy and pointed, rather like bay leaves, while the fruits grow in thick upright clusters or panicles, ripening from green to yellow to vibrant pinky red. The French call them 'baies roses', 'poivre rose' or 'poivre de Bourbon', the old name for Réunion. Other common names are Brazilian pepper, Christmas berry, Florida holly. These are the pink or red peppercorns normally found in the shops

The less familiar *Schinus molle* is native to Peru and Mexico. Introduced into Southern California in the mid 16th century, it also found its way to Spain and from there to other Mediterranean countries where it grows prolifically. A sub-variety (*Schinus molle var. areira*) is rampant in dry areas of Southern Australia, New South Wales and Victoria where it is subject to an eradication programme, although its shade is appreciated by humans and livestock alike. With a willowy demeanour and long frond-like leaves, the tree is easily distinguishable from *Schinus terebinthifolius*. The fruits, which hang in loose downward-facing bunches, have a similar flavour but possibly with a more pronounced turpentine aftertaste.

pink pepper panic

In the 1970s, when chefs used pink pepper with reckless abandon, there were reports in the United States of it causing respiratory and intestinal irritation due to allergens and terpenes found in the essential oil. Imports of pink pepper were banned, resulting in howls of protest from chefs and foodies. Following extensive analysis, the spice was subsequently reinstated. Scientists agreed that the levels present in *Schinus terebinthifolius* were too low to be a hazard in the amounts that would normally be used in a recipe, although some cookbooks still recommend caution.

pink pepper in the kitchen

A distinctive seasoning in its own right, pink pepper shouldn't be thought of as a substitute for true pepper or even as a partner; the flavours simply do not sit easily together. It is at its best with lighter foods – poultry, fish and vegetables, for example. Try crushing the berries with sea salt and diced ginger to make a coating for butter-sizzled salmon steaks. Or use it instead of juniper in marinades for pork and game. Just a few lightly crushed berries taste and look excellent sprinkled over slices of creamy buffalo mozzarella, along with sea salt flakes and a dribble of golden olive oil.

With its sweet hint of pine and aniseed, pink pepper adds a certain something to syrups, fruit sauces and jellies. The berries are stunning in a sparkling rosy pink quince jelly (page 189), adding just the right amount of warm spiciness. They are also good in biscuits and cakes – try them with white chocolate in irresistible Pink Pepper Blondies (page 212), or instead of black pepper in Cantucinni (page 220).

buying and storing

You often find pink pepper cured in brine or vinegar which I think overwhelms the flavour and dulls the colour. If you do buy the brine-cured berries check the label to make sure they are not true red peppercorns (*Piper nigrum*).

For the best colour and flavour look for organic freeze-dried berries, easily recognisable by the brittle skin. Being slightly soft and naturally oily, dried berries tend to clog the pepper mill, so they are better crushed with a mortar and pestle or the blade of a large knife. Keep them in an airtight container away from heat and light.

See also
Red Peppercorns, page 32
Sources, page 248

allspice

(also known as pimento, Jamaica pepper, English pepper, myrtle pepper)
Pimenta dioica

p e p p e r

Though not a member of the pepper family and not particularly peppery, allspice played a key role in the early Spanish explorers' quest for pepper, and as such, deserves a mention. It is unique in that it is the only spice grown almost exclusively in the western hemisphere, and, as a pepper look-alike, it lies at the heart of the confusion between peppercorns and chillies.

As most people know, Columbus's voyage of 1492 culminated in the discovery of the New World rather than a westerly route to the Spice Islands. The story goes that on reaching Cuba, Columbus showed a bag of peppercorns to the natives and they, in turn, pointed him towards an allspice tree. Thinking he had discovered the much-coveted pepper he was after, Columbus named the tree and its berries *pimienta*, the Spanish word for pepper. (Adding to the confusion, he, and fellow Spanish explorers, referred to all natives as 'Indians' regardless of the country in which they were encountered.) *Pimienta* was eventually corrupted to *pimento*, although nowadays this is a term more often used in reference to the leaf rather than the berry.

The name allspice reflects the complex flavour of the berry, said to resemble a mixture of cloves, cinnamon, nutmeg and black pepper. The clove element is unmistakable since both cloves and allspice contain the essential oil eugenol. There is certainly a hint of pepper, but cinnamon and nutmeg are barely obvious in the whole berry, although slightly more so in the ground spice. There is further confusion over allspice and 'mixed spice', a ground spice blend used in baking. The blend includes allspice, but contains other sweet spices as well.

pimenta, pimienta or pimiento?

The confusion is ongoing and stems from the Spanish explorers' erroneous belief that pimento (allspice) berries were the same as pepper. The following list (in Spanish) is an attempt to put the record straight:

Pimento, pimenta allspice
Pimentón paprika (powder)
Pimienta (fem.) peppercorn (*Piper nigrum*)
Pimienta dulce (fem.) sweet pepper (but also means allspice)
Pimienta inglesa allspice
Pimienta picante (fem.) hot pepper, chilli
Pimiento (masc.) sweet and hot peppers (*Capsicum annuum*)
Pimiento dulce (masc.) sweet paprika

Allspice is indigenous to Central America and the West Indies, particularly Jamaica – home to the best quality and quantity, and the reason for yet another name, 'Jamaica pepper'. Unlike true pepper (*Piper nigrum*), allspice grows on a bushy evergreen tree rather than a climbing vine, and the flowers and fruits grow in clusters rather than spikes. Once dried though, the fruits look very similar to peppercorns albeit more buxom and with fewer wrinkles.

The trees are a magnificent sight, particularly in summer when they are blanketed in aromatic white flowers. They grow in the wild in coastal regions of Jamaica, but, since allspice is a major export, they are also cultivated in plantations. The plantations were traditionally called 'walks'; to take a 'pimento walk' was to stroll through a plantation. Botanist Patrick Browne wrote in 1755: 'nothing can be more delicious than the odour of these walks, when the trees are in bloom, as well as other times; the friction of the leaves and small branches even in a gentle breeze diffusing a most exhilarating scent'.

Europe started importing allspice soon after discovery of the New World but the spice never really caught on. Despite the distinctive flavour and large berries, people simply did not covet it in the same way as pepper and other spices from the exotic east. And in the years to come, New World products such as coffee and tea became the latest 'must-haves' and eclipsed any hope of allspice achieving the same status. That said, allspice had and still has its loyal fans.

allspice in the kitchen

It goes without saying that the spice features strongly in Jamaican cuisine, though you'd be hard put to find it in the shops. It is an essential ingredient in *escabeche* – a palate-tingling dish of raw fish preserved in lemon juice or vinegar with onions, chillies and spices. It is also used in jerk seasoning, a fiery paste for rubbing into goat, mutton and other hearty meats before barbecuing.

In the UK and North America, a jar of allspice is usually tucked away in every spice cupboard, ready for sprinkling into cake mixtures, desserts and pies. Wary though they may be of spices, the French include allspice in Quatre Épices (page 230), a traditional seasoning for sausages, pâtés and cured meats.

The Scandinavians add it to pickled herrings and the Germans to *sauerkraut*. Allspice even turns up in the Middle East – it is an essential flavouring in Turkish and Lebanese cuisine, adding unmistakable fragrance to stuffed vegetables, rice, meat dishes and desserts. Going further east still, allspice is a standard ingredient in *berbere*, a traditional Ethiopian spice blend.

Allspice is strongly aromatic, slightly peppery and woodsy. Chewing a whole berry produces a strong flavour of cloves and a slight anaesthetised feel in the mouth, reminiscent of childhood toothache. Mixed with different types of pepper, allspice makes a tasty addition to the spice mill. On its own, it adds a delicious warm spiciness to sweet dishes, cakes and biscuits.

buying and storing

Like pepper, allspice is best bought whole and freshly ground when needed. Ready-ground allspice quickly loses its flavour and tastes stale. Kept in an airtight container away from heat and light, the berries should last for a year or two.

the greater pepper family

The *Piperaceae* family is a truly extended one with exotic and little-known relatives scattered in far-away places. The family includes more than two thousand species in addition to ordinary pepper (*Piper nigrum*). The better known, such as long pepper and cubeb pepper, are discussed in greater detail on the preceding pages; some of the more obscure types are described below.

In many cases it is the aromatic leaves, rather than the berries, that are used, either chopped up as a seasoning, or left whole and used as a wrapper for other foods. Some are used in medicines and herbal tisanes, or even to make snuff. Most of these species are uncultivated; they grow locally in the wild and are hard to find outside their region of origin. However, they occasionally show up in stores selling Asian, Indian and African groceries. Fresh leaves can be

Species	Common name	Habitat	Description
Piper amalago	Rough-leaved pepper	Jamaica	Minute seeds have the same flavour and pungency as black pepper. Used as a seasoning and a herbal medicine.
Piper auritum	Mexican pepperleaf, sacred pepper, false kava	Central America	Leaves slightly pungent with hint of mint and aniseed. Good for seasoning tamales, sauces, and as a wrapper for steamed or baked fish and chicken. Cinnamon-scented berries make an aromatic condiment.
Piper betle	Betel pepper	India, Indonesia, Malaysia, Africa	Leaves wrapped round betel nuts and chewed to sweeten the breath. The practice of continual chewing can cause tooth loss, mouth cancer, digestive upsets.
Piper guineense	Ashanti pepper, false cubeb	West Africa	Milder flavour than black pepper, used in same way as a versatile seasoning. Ashes from the burning plant used as a salt substitute.
Piper methysticum	Kava-kava	Micronesia	Euphoria-inducing drink is made from the roots for use in political and religious rituals.
Piper pellucidum	Cresson	Central America, West Indies	Pungent leaves chopped and added to an oil and vinegar dressing for green salads.
Piper sarmentosum	Lá lót	Thailand, Vietnam	Leaves make a wrapper for small tasty snacks, spring rolls, and strips of beef for the barbecue. They are also chopped and added to soups.
Piper umbellatum	Santa Maria leaf	Jamaica	An ingredient in a syrup to treat colds and catarrh. Roots are an antidote to poison.

frozen and are worth buying if you come across them.

As well as the *Piperaceae*, there are other families whose species have similar flavours to ordinary pepper. A member of the *Zingiberaceae* (ginger) family is the evocatively named grains of paradise, while the A*nnonaceae* (custard apple) family includes the negro pepper, otherwise known as grains of Selim, Senegal pepper and Guinea pepper – causing potential confusion with *Piper Guineense* (Ashanti pepper – see table opposite).

In a class of their own are those that produce a pleasant tingling on the lips followed by a curious numbing sensation that is usually short-lived. The best known is Sichuan pepper but there are others such as mountain pepper and water pepper.

Dried mountain pepper leaves and berries are reasonably easy to find in food halls and specialist spice shops, but you will have to go to Australia for the fresh leaves and berries. There, mountain pepper is an up-and-coming native bush food, popular with macho chefs; they like to use the intensely pungent berries in a power-packed seasoning for emu and kangaroo steaks. Water pepper, though its habitat is wide ranging, is rarely used in cooking outside Japan.

See also
Cubeb Pepper, page 38
Grains of Paradise, page 42
Long Pepper, page 34
Sichuan Pepper, page 46

Species	Common name	Habitat	Description
Polygonum hydropiper	Water pepper, marsh pepper	Europe, Asia, North America, North Africa	Leaves are slightly pungent with pleasant seaweedy smell. In Japan, they are sliced and mixed with soy sauce to garnish *sashimi*. Numbingly pungent seeds were a substitute for black pepper during shortages after world war two.
Tasmannia lanceolata	Mountain pepper, Tasmanian pepper	Tasmania, southeast Australia	Leaves and berries used fresh or dried. Leaves have a woody lemony flavour. Berries are sweet at first then intensely pungent and numbing – to be used with care.
Xylopia aethiopica	Negro pepper, grains of Selim, moor pepper, Senegal pepper	Tropical Africa	Berries are encased in curved pods 2.5–5cm long, about 5–8 per pod. They are aromatic, fairly pungent and slightly bitter. Immature pods are green, and grow in finger-like clusters, becoming dark brown when dried. Used locally in meat and vegetable dishes. Was also a substitute for black pepper during shortages after World War Two.

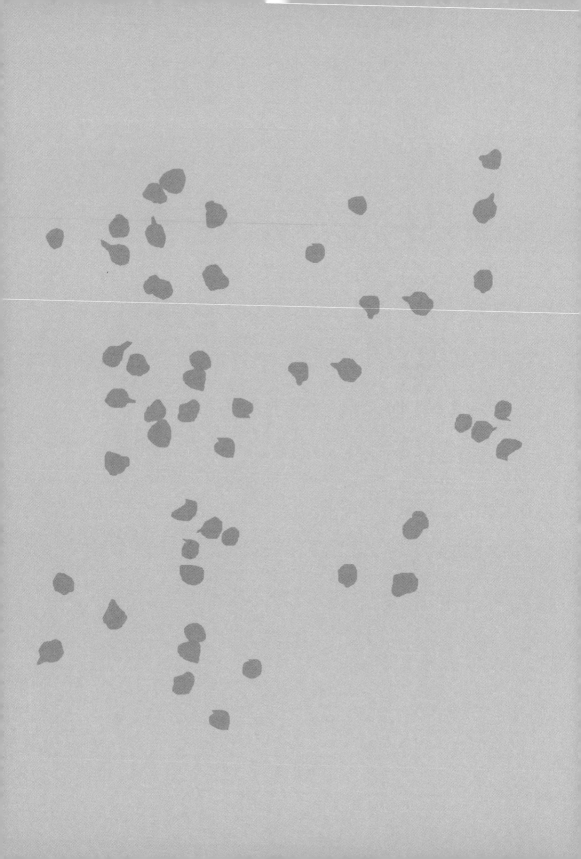

the pepper trade

62   pepper as a commodity

64   pepper names

pepper as a commodity

Though pepper has lost its historic charisma and is traded on the stock market just like any other commodity, it is still witness to the dramas of stiff competition, production problems and stomach-churning price fluctuations.

Pepper production shot up in the last fifteen years once Vietnam entered the market and, along with Brazil, established acre upon acre of new plantations, ripping up forests and farmland in the process. Vietnam is now the world's largest pepper producer (estimated production 100,000 tons for 2004), followed by India (62,000 tons) and Indonesia (55,000 tons). China and Indonesia also stepped up their output, and at the same time there was a worldwide steady increase in the overall area of land devoted to pepper cultivation. Encouraged by the high prices of the late 1990s, countless small farmers expanded their plantations in the hope of easy riches. As a result, global pepper production peaked at 362,160 metric tons in 2003 – an increase of just over 100% since 1991 – with a consequent glut and decline in prices.

A surplus in supply results in the build up of 'carryover' stocks – farmers and traders can stockpile pepper until market conditions become favourable again. However, this has to be weighed up against the risk of loss of quality; even when peppercorns are properly stored, piperine and essential oil levels drop after a few months.

Since peaking in 2003 world pepper prices and output have continued to fluctuate. Because of good carryover stocks, Indonesian output is on the increase, and Vietnam continues to lead the field. However, a substantial shortage in overall world supply is expected for 2007 as erratic weather and persistent diseases continue to wreak their havoc.

exports and imports

Over the past twenty years black pepper exports have seen an annual growth rate of 5%, with Vietnam, Brazil and Indonesia leading the field.

The United States is the world's largest importer and consumer of pepper. Curiously, India also imports significant amounts even though it is the longest-established pepper-producing country. Output per hectare remains relatively low, partly because farming techniques are less intensive than elsewhere; meanwhile, domestic demand continues to increase and imports become necessary.

The biggest importers in Europe are Germany and the Netherlands where a high proportion of pepper is used in commercial processing.

modern technology

In an age of fast-track free-flowing information, market prices are no secret – mobile phones and access to the internet are commonplace even in far-flung areas. Indeed, one of the unusual things I noticed while visiting plantations in India was the plethora of mobile phone masts and ISD phone booths in remote corners of the jungle. It was only later that I discovered that they had been installed to make sure that farmers have easy access to vital trading information.

Modern technology has made its mark on the epicentre of the Indian pepper trade, The Pepper Exchange at Fort Cochin. The faded building is situated in the historic Mantancherry district, a vibrant area of narrow streets crammed with spice shops and warehouses.

It was here that I met Mr Samson, Secretary of the Exchange, in his blissfully air-conditioned office. He explained that the Exchange is the only trading centre in the world where pepper is exclusively traded. At one time trading took place using the 'open outcry' system in which wildly gesticulating brokers bellowed their bids in native Malayalam over the phone. Once computers were installed in 2003 and trading subsequently carried out on-line, the cacophony lessened somewhat, but the Exchange is still a lively place. Trading had finished on the afternoon of my visit, and the trading area was cool and quiet. Even so, it was not hard to imagine the hubbub and excitement when the brokers start negotiations.

ancient trading techniques

In complete contrast to the computerised Exchange, a noisy pepper market takes place each morning in the blistering heat of a nearby street. Here, all trading is done with cash, and buyers and sellers 'negotiate' using ancient trading techniques. Hands are hidden under a cloth to escape the prying eyes of onlookers. Deals are done with subtle tapping and significant finger movements – a system that is impossible for an outsider to understand.

pepper products

Pepper is a spice from which other products are made. This makes sensible use of inferior grades of pepper, leaving the top-notch varieties for the export market.

pepper oil
This is a volatile essential oil extracted from black peppercorns by steam distillation. The oil has a wonderful peppery aroma but no pungency. It is mainly used as a food flavouring, particularly for sausages, soups and canned meats, but it has other interesting uses too. It goes into carnation-perfumed soaps and popular perfumes such as 'Charlie' by Revlon and 'Poison' by Christian Dior. Chemists at the Pepper Marketing Board in Sarawak have also developed two special pepper fragrances – 'Yang' and 'Rhea' – that are snapped up by tourists. As an essential oil, it is also used in the aromatherapy industry – black pepper oil is wonderfully potent and warming when added to a hot bath or used in a massage oil.

pepper oleoresin
As the name suggests, oleoresin is a blend of essential oil and resinous matter, including pungent components such as piperine. It possesses all the sensory properties of the spice – flavour, aroma, pungency – but in the form of a concentrated extract.

Oleoresin is mainly used for flavouring processed foods and is often preferred to the whole or ground spice. You'll find it in a remarkable number of products – pepper sauces, pepper mayonnaise, pepper tofu, pepper-flavoured crisps and crackers, and even in certain beverages and liqueurs.

The ever-inventive product developers at the Pepper Marketing Board in Sarawak have even come up with pepper candy made with glucose syrup, sugar and pepper oleoresin.

pepper and the food industry

It's probably true to say that pepper is used more than any other spice in the food industry, particularly in processed meat products, pickles and sauces.

Italian sausage-makers like to use Tellicherry pepper in their salamis – not just for flavour but for its distinctive appearance. The Germans, meticulous as ever, insist on the ultra-clean fast-dried peppercorns from Sarawak for their unique cold-cured sausages.

Pâtés and quiches come topped with peppercorns as does smoked mackerel. Green or black peppercorns add flavour to certain cheeses. White pepper gives bite to light-coloured sauces, soups and mayonnaise where dark flecks are considered undesirable. Cracked black pepper has become the ubiquitous seasoning for crisps, savoury biscuits, and, as product developers become more daring, certain sweet foods. Pepper chocolate has become *de rigueur* in certain circles as has pepper ice cream.

pepper names

The mysterious and evocative names used in the trade are an aspect of pepper that has always attracted me. Names like Muntok White, Tellicherry Extra Bold or Malabar Garbled were, and still are, deeply fascinating. They evoke images of far-away ports, shouting traders, sacks of spices and dimly lit warehouses. They are also a valuable lesson in geography, for pepper often takes the name of the region of origin, or the port from which it is exported, or the regional capital. Locate these places in an atlas and you will start to get an idea of pepper's far-reaching influence.

As with any crop where flavour is paramount, *terroir* – the local conditions of soil and climate – makes a difference to the peppercorn's physical and chemical make-up. There are variations in colour, size and skin texture, as well in the piperine and essential oil levels so vital for flavour and aroma.

The following list is not exhaustive but describes the key features of pedigree peppercorns named after their place of origin. They are described in more detail in Tasting Pepper, page 76.

lampong (1)
Indonesian black pepper from the Lampong/Lampung region on the southern tip of Sumatra. Uniformly small berries, dimpled, dark brown to black, highly pungent but not particularly aromatic.

malabar (2)
Good quality black pepper from Kerala's Malabar coast, in southwest India. Once known more precisely as Alleppey pepper, named after the picturesque backwater region south of Cochin where pepper trading takes place. Slightly wrinkled good-sized berries, dark brown, strongly pungent with a rich complex aroma.

muntok (3)
Indonesian white pepper from the tiny island of Bangka, east of Sumatra, named after the island's principal port, Muntok. The most important source of white pepper today. Good-sized berries ranging from cream to pale biscuit colour. Strongly pungent with a slightly fermented aroma.

sarawak (4 and 5)
Malaysian black and white pepper from the Sarawak region of northwest Borneo. Sarawak produces top-quality speciality pepper 'Sarawak Naturally Clean Black Pepper' and 'Sarawak Creamy White'.

Black peppercorns are small and wrinkled, ranging from mid-brown to black, fresh peppery aroma and mild pungency. White peppercorns are large, creamy white, strongly pungent with a clean aroma.

tellicherry (6)
Malabar black pepper grown near the port of Tellicherry (Thelassery). Widely accepted as the Rolls Royce of black pepper. Berries uniformly large, very dark brown and wrinkled, with mellow pungency and complex flavour. Aroma not very noticeable until peppercorn crushed.

1

2

3

4

5

6

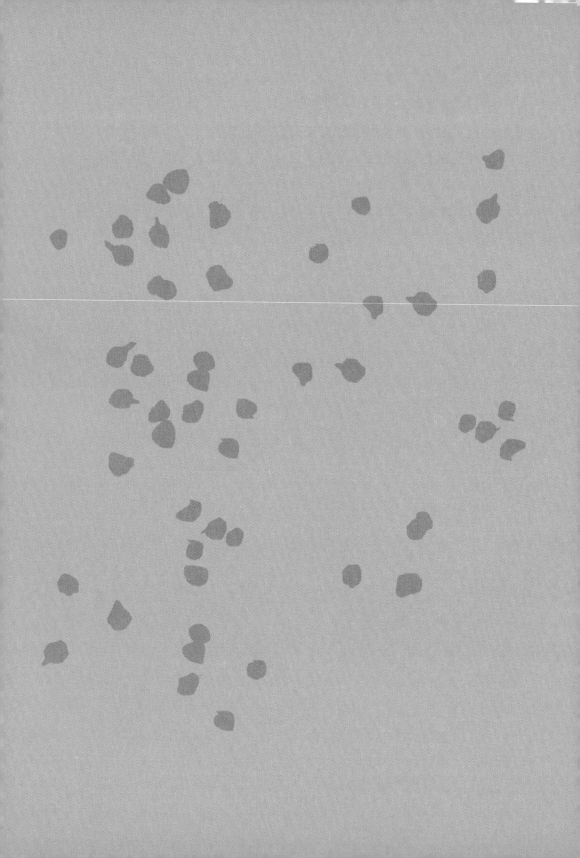

pepper and pungency

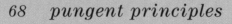

68   *pungent principles*

70   *pepper and health*

72   *pepper and passion*

pungent principles

The typical dictionary definition of pungency, 'having an acrid smell or sharp bitter flavour', does not sound particularly appetising. However, if we bear in mind that it is pungency which makes so many foods desirable, descriptions become more mouth-watering – tangy, zesty, spicy and piquant, for example. Nevertheless, pungency is still hard to define. Is it a flavour, a taste, or some other gustatory experience?

taste, aroma and flavour

To fully understand the pungent principle, as scientists call it, we must first consider the concept of taste, aroma and flavour. The three are closely connected, taste and flavour often being used interchangeably, but they are not the same. We experience the taste of food – sweet, salty, sour and so on – through thousands of taste buds on the tongue, inside the cheeks and at the back of the mouth. We detect aroma when we chew food. The cells in the lining at the back of the mouth capture the aromas and transmit them to the olfactory bulb, an organ behind the bridge of the nose. These chemical messages, and those from the taste buds, are transmitted to the brain which interprets them as flavour. If you have a cold and your sense of smell is reduced, your food will have little flavour although you may still be able to 'taste' it.

According to Dr John Prescott of the Sensory Science Research Centre in Otago, New Zealand, pungency is an important but often overlooked component of flavour. We experience it as a physical irritation produced by stimulation of the trigeminal nerve in the nose and mouth – think how pepper makes us sneeze, or onions make us cry. In many respects, pungency is as essential as the sense of taste in our appreciation of many foods, not just pepper and chillies. Think of ginger beer without the bite, a glass of wine without the sharpness, or horseradish and mustard without the heat; such foods would lose much of their defining qualities if they weren't pungent.

the slow burn

Pungency isn't an immediate sensation; it has a slow onset and a lingering effect ranging from mild sensations of warmth or irritation to blistering noxious pain. If you try White Pepper Shortbread (page 218) or Strawberry and Black Pepper Ice Cream (page 198) you might be lulled into thinking the pepper has been left out, but after a mouthful or two you'll notice a slow and delicious after-burn.

So what is it in pepper and chillies that causes the heat? In pepper it's a substance called piperine; in chillies it's capsaicin. The two produce different 'heat' sensations. Piperine seems to have more of a bite and its oral burn is relatively short-lived. Capsaicin is burning, lingering and invasive, sometimes bordering on sensory overload – any part of the body that comes in contact with it will feel the long-lasting effect. Measured in Scoville Units (the official measurement for determining the heat of capsaicin), the pungency of piperine is 'only' 200,000 SU, compared to 30 million SU for capsaicin from chillies.

need or addiction

Why do we like pungent foods? Is it need or addiction? As far as need goes, we read that pepper was used in pre-refrigeration days to mask the unwholesome flavour of less-than-fresh food (an issue hotly disputed by food historians). We also know that pepper was, and still is, traditionally used as a medicine, that it gets the digestive juices going and helps control unwelcome bacteria and moulds. The chilli has similar health-giving properties.

Both piperine and capsaicin promote sweating which in turn has a cooling effect. The typically pungent dishes of hot countries are therefore not only cultural – the beads of sweat they bring to the brow are essential for comfort. It's no accident that street vendors in India and Mexico sell cooling snacks of sliced fruit sprinkled with pepper or chilli.

Addiction comes into play once we move into the kitchen and there may well be a valid biochemical reason for this. When the body experiences the numbing bite of pepper or the lingering burn of chilli, it interprets this as pain. It reacts by secreting natural analgesics called endorphins. As well as controlling pain endorphins elevate the mood, producing a natural 'high', which may well explain the attraction. Pungent foods also satisfy the natural human craving for excitement, for the new and exotic, and they compensate for jaded palates.

piperine and essential oil

Pepper owes its pungency to piperine and its aroma to essential oil. It is the balance between the two that is key to distinguishing pepper of different qualities and from different sources. As I learned from tasting sessions, peppercorns from India's Malabar coast are wonderfully aromatic, thanks to an abundance of essential oil, whereas those from Malaysia and Indonesia tend to contain less essential oil and more piperine, making them pungent rather than aromatic.

To the scientists, piperine is an alkaloid with a formula of CHNO (interestingly, morphine shares the same formula but has different properties). Put more simply it is a chemical substance that gives pepper its pungent bite. It is found predominantly in the main body of the peppercorn rather than the outer husk. Weight for weight, white pepper, devoid of its husk, contains more piperine than black – up to 8% in some cases.

Unlike essential oil, piperine is non-volatile and doesn't evaporate when exposed to air or heat. For the cook, this means that the pungent flavour will last during cooking whereas the aroma is more fleeting. However, piperine is essentially tasteless until mixed with a liquid – saliva or cooking liquid, for example. With freshly milled pepper, you have to chew for a few seconds before piperine starts to make itself

felt. This delayed action is something not fully appreciated, but, to my mind, the slow burn makes pepper a more enjoyable gustatory experience than the full-blown assault of chillies.

Though known mainly for its pungency in food, piperine has other uses. A few drops go into brandy to give it a little kick, and it's also used in insecticides. Its health-promoting properties are the basis of several nutritional research studies.

Found mainly in the peppercorn's outer husk, essential oil is a chemical maze of terpenes, acids and aldehydes which gives pepper its unique aroma. Black pepper contains up to about 5% essential oil and long pepper 6%, whereas white pepper, lacking the outer husk, contains less than 1%.

The oil is volatile which means it evaporates when exposed to air or heat. An extra twist of the pepper mill just before serving will make up for aroma and flavour lost during cooking.

Of the oil's hundred different components, the main ones, regarding aroma, include pinenes, phellandrine, myrcene, and limonene. These names don't mean much to the non-scientist until you consider how pepper sometimes has a lemony, or pine-like flavour; then the complex business of flavour starts to make sense.

The relative proportions of chemicals in the oil depends on the type of pepper, where it is grown and the environmental conditions during the growing season and harvesting. Storage conditions have an effect too. This means that the aroma and flavour of a particular type of pepper may vary slightly from sample to sample, although the main characteristics remain broadly recognisable.

See also
Pepper and Health, page 70
Tasting Pepper, page 76

pepper and health

Unlike salt, pepper has not yet received bad press from the nutritional experts. Within reason we can use as much or as little of it as we want without risk of high blood pressure, heart disease, nutritional deficiency and so on. Yet, as we reach for the pepper mill and 'season to taste', how many of us are aware of the part pepper has played, and continues to play, in contributing to our well-being and good health?

traditional medicine

For thousands of years herbalists and traditional healers have relied on the dried fruits of the pepper vine (*Piper nigrum*) to treat a remarkable assortment of ailments. The weighty compendium *Indian Medicinal Plants* lists pepper's multi-faceted properties as 'antihelmintic, aphrodisiac, carminative, diaphoretic, diuretic, rubefacient, stimulant and stomachic'. To you and me this means pepper is traditionally used to treat intestinal worms, stimulate sexual desire, relieve flatulence, promote sweating, reduce fever, increase urine flow, redden the skin, perk up the appetite and soothe stomach cramps.

Nicholas Culpeper, 17th-century astrologer-physician, bears this out. Describing the 'Government and Virtues' of pepper in *Culpeper's Complete Herbal* he states: 'It comforts and warms a cold stomach, consumes crude and moist humours, and stirs up the appetite. It dissolves wind in the stomach or bowels, provokes urine, helps the cough and other diseases of the breast, and is an ingredient in the great antidotes.' He goes on to say that white pepper and long pepper (*Piper longum*) were more effective than black pepper, the long variety 'being used for agues, to warm the stomach before the coming of the fit'.

Dr Malcolm Stuart, contemporary medical herbalist and one of the first eminent scientists to promote beneficial uses of plants, explains that pepper stimulates the taste buds causing a reflex flow of gastric secretions which improve digestion. Pepper also stimulates parts of the nervous system and the mucous membranes – which explains the pepper-engendered sneeze – and is widely accepted as having antifungal and antibacterial properties.

Pepper crops up time and again in most traditional healing doctrines. In Indian Ayurvedic medicine, which teaches that every taste and aspect of food has a specific effect on the physiology and psychology of the person eating it, pepper is valued for its pungent, warming and light properties. It is said to kindle 'agni', a term which refers to the concept of digestive fire and cosmic transformation, and is also the name of the Hindu god of fire.

Many Indian home cooks hold fast to their traditional beliefs about food and its effect on mind and body. Daily menus are constantly fine-tuned to achieve the optimum balance of heating, cooling, light, heavy, damp and dry foods necessary for the family's wellbeing. It follows, therefore, that pepper is a key ingredient in the spice mix *Garam Masala* (page 226), literally meaning 'heating spices', and routinely added to balance numerous dishes in the final stages of cooking.

In traditional Chinese medicine knowledge of the 'temperature' of food, its flavour and its effect on metabolism is intrinsic to traditional cooking. Pepper is considered a hot food, driving energy upwards and outwards from the body's core. As far as flavour goes, black pepper is classified as sweet and pungent, white pepper as pungent and bitter. Given that sweet foods are considered strengthening and moistening, pungent foods help shift stagnant energy, and bitter foods drain and counteract excessive 'dampness', the combination of black and white pepper in the diet would indeed appear to be a beneficial mix.

Pepper features in Unani medicine, based on the teachings of the Ancient Greek philosopher/physician Hippocrates and widely practised in the Muslim world. Unani doctrine follows similar precepts to Ayurveda based on heating and cooling foods. Pepper is prescribed to relieve colic and other digestive ailments.

It is also considered an aphrodisiac; somewhat alarming instructions for its use are given in the Kama Sutra.

No doubt mindful of pepper's capacity to stimulate, Mrs Beeton, 19th-century cookery writer and housekeeper supreme, warns us that '...even in small quantities, it produces detrimental effects on inflammatory consti-tutions'. She goes on to cite the warning of a Dr Paris who states ' Foreign spices were not intended by Nature for the inhabitants of temperate climes; they are heating, and highly stimulant.'

western medicine

Although pepper is not as widely used in modern western medicine as it is in traditional medicine, it is interesting to note parallels and possible links between the two approaches.

For example, scientific research cites piperine, the alkaloid responsible for pepper's pungency, as a factor involved in the process of transforming the chemical energy we get from food into the thermal (heating) energy that keeps us warm; in traditional medicine the heating and transforming properties of pepper are taken as read.

In Nicholas Culpeper's day piperine had yet to be discovered, but, as we already know, he thought that white pepper and long pepper (*Piper longum*) were more effective than black for healing certain ailments. Modern research bears this out – both white and long pepper are known to contain more piperine than black, which could account for the greater potency that Culpeper noticed.

It's well known that pepper titivates the taste buds – think how the mouth waters when we grind flakes of aromatic black pepper over a juicy steak. This reaction has the knock-on effect of upping the amount of hydrochloric acid secreted in the stomach. Without sufficient hydrochloric acid the body cannot easily digest proteins and other food components, causing unwelcome symptoms of flatulence, diarrhoea or constipation.

A number of studies suggest that piperine also has a beneficial affect on the lining of the gut, increasing the rate at which valuable nutrients are absorbed. It is particularly encouraging that the absorption rates of selenium, vitamin C, beta-carotene, vitamin A, vitamin B6 and co-enzyme Q10 all appear to be improved by piperine. These nutrients are part of a powerful group known as anti-oxidants which protect the body cells from oxidative damage and the host of modern diseases, such as heart disease and certain cancers, that such damage causes. Piperine itself is an anti-oxidant and could play an important part in lowering the risk of hardening of the arteries.

As well as piperine, pepper contains several useful nutrients including manganese, iron, calcium and potassium, albeit in extremely minuscule amounts. Pepper also provides dietary fibre or 'roughage' as our grandmothers used to call it. Bear in mind that we don't consume huge amounts at one sitting – two teaspoons of peppercorns represent about a hundred turns of the pepper mill – but many of us routinely season our food with pepper and may well benefit from this small but regular intake.

See also
Long Pepper, page 34
Pepper and Passion, page 72
Piperine and Essential Oil, page 69
Pungent Principles, page 68

pepper and passion

In biblical and medieval days, spices and sex went hand in hand – as they still do in some parts of the world. Spices were regarded as potent aphrodisiacs, and, as such, were an important ingredient in heady perfumes and unguents, and in lotions and potions designed to revive a flagging libido or boost an already vigorous one.

The aphrodisiac effect was based on the doctrine of humours, a theory that formed the basis of medical and philosophical thinking from the days of Hippocrates (460-370BC) until the biological revolution of the seventeenth century. The theory postulated that a healthy body depended on an optimum balance of four humours or body energies: hot, cold, moist and dry. Spices, which were more often found in the apothecary's shop than the kitchen, were believed to possess the same qualities and could therefore counteract imbalances. The early physicians, who looked on sexual matters as they would any other branch of medicine, dispensed suitable remedies accordingly.

As discussed in Pepper and Health (page 70), pepper was classified as 'heating' and 'drying'; perfect, then, for loss of libido – a symptom of excessive coldness – and for the genital area as a whole since this was thought to be naturally cold and damp.

De Coitu, a medieval sex manual written by the Benedictine monk Constantine (supposedly celibate), includes long pepper along with cloves in a remedy for flagging sex drive. Long pepper was believed to increase the amount and potency of semen; and there is in fact a modern Saudi Arabian study demonstrating that long pepper increased the sperm count and weight of reproductive organs in mice. Like black pepper, long pepper contains piperine, a substance responsible for the biting heat, which may indirectly cause a natural 'high'. It's also no coincidence that cloves contain eugenol, a chemical substance with a numbing effect. As such, it could prolong male sexual performance.

Long pepper appears to be the spice of choice in this context. In Dangerous Tastes: the story of spices, food historian Andrew Dalby quotes the Carakasamhita, an ancient work on the Indian system of ayurvedic medicine. This cites the special properties of dried long pepper as 'pungent and hot, it is capable of increasing the semen. Foods of pungent flavour do not generally increase the semen but long pepper and dry ginger are exceptions to the rule'.

Unsurprisingly, pepper is mentioned several times in the Kamasutram, the ancient Hindu text on erotic pleasure. It is crops up particularly in suggestions for prolonging sexual stamina – a latter day viagra, as it were. One remedy that sticks in the mind includes black and long peppers and the prickly thorn apple (datura) mixed with honey. It comes with the guarantee that this will 'utterly devastate your lady' when used to anoint the penis.

The Chinese were more concerned with the nourishing aspects of aphrodisiacs. To improve general health and therefore sexual capacity, they thought it vital to nourish yang energy in the kidney. The opposite to the 'external' and outgoing energy of yin, yang energy is believed to be the internal force behind the fire that kindles the spirit and animates creative processes, including sexual appetite. Although not a feature of Chinese cuisine, black pepper was among the recommended warming spices along with cloves, ginger and cinnamon.

Harem-maintaining sultans of the Ottoman Empire relied on 'Sultan's Paste', a potent mix of more than forty ingredients. The 'heating' constituents included long pepper, cubeb pepper, ginger, cloves, mustard seed, pimento and nettles. The product is still available today – one Turkish web site discreetly claims that it prevents 'sexual inefficiency' and provides 'self-trust'. Another is more straightforward, stating that the paste promotes 'strength, energy, sexual desire and a general sense of well-being'.

Back in Europe, long after sex therapy had moved on from the humoral theory, pepper was still valued for its supposedly aphrodisiac effect.

Meanwhile, tub-thumping evangelists continued to fret about overdose; clergyman-physician Sylvester Graham (1794-1851), father of the American Graham cracker, was adamant that excessive use of pepper would cause insanity. Isabella Beeton (1836-1865), of household management fame, warns 'it should never be forgotten, that, even in small quantities, it (black pepper) produces detrimental effects on inflammatory constitutions'.

Meanwhile, Eastern Europeans displayed a more relaxed attitude. In Slovenia, pepper was used to spice *mali kruhki*, delicious heart-shaped biscuits that young girls and boys gave to each other as love tokens. Maria Keneva-Johnson, food writer and Balkan cooking expert, explains that the biscuits were always made with pepper and honey, a combination considered highly erotic in Slovenia but, strangely, not in neighbouring countries.

Despite widespread and long-term use as an aphrodisiac, it's hard to say whether the effect of pepper and other spices was sustained by the repetition of strongly held beliefs, and therefore existed in the mind rather than the body, or was based on a genuine physiological response. Perhaps if we accept that pepper and other spices exist not for necessity, as is the case with salt, but for enjoyment, we could argue that by extension they contribute to sensual pleasure and, as such, may have aphrodisiac properties.

The scientific take on the subject is that certain supposedly aphrodisiac foods simply provide a shot of nutrients that improve well-being, and, as a result, sexual performance. Some have physiological effects that may affect blood flow or cause numbing. Applied externally, others cause a burning sensation in the genital area, mimicking the 'heat' of sex. As a rubefacient (a substance that reddens the skin), pepper may well come into the last category.

In general, though, the scientific community tends to refute the idea that any foods are directly responsible for an aphrodisiac effect, possibly because the research relating to food and sexual arousal is in any case slim, but also there is perhaps an unwillingness to delve into a topic so loaded with legend.

See also
Cubeb Pepper, page 38
Long Pepper, page 34
Pepper and Health, page 70
Pungent Principles, page 68

pepper in the kitchen

76   tasting pepper

80   cooking with pepper

83   grinding, crushing, cracking

89   the recipes

tasting pepper

Very few people 'taste' pepper in the way that connoisseurs taste wine or olive oil, meticulously assessing 'nose', 'finish', 'bouquet' and so on. Given patience and the necessary enthusiasm, I believe it is possible to do the same with pepper. The idea may seem bizarre and begs the question of how to taste a peppercorn, but it is certainly worth trying. Your palate will become receptive to pepper's fascinating nuances of flavour and you'll be able to use pepper in your cooking with greater discernment and confidence.

setting up a tasting session

A pepper-tasting session needs a bit of planning and timing. My preference is an hour or so after breakfast but before morning coffee. At that time of day I have a clear head, a clean palate and a fairly empty stomach. Serious tasting requires concentration so make sure there will be no disturbances for an hour or so.

It's essential to have some sort of starchy plain food to refresh the palate between samples; unsalted plain crackers are fine, but I think cold mashed potato (without salt or butter) does a better job. Its neutral flavour doesn't detract from the pepper, and the floury texture soothes the mouth and the stomach.

It's best not to attempt to taste more than five or six types of pepper in one session. If you try to do more you'll suffer from 'palate fatigue' and the inevitable sneezing fits will get out of hand. For the first session it makes sense to start off tasting just a black, a white and a green peppercorn. When you're clear about the differences in their aroma and flavour, you can move on to different types of black and white, and then to the exotic varieties.

Before you begin, gather together the following:
- electric coffee grinder or large pestle and mortar
- paper and pen
- small plastic bags
- self-adhesive labels
- tissues
- water
- unsalted crackers or cold mashed potato

Once you've assembled the kit, coarsely grind a couple of tablespoons of each kind of peppercorn, using an electric coffee grinder for speed, or failing that, a pestle and mortar. Be sure to wipe out the grinder with damp paper towel each time to avoid contaminating the next sample.

Tip the ground pepper into the corner of a small plastic bag, and tie a knot in the bag close to the pepper, eliminating as much air as possible. Label each bag with the name of the pepper.

When you're ready to go, hold a sample in your palm, still in its sealed bag. Massage the pepper to warm it and release the essential oils, then open the bag, put your nose inside and inhale gently. Describe the initial aroma. If words fail, use the descriptions opposite, or try and relate it to the natural environment or your memory of similar aromas. Inhale two or three times more – different aromas will present themselves each time. You might want to rub a pinch of pepper between your finger and thumb and then inhale. The aroma will be different again. Write down all your impressions of the aroma.

Next, put a tiny pinch on your tongue and hold it for a few seconds. Is it numbing, biting, bitter, astringent or none of these? Write down your description. As discussed on page 68, taste, aroma and flavour are closely linked, so it's likely that some of the tastes and flavours will be similar to those you experienced when you inhaled.

an inexact science

It's worth bearing in mind that tasting is an inexact science; there are simply too many variables. For example, had the samples I tasted been grown on another plantation, harvested later in the season or in another year, or stored under different conditions, the results might be different. To limit such variables, one would need armies of professional tasters stationed in hundreds of locations, tasting at regular intervals throughout the year. That said, most varieties of pepper do have broadly recognisable characteristics that nevertheless remain consistent. The full-bodied flavour of Tellicherry peppercorns is instantly recognisable, for example, as is the hint of coconut in grains of paradise and tobacco in Madagascan black.

Minty	Oxidised lime	Piny, resinous
Pungent	Musty	Terpene
Soapy	Warm	Floral
Barnyard	Astringent	Biting
Cedarwood	Cardboard	Bitter

the language of tasting

As yet, there is no official language for tasting pepper, as there is for wine or olive oil. However, the following terms are used by experienced pepper tasters at major spice companies:

See also
Piperine and Essential Oil, page 69
Pungent Principles, page 68

black pepper tasting notes

Name	Source	Comments
Brazilian	Brazil	Brownish black berries. Good all-round pepper. Strong, well-balanced, complex. Fruity flavour with hint of orange zest, some cedar wood. Biting and slightly bitter.
Ecuador	Ecuador	Dominant liquorice aroma. Hint of cinnamon. Bitter and harsh.
Lampong	Indonesia	Slightly floral aroma and flavour with warm nutmeg and a touch of menthol.
Madagascan	Madagascar	Dominant aroma of tobacco, stale pipes. Rich but not floral. Some cedar wood.
Malabar	Kerala, India	Complex aroma and flavour. Well-balanced, floral, soft, with a hint of mint. Biting but not bitter.
Organic	India, Sri Lanka	Excellent all-round pepper. Slightly medicinal, hint of menthol. Good bite on the tongue.
Penja	Cameroon	Floral, resinous, cut-grass aroma. Cardboardy taste. Slightly bitter.

black pepper tasting notes (cont.)

Name	Source	Comments
Rimbàs	Malaysia	Warm spicy aroma with slight hint of acetone. Slightly fruity. Strongly pungent, lingering bite, slightly sharp.
Sarawak	Malaysia	Smells of sap and Christmas trees. Mild pungency with hint of menthol. Warm and enveloping.
Sri Lankan	Sri Lanka	Good earthy pepper with high piperine content. Not complex.
Tellicherry	Kerala, India	Large berries, slightly red hue. Complex flowery, fruity aroma. Excellent well-rounded clean flavour, with hints of lapsang tea, mace, nutmeg. Glowingly warm slow burn, not biting.
Vietnamese	Vietnam	Very sharp and biting. No warmth or depth of flavour. Tastes like chewed tobacco.
Wynad	Kerala, India	Excellent, well-rounded aroma and flavour. Warm bite. Slightly resinous aftertaste. Would be good with pasta or aubergines but might overpower chicken or fish.

white pepper tasting notes

Name	Source	Comments
Muntok	Indonesia	Pale biscuit colour. Trace of barnyard aroma with some eucalyptus. Warm and welcoming. Good clean biscuit flavour. Hot, tingly on the tongue.
Penja	Cameroon	Barnyard aroma.
Rimbàs, decorticated	Malaysia	Dark beige colour. Spicy cinnamon aroma. No trace of barnyard. Bitingly hot with no particular flavour.
Sarawak	Malaysia	Cream colour. Very mild barnyard aroma. Clean pine flavour. Pleasant hot bite.
Thai	Thailand	Dark beige colour. Moderate barnyard aroma. Fresh slightly resinous flavour.
Wynad	Kerala, India	Pale creamy white. Superb strong resinous clean aroma with barest trace of barnyard. Slow gentle burn. Perfect with chicken and fish, leafy green vegetables and cabbage.

green pepper tasting notes

Name	Source	Comments
Air-dried	Kerala, India	Dull khaki green. Mildly pungent with fresh clean hint of pine.
Freeze-dried, biodynamic	Kerala, India	Excellent colour – bright yellowish green. Subtle herbaceous flavour with hint of spearmint. Mildly pungent.

exotics tasting notes

Name	Source	Comments
Cubeb	Indonesia	Less red than Madagascan. Strong nutmeg flavour. Bitter. Mildly pungent.
Grains of Paradise	West Africa	Glossy terracotta pyramid-shaped grains. Lovely sweetish coconut aroma when ground – like Bounty Bars. Warm chocolate, nutmeg flavour. Biting on the tongue.
Long pepper	Indonesia	Sweet spicy aroma, like dried ginger. Good peppery bite on the tongue.
Pink pepper (*Schinus terebinthifolius*)	Isle of Réunion	Sticky and resinous when ground. Distinct floral resinous taste, with hint of turpentine.
Red pepper, freeze-dried, biodynamic (*Piper nigrum*)	Kerala, India	Reddish beige colour. Strong toffee aroma with hint of acetone, sherbet, sweets. Intense warm cereal flavour at first. Becoming salty. Glowing well-rounded heat that spreads and lingers.
Sansho	Japan	Sweetish but also bitter and biting. Stays in the mouth. Hint of cloves and carbolic soap.
Sichuan	Sichuan, China	Smells of doctor's surgery, carbolic soap. Bitter menthol taste. Tingling and numbing in the mouth, like lemon sherbet.
Tsiperifery	Madagascar	Brownish red when ground. Gingery aroma with hint of cloves. Complex flavour – woody, resinous, sweetish. Pungent bite.

cooking with pepper

As the late French chef Louis Diat once commented, no other spice can do so much for so many different types of food. He was right – pepper starts to work its magic even before cooking begins. Added to marinades and dry-rubs, sauce bases and stocks, it will round out the basic flavour of the finished dish remarkably well. Added during cooking, pepper is a stock-in-trade seasoning; whereas a final dash at the end adjusts the flavour. At the table, the diner can add a discretionary turn or two of the mill for extra piquancy and aroma; there are few who can resist doing so.

some kitchen chemistry

Without going too deeply into the nuts and bolts of food science, it's worth having a look at different ways of cooking pepper and the effect these have on flavour and heat. As Indian cooks instinctively know, when pepper (or any spice) is simmered or boiled in 'wet' dishes – soups and stews, for example – the intensity and staying power of its flavour is different from that found in fried or roasted dishes.

As already discussed, the biting pungent taste of black peppercorns comes from piperine, an alkaloid found in the inner part of the berry, and the unique flavour and aroma come from volatile oils embedded in the outer husk. White peppercorns, which are the kernel that has had the oil-bearing husk removed, are therefore pungent but not particularly aromatic.

Once the husk is broken by crushing or grinding, the fragrant oils are released and gradually disperse through the dish. However, being volatile, the oils evaporate during cooking – the pungent heat from the kernel is still there but the fresh peppery aroma eventually disappears, especially during lengthy simmering. This is easily corrected by adding an extra hit of pepper at the end, as Indian cooks do when they 'temper' a dish with spices before serving. Lamb Pepper Fry (page 152) is a good example of this technique.

Another culinary trick is to use white pepper to season the dish while it cooks, then finish off with a grinding of black.

Being neither sweet nor savoury, pepper complements both. It is used in practically all savoury dishes, and is the third most added ingredient, water and salt coming first and second respectively. Pepper works with sweet dishes too. It brings out the best in strawberries warmed through with kirsch (page 201) and it certainly adds an extra something to rich dark chocolate ice cream (page 200). In baking, it imparts a warm bite to cakes and biscuits, rounding out the flavour of other spices and cutting through sweetness.

Containing essential oils itself, pepper mixes easily with other oils, and the cook can put this to good use. A few lightly cracked peppercorns briefly sizzled before adding other ingredients will help disperse the peppery flavour through the dish. Left to infuse in olive oil for a few weeks, a tablespoon of crushed peppercorns (with some cardamom, chilli and other spices) slowly release their flavour in Olio Santo (page 237) – a superbly fragrant and spicy oil for drizzling over vegetables, fish or crusty bread. A simple way of livening up steamed vegetables is to anoint them with clarified butter or ghee that has been simmered with lightly cracked black, white or green peppercorns tied in a muslin bag. Use about 1 teaspoon of pepper-corns to 250g/9oz butter. Chilled unsalted butter pounded with the best peppercorns you can lay your hands on is unbeatable for slathering over steaks and chops.

The bite and aroma of pepper will permeate water as well as oil, as we know from peppery soups like Tomato Rasam (page 112) and Mulli-gatawny (page 110). Indian food expert Camilla Punjabi writes that an infusion of peppercorns boiled in water with Indian basil leaves is drunk to cure asthma or a chest cold. Peppercorns also go into spicy Indian cha (tea) and chilled Lime and Pepper Refresher (page 184).

Even a very few peppercorns make a difference to a stock or sauce. I was not convinced that steeping five unbroken black peppercorns in warm milk prior to making white sauce would affect the flavour in any way. True to form, though, they changed the sweetish flavour of milk to something definitely more savoury. Similarly, a few peppercorns simmered in a reduction of tarragon vinegar and shallots contribute to the faintly sharp and spicy flavour of *Béarnaise* sauce.

to roast or not to roast

A contentious issue arises over whether or not to roast peppercorns before adding them to a dish. While it's true that most spices benefit from a few seconds in a hot dry pan – the heat releases the essential oils that create aroma and flavour – it's not so with pepper. I find that roasting or dry-frying makes black and green pepper taste slightly bitter and drives away the fragrance; white pepper becomes intensely hot and develops a dry cardboardy taste.

On the other hand, Sichuan pepper and pink *schinus* pepper seem to be noticeably improved by dry heat. Pink pepper loses its somewhat antiseptic taint, becoming sweeter and more intense, while Sichuan pepper develops a mellow flavour but keeps its pleasantly numbing tingle.

choosing pepper

black pepper
There are few dishes that aren't improved by black pepper but it is at its best with red meat, and game. Classics like Steak au Poivre (page 151) and gutsy stews such as Peppered Beef with Balsamic Vinegar and Molasses (page 148) allow it to really shine. Black pepper is good with fish, too, as long as the fish is robust enough to match its aroma and pungency. Oily fish such as sardines and mackerel cry out for pepper, but delicate white fish like plaice and sole usually need a lighter touch.

A good hit of black pepper brings rice and pasta to life. Without it, Black Pepper Rice (page 181) or Pasta with Pecorino and Black Pepper (page 178) would be disappointingly pallid. Vegetables benefit too, particularly those with a sweetish flavour such as parsnips, carrots and squash, or strongly flavoured chard and spinach. It would be unthinkable to serve a leafy salad or a simple dish of sliced tomatoes without a few aromatic black flakes to provide a zesty edge. The simplest dressing of all is made with olive oil, a squeeze of lemon, sea salt and cracked black pepper.

white pepper
Traditionally, white pepper is recommended for pale foods such as *béchamel* sauce, the theory being that black is unsightly. This doesn't bother me – if anything, black or green peppercorns look more appetising especially with pallid food. However, I use white when I want a clean peppery hit without the assertive aroma of black, and sometimes I use a bit of each – white for bite and black for aroma. On its own, though, white pepper seems exactly the right seasoning for a simple dish of buttered cabbage (page 158), or the Chinese classic Hot and Sour Soup (page 107).

green pepper
Green peppercorns are fresh-tasting and pungent, and also slightly lemony. They lack the strength of white and the aroma of black, but complement both. You'll invariably find them in a colourful mix with black, white and pink peppercorns – lovely for coating fish or meat. On their own, green peppercorns go well with light meats such as pork or turkey, particularly when added to an accompanying sauce. They are especially good mixed with butter and pushed under poultry skin before roasting (page 142). I like them with leeks and cannellini beans in a soothing creamy soup (page 106).

Fresh green peppercorns, if you can get them, are delicious in Thai-style curries and stir-fries. Freeze-dried berries are a reasonable alternative as they soften quite quickly and the flavour is good. Brine-cured green peppercorns are better kept as a piquant garnish for cream cheese or egg-based dishes like quiches and omelettes. Drain and rinse them first to get rid of excess saltiness.

red pepper

Fresh red peppercorns are almost impossible to get hold of in the west; they are usually cured in brine or vinegar. However, Bart Spices biodynamic freeze-dried red peppercorns from Kerala are a good substitute. They have a delicious toffee-like flavour and a wonderfully rounded lingering heat. Use them in the same way as green peppercorns.

See also
One Plant, Four Peppercorns, page 31
Pungent Principles, page 68
Grinding, Crushing, Cracking, page 83

p e p p e r

grinding, crushing, cracking

Once ground or crushed, peppercorns release the volatile oils which produce the distinctive flavour and aroma. When exposed to the atmosphere these oils quickly oxidise and lose their potency. Whole peppercorns are therefore a must if you want your cooking to have bright zesty flavours. You have only to smell the heady aroma of freshly ground pepper to appreciate the difference in the grey dust that passes for ready-ground pepper.

Equally important are tools for grinding, crushing and cracking. They enable you to process your peppercorns and other spices at exactly the right moment for maximum flavour and minimum deterioration. A couple of peppermills are essential – one for black, one for white – as are mortar and pestle. For grinding large amounts of pepper it's worth investing in an electric coffee grinder and keep it especially for the purpose.

peppermills

'The world is full of broken peppermills,' says Jeff Riley, marketing manager at T&G Woodware, manufacturers of top-notch mills. Jeff goes on to comment how a surprising number of us continue to opt for a cheap and cheerful mill even though we already have a collection of defunct mills at the back of the kitchen cupboard. Don't be seduced by good looks; some of the most stylish mills aren't necessarily the best performers. If you take cooking seriously it's essential to invest in one that's going to last, and with the growing choice of pepper on the market, it's important to choose carefully – not all mills can cope with large peppercorns.

grinding mechanisms
A reliable grinding mechanism is far more important than the mill's casing. The best are made from stainless steel, high-carbon steel or ceramic. The quality of the components and how they are put together are crucial.

The traditional mechanism is based on a steel spindle running through a central chamber. The spindle is connected to a rotating grooved 'male' head that fits into a fixed 'female' ring, also grooved. Large grooves cut into the top of the male part nudge the peppercorns towards the rotating spindle that cracks them into fragments. The fragments then fall between the finer grooves of the male and female parts and are further ground into particles.

An adjustable mechanism – usually a knob or a small dial on the outside of the mill – increases or reduces the space between the male and female parts. The greater the distance, the larger the fragments and the coarser the grind – and vice versa.

The most coveted of spindle-operated mills are made by Peugeot. The grinding mechanism was developed in 1842 and the large grooves are still cut by hand using the original techniques. Unlike many mills, the number of grooves on the 'male' grinding head is different to the number on the 'female' outer ring, so they do not lock together. This produces the unique ultra-fine grind characteristic of Peugeot mills. The mills have a lifetime guarantee even for commercial use, but are not covered for rusting.

Thought to be the most long-lasting mechanism and certainly rivalling Peugeot, is the ceramic CrushGrind® system. Originating in Denmark and now licensed to T&G Woodware in the UK, the system is unique in that it contains no spindle, allowing the entire cavity of the mill to be filled with peppercorns. Since ceramic is harder and sharper than steel and also non-corrosive, the mechanism can cope with large peppercorns, salt, herbs and rock-hard spices too. Best of all, it is simple to take apart for cleaning or repair. You simply loosen the adjustment wheel and remove the grinding cone.

appearance and style
There is an increasing range of shapes, materials and sizes to choose from, some of which are described below. For kitchen use I recommend highly functional, easy to grip and wipe clean mills in wood, aluminium or

stainless steel; keep the glitzy chrome and perspex models for the table. Remember that giant peppermills belong in restaurants and not in your kitchen. They hold industrial amounts of peppercorns that will become stale before you use them. They are also heavy and awkward to use although perfect for waiters who need to reach across the table to season your pasta.

choosing a peppermill
- Look for a mill that holds at least three tablespoons of peppercorns otherwise you will be constantly refilling it.
- Check how comfortable it is to hold. If you have large hands you won't find it easy to grip a dainty mill.
- Inspect the filling mechanism and see how convenient it is to use.
- Make sure you can adjust the size of grind

from fine to coarse and that the setting stays in place without slipping.
- How easy is it easy to grind? Look for an even grind that produces a decent output after a two or three turns. (A good kitchen shop should have filled mills on hand for you to try.)
- Check that the fine grind is consistently fine without any larger particles, and that the coarse grind produces uniformly large fragments without any dust. Check that the coarse grind setting can cope with large peppercorns.
- Check the precision of machining on a metal grinding mechanism; sharper teeth give a better grind.

mill maintenance
- Don't be tempted to use salt in a mill intended for pepper; salt will corrode the grinding mechanism if it's made of metal.

types of mill

traditional capstan mill
These mills come in wood or acrylic, and have a mushroom-shaped top that you turn to grind. The knob on top adjusts the grind size. However, if the knob is tightened enough to produce a fine grind, the top itself becomes more difficult to turn. Another drawback is that the knob has to be completely unscrewed in order to remove the top and refill the mill, which means you have to reset the grind size each time.

Perfex® crank-key mill
Turning a crank-key doesn't feel quite so easy as rotating a mushroom-shaped top. However, the mill has a pull-down laundry chute refilling system that is convenient and saves unscrewing and dismantling the top.

T&G Crushgrind® upside-down spice mill
This is such a simple idea I wonder why it has taken so long for someone to think of it. The mill is designed with the grinding mechanism at the

top, putting an end to pepper residue left on the work surface. The CrushGrind® mechanism allows the entire top to unscrew for easy refilling with no central spindle to get in the way.

battery-powered mill with spotlight
This concept of a battery-powered, illuminated mill may seem frivolous but is actually extremely functional. The mill has an easily pressed push-switch that activates the grinding mechanism and turns on the light in the base. Fragments of pepper are beautifully illuminated as they drift down onto your plate. Wonderful for candle-lit dinners or barbecues, and a boon for anyone with painful or weak hands.

single-handed mill
This type of mill has two handles that you squeeze together with one hand, leaving the other free for stirring the pot. Convenient to use for light seasoning but tiring if you have to measure out a specific amount of pepper.

- Lubricate the top of the spindle, where it meets the adjusting screw, with a drop of cooking oil. This will prevent rusting and keep the thread in good working order.
- Brush the grinding mechanism clean when refilling your mill.
- Get into the habit of milling into a large spoon or over a plate or piece of paper, then tip the grounds into the pan. If you mill directly over an open pan the steam causes rusting and dampens the grounds which may then clog the mechanism.
- Keep mill bodies clean by wiping with a damp cloth. To keep chrome or stainless steel mills smear-free, spray with vinegar-based glass cleaner and wipe with paper towel.
- Rub wooden mills with vegetable oil occasionally to prevent the wood drying out.

mortar and pestle

Once you've tried a mortar (that's the bowl) and pestle you'll understand why cooks the world over rely on this versatile kitchen duo. You can use it for grinding dry spices, crushing and pounding wet spices such as ginger, garlic and chillies, and for blending sauces and pastes. The friction of the pestle against the rough surface of the mortar coaxes out the freshest possible flavours, and also allows you to control texture. I use a mortar and pestle rather than a food processor for making spice blends such as Sichuan Spiced Pepper and Salt (page 229), or the zesty ginger and garlic paste that goes into Tandoori-Style Chicken (page 132).

Mortars and pestles come in a fascinating range of shapes, sizes and materials each bringing their particular quality to the food prepared therein. There are gigantic stone bowl-shaped models from Thailand, big enough to toss a salad in, and rough and ready Mexican *molcajetes* made from volcanic rock. In Britain, cooks and chemists have traditionally used ceramic mortars with either a wooden or ceramic pestle.

I own a shiny cast-aluminium model from India, specially designed for grinding spices and seeds. The interior of the mortar has a completely flat base and straight outward-sloping sides instead of the usual rounded bowl shape. The pestle has a flat tip that mirrors the flat bottom of the mortar and increases the surface area available for grinding.

Another kitchen treasure is a tall wooden mortar and pestle from Africa that I use for relishes and pastes. I enjoy the soft thud of the wood as I pound and I like the way the tall sides stop the contents from jumping out.

For everyday use I prefer a capacious bowl-shaped mortar made of dark unpolished granite. The rough surface and hefty pestle make light work of reducing whole peppercorns to coarse fragments or down to a fine grind.

choosing a mortar and pestle
For grinding whole spoonfuls of peppercorns you'll need a fairly large mortar about 13cm/5in across with a reasonably deep bowl; the corns will bounce over the sides if it is smaller. A rough interior produces good friction, so if you choose ceramic or marble make sure the inside has enough abrasion, otherwise dry ingredients will skid over the surface.

electric grinder

It's convenient to have a dedicated coffee mill for grinding large amounts of peppercorns. Working on the same principle as a blender, the two-armed blade pulverises peppercorns in seconds. Though compact and easy to use, electric grinders produce uneven grounds and you have to guess how long to whiz for. They are also noisy but they are useful for reducing a large quantity of peppercorns to a medium or fine grind.

techniques

The recipes in this book usually specify the fineness or coarseness of grind required, or whether peppercorns are to be crushed or cracked. This level of detail is important because the way you prepare peppercorns affects the flavour, colour and texture of the finished dish.

Peppercorns release very little flavour until the hard outer husk is broken. The actual strength of flavour depends on the way the corn has been ground or crushed. For example, cracked pepper releases pungency and flavour slowly because the fragments are relatively large. There is a slow build of heat after the first mouthful, and you taste it towards the back of the mouth after you have chewed the food and are on the point of swallowing. At the other end of the scale, finely ground pepper disperses more evenly through a dish, so its spicy heat makes itself felt throughout your whole mouth as soon as you start to chew.

bruising and cracking

To bruise or crack peppercorns put the required amount in re-sealable clear plastic bag (you need to see what's going on). Seal the bag and pat the berries into a single layer. To bruise, tap gently but firmly with a rolling pin, just enough to dent the berries (1). To crack, use a bit more force – enough to shatter the berries into three or four fragments (2).

crushing

To crush peppercorns, use the technique for cracking but keep on bashing until you have coarse fragments (3). If you're crushing a large amount, it's quicker and easier to use the base of a saucepan or frying pan. Alternatively, use a pestle and mortar and pound the berries into coarse fragments (4). Don't forget to sieve out the dusty chaff (see below) especially for dishes like Steak au Poivre (page 151).

grinding

If you use a pestle and mortar for grinding, bash the corns into rough fragments with the end of the pestle. Then grind in a circular direction to create friction, which in turn produces the necessary grounds (5).

dealing with dust

When you crack, crush or coarsely grind pepper there is likely to be a dusty residue mixed in among the larger fragments. It would look unsightly if you included this dust in a cracked pepper crust or in a seasoning for pale food, so it's worth sieving it out. It makes a difference not only to appearance but also to flavour.

See also
Tasting Pepper, page 76
Pungent Principles, page 68

p e p p e r

pepper

the recipes

93   salads

103   soups

115   fish

131   poultry

143   meat

157   vegetables

173   pulses, pasta and rice

183   drinks, dips and relishes

197   desserts and sweetmeats

211   cakes and biscuits

225   spice blends, seasonings and sauces

Given our predilection for spicy foods, I am surprised how few dishes exist in which pepper is brought into play as a key ingredient. We mainly use it out of habit as in 'season to taste with salt and pepper'. Pepper is more than a mere partner to salt, though, as Roman and medieval cooks well knew and today's cooks are beginning to appreciate. It is a valid ingredient in its own right with a full spectrum of flavours equal in nuance to those found in good olive oil, chocolate or fine wine.

The recipes that follow are a broadly based collection that shows off these qualities. They are recipes in which pepper makes a real difference, where its absence would be noticeable however small the amount used. Many of them are my own creation, the result of long hours spent tasting and testing; others are from chefs and food writers whose passion for pepper matches my own.

You'll also find familiar pepper classics such as *steak au poivre*, as well as modern Mediterranean-style dishes, palate-challenging curries and zesty stir-fries. There are some surprises too – irresistible desserts where pepper adds a subtle but unmistakable sparkle. And the bakers amongst you will enjoy making cakes and biscuits with a subtle peppery bite.

Whatever the recipe, I have tried to show you how to make good use of this valuable spice and help you understand why it is that pepper and certain foods make such excellent culinary partners.

the pepper pantry

In the same way that I keep several oils and vinegars to hand, I like to have a choice of pepper in the spice cupboard. In most situations it's fine to use good quality ordinary black or white pepper, but now and again something more is called for, such as an exotic or single estate variety, to make a dish really special.

For general use I recommend organic black peppercorns from India or Sri Lanka. The dark brown berries have a good peppery aroma and flavour with the necessary bite. For special dishes it's hard to beat Tellicherry peppercorns – acknowledged by many devotees as the finest. The voluptuous berries have a fruity aroma and a deep mellow intense flavour, best appreciated if you add the pepper just before serving.

I must confess to having a bit of a problem with white pepper. Put politely, it often has a dubious barnyard-like whiff that I am told is to do with the method of curing the peppercorns in water. The unwelcome aroma is less obvious if you use white pepper in combination with black or green. For using alone, when you want the typical bite of white pepper, my peppercorn of choice is a good quality white Sarawak, preferably double washed (DW),

or a single estate variety from Wynad in Kerala. Both have a clean, strong, slightly resinous flavour with little trace of mustiness.

It's useful to have green peppercorns for sauces, vegetables and pork dishes. The best are freeze-dried; unless you live near an Asian grocery shop, you'll rarely find them fresh. Freeze-dried berries have a clean fresh flavour and although slightly brittle, they soften easily when cooked. Bart Spices biodynamic green peppercorns are well worth seeking out. Produced on an organic estate in Kerala, they are freeze-dried immediately after harvest. This rapid processing gives them a superb flavour and fresh green colour almost equal to that of fresh green peppercorns.

Lip-tingling Sichuan peppercorns are handy for spicy stir-fries and vegetable dishes. I also keep one or two exotics for days when I get the urge to experiment. Long pepper and grains of paradise are the most interesting and can be used to replace ordinary black pepper. Rare peppercorns like these are becoming much easier to find. I buy mine from Seasoned Pioneers who market a remarkable range of esoteric spices for the adventurous cook.

There are more varieties of pepper, both black and white, than you would imagine, each with its own subtle characteristics. I encourage you to seek them out and expand your pepper repertoire. I have included brief descriptions and tasting notes on page 77 and there are details of suppliers on page 248.

a word about storage...

Once ground, pepper quickly loses its volatile oils, and the aroma and flavour start to deteriorate. It should go without saying that whole peppercorns are the ones to use, rather than pre-ground pepper. If you're not convinced, try tasting them together and compare the flavours.

Stored in a sealed container, peppercorns will keep for up to two or three years. But bear in mind that they may spend a good part of that time on the supermarket shelf. Buy them a little at a time from shops with a quick turnover, and store away from light and heat. Check sell-by dates regularly and ruthlessly chuck out any that are past their best.

...and measurements

In most of the recipes I have specified whole peppercorns rather than an amount of freshly ground pepper. This is partly because I have used several types of peppercorns and you might not necessarily have these in your mill, but it is mainly because the amounts tend to be on the generous side. Since it takes nearly 30 turns of the mill to fill a mere 1/2 teaspoon with ground pepper, it's easier to use whole peppercorns and grind them in an electric mill or with a mortar and pestle. However, if you're dealing with a 1/4 teaspoon or less, grinding pepper straight from the mill is not too arduous.

When using ground pepper from a mill, you should use the same number of spoonfuls specified for whole peppercorns. Believe me, one teaspoon of whole peppercorns still measures one teaspoon even when ground, though you might expect ground pepper to occupy less space once packed in the bowl of a spoon.

Some cookery writers specify the number of peppercorns to be used. Unless the amount is very small I see little point in this – it's more convenient to measure by volume rather than by individual peppercorns, and it's usually not necessary to be so precise. However, for what it's worth, the following table shows the number of average-sized peppercorns per spoonful, and, for comparison, the number of larger Tellicherry peppercorns per spoonful.

	Average black peppercorns	Tellicherry peppercorns
⅛ tsp	8–10	4–5
¼ tsp	12–14	7–8
½ tsp	26–30 (1g)	16–18 (1.5g)
1 tsp	60–68 (3g)	38–40 (3g)
½ tbsp	98–100 (4.5g)	56–58 (4.5g)
1 tbsp	200 (9g)	128–130 (8g)

To get the best results from the recipes use either metric measuring spoons and scales or imperial; do not mix two sets of measurements. Unless otherwise stated, all spoons are level.

Where I specify 'a handful' or 'a good pinch' or no measurement at all, I want to encourage you to use your own judgement and taste buds.

Oven temperatures and timings are for non fan-assisted ovens. Fan-assisted ovens, or ovens that combine grilling with circulated air, tend to cook food more quickly. As a rough guide, reduce the temperatures stated in the recipe by 10°C/50°F, but it's best to follow the manufacturer's manual for greater accuracy.

salads

One of the most pleasurable kitchen activities I know is creating salads. I'm inspired by the way the colours, textures and flavours of three or four raw or cooked ingredients combine to make an instantly and effortlessly beautiful dish. I particularly appreciate the fact that salads are relaxing to make, 'requiring neither fire nor attendance', as pioneering vegetarian Albert Broadbent wrote in the early 1900s.

I enjoy the leisurely process of assembling the components and deciding what will go with what. A few crisp leaves, vinegar or lemon juice, top quality oil, salt and freshly ground pepper make up the basics – and, of course, the ability to see whatever you happen to have in your fridge or store cupboard in terms of a salad. The recipes in this chapter demonstrate just that and I hope they will encourage you to experiment.

Of vital importance is seasoning. Salt is essential – after all, the Italian word for salad, *insalata*, is based on the Latin *sal* meaning salt. Salt heightens and rounds out other flavours. Without it, and an acidic dressing of some sort, a salad is merely a collection of disparate components. Try eating an unadorned lettuce leaf or cucumber slice and see how bland they taste.

Essential though salt may be, it is pepper that adds the final flourish to a salad. The aromatic flakes impart minuscule but potent nuggets of flavour and texture to oil-slicked leaves, complementing the gentle pungency of peppery greens such as watercress or rocket, and of the oil itself.

Just a few turns of the mill are enough to season a simple leafy salad, but don't hang back when it comes to more complex salads; they need a full-on pungent bite to draw together all the components and balance richness, sweetness and acidity.

It's worth experimenting with different kinds of pepper, too. A numbing and pungent mix of Sichuan and white peppercorns is good with an Asian-style Numbing Chicken Noodle Salad (page 94), while citrusy green peppercorns work well in a creamy dressing for a salad of pear with green beans, blue cheese and walnuts (page 100). If you happen to have exotics such as grains of paradise or long pepper, try them instead of black pepper and enjoy the spicy tropical flavours.

numbing chicken noodle salad

boneless, skinless chicken breasts 3 organic, each weighing about 150g/5^1/$_2$oz
thin rice noodles 100g/3^1/$_2$oz
cashew nuts 3 tbsp, roughly chopped
muscovado sugar ^{3}/$_4$ tsp
sea salt ^{3}/$_4$ tsp
lime finely grated zest of 1
groundnut oil 2 tbsp
Sichuan pepper 1 tsp, crushed
white peppercorns ^{1}/$_2$ tsp, crushed
cucumber ^{1}/$_2$
spring onions 3 large, thickly sliced diagonally
Chinese leaves ^{1}/$_3$ of a head, thickly sliced diagonally
mint handful of leaves, stems discarded
coriander handful of leaves, stems discarded

for the marinade
sugar 2 tbsp
dry sherry or **rice wine** 2 tbsp
soy sauce 2 tsp
ginger root 2.5cm/1in chunk
hoisin sauce 3 tbsp
salt ^{1}/$_4$ tsp

for the dressing
Sichuan pepper 1 tbsp, crushed
light soy sauce 2 tbsp
rice vinegar 2 tbsp
cold-pressed sesame or **sunflower oil** 3 tbsp

Serves 4–6 as a starter or light meal

This is a glorious mix of contrasting textures and flavours – numbing and tingling Sichuan pepper, cooling cucumber and mint, sweet crunchy nuts, zesty lime and tender noodles. A mellow sesame and soy dressing rounds out the flavours.

First make the marinade: dissolve the sugar in the sherry and soy sauce. Squeeze the ginger in a garlic press and add the juice to the mix. Stir in the hoisin sauce and salt.

Halve the chicken breasts horizontally, then cut them as evenly as possible into neat strips about 1cm x 4cm/^{1}/$_2$in x 1^1/$_2$in. Mix these with the marinade and leave at room temperature for 30 minutes or in the fridge for up to 2 days.

Boil a kettleful of water and leave to stand for 5 minutes. Pull the rice noodles apart and break into shorter lengths. (Do this in a large deep bowl to stop bits of noodle flying about.) Pour the just-boiled water over the noodles and leave them to soften for 8–10 minutes. Swish with tongs now and again to separate the strands. Drain under cold running water for about a minute. Shake off as much water as you can, then spread the noodles out on a tray to dry off a bit.

Whisk all the dressing ingredients until well blended. Combine the cashews, sugar, sea salt and lime zest in a small bowl.

In a frying pan or wok, heat the oil with the two kinds of pepper until almost smoking. Add the chicken and the marinade and stir-fry for 4–5 minutes or until cooked through. Drain on paper towels.

Trim the ends from the cucumber, cutting at a sharp angle. Halve lengthways and scoop out the seeds with a teaspoon. Slice diagonally into thin crescents.

Mix the cucumber with the spring onions, Chinese leaves, mint, coriander and noodles in a large bowl. Whisk the dressing again and pour two-thirds of it over the salad. Toss with your hands to distribute the noodles, then tip into a shallow serving dish.

Sprinkle with the nut mixture then scatter the chicken over the top. Pour over the rest of the dressing.

cook's note
• This is actually quite easy despite the long list of ingredients. Prepare the chicken, noodles and nut mixture in advance, then the final assembly will take very little time.

chicken liver, pancetta and mangetout

mangetout 150g/5^1/$_2$oz,
   trimmed
extra-virgin olive oil 2 tbsp
balsamic vinegar 1^1/$_2$ tbsp
pancetta or **streaky bacon**
   5 rashers
vegetable oil for frying
ciabatta or **sourdough bread**
   2 thick crust-less slices,
   cubed
chicken livers 225g/8oz,
   cleaned and chopped into
   bite-sized pieces
lemon juice of ^{1}/$_2$
mustard powder a large pinch
oregano or **thyme** chopped to
   make 1 tsp
sea salt flakes a pinch
black peppercorns ^{1}/$_2$ tsp,
   crushed
frisée (curly endive) 2 generous
   handfuls

**Serves 2 as a starter or light
meal**

This salad should be served warm. It is quite filling so portions are small, but the bitter leaves and pungent cracked pepper counteract the richness of the livers.

Plunge the mangetout into a pan of boiling water and leave for 1 minute exactly. Drain, then spread out on a board to cool slightly. Slice in half diagonally and put in a bowl. Whisk the olive oil with ^{1}/$_2$ tablespoon of the balsamic vinegar and toss with the mangetout.

Fry the pancetta in a non-stick pan for 3–4 minutes or until crisp. Remove with tongs, drain on crumpled paper towels and keep warm in a bowl.

Heat 1 tablespoon of vegetable oil in the same pan and fry the bread cubes until golden on all sides. Drain on paper towels and add to the pancetta.

Put the livers in a bowl and mix with the lemon juice, mustard powder and oregano. Heat another tablespoon of oil over medium-high heat. Add the liver mixture and fry for 3 minutes, turning, until the livers are no longer pink. Season with a pinch of crumbled sea salt flakes and most of the peppercorns.

Stir in the remaining tablespoon of vinegar, scraping up any sediment. Add the contents of the pan to the pancetta and bread mixture.

Arrange the salad leaves in a serving dish. Add the chicken liver mixture and scatter over the mangetout. Sprinkle with the oil left in the bowl and the last of the peppercorns.

peppered figs, air-dried ham and celery

celery 2 tender stalks
sea salt flakes a pinch
freshly ground black pepper
to taste
extra-virgin olive oil 2 tsp
marjoram or **flat-leaf parsley**
finely chopped to make 2 tsp
lemon juice a squeeze
semi-dried figs 3
black peppercorns preferably
Tellicherry, 2 tsp, cracked
air-dried ham (such as San
Daniele, Serrano or Parma)
4 slices
baby chard or **spinach** a small
handful
celery leaves a few snipped,
to garnish

**Serves 2 as a starter or light
meal**

Figs with cracked peppercorns are such a good combination of flavour and texture – intense sweetness balances heat, and crunch counteracts soft figgy goo. The ham provides mild background sweetness while crisp celery ribbons add a refreshing cleanness to the dish.

Remove the strings from the celery stalks with a swivel peeler. Cut the stalks in half crossways. Using the peeler and working from alternate sides, shave each piece into thin ribbons. Put in a bowl and toss with a pinch of crumbled sea salt flakes, a few twists of the pepper mill, the olive oil, marjoram and a squeeze of lemon juice.

Slice the figs in half from top to bottom and gently press the sides to plump them up. Press the cut surface onto the cracked peppercorns so that they stick and mingle with the fig seeds.

Arrange the ham on individual plates. Place three peppered fig halves on top, with a small mound of chard leaves and celery ribbons to one side. Drizzle with the juices left in the celery bowl. Sprinkle with snipped celery leaves.

cook's note
- If you happen to have made some of the luscious Greek Peppered Dried Figs on page 196, use these instead of the dried figs. You won't need to dip them in extra black pepper.

peppered figs, air-dried ham and celery (page 97)

pear, green beans, blue cheese and walnuts with green peppercorn dressing

green beans (preferably slim French ones) 125g/4$\frac{1}{2}$oz

pear 1, plus $\frac{1}{4}$ leftover from the dressing

lemon juice a squeeze

sea salt flakes to taste

rocket or **watercress** 4 small handfuls, coarse stalks removed

walnuts shelled and roughly chopped to make 4 tbsp

blue cheese 50g/1$\frac{3}{4}$oz, crumbled

for the dressing
pear 1
lemon juice 1 tbsp
olive oil 2 tbsp
dried green peppercorns 2 tsp, crushed
sea salt a pinch

Serves 4 as a starter or 2 as a light meal

Green peppercorns add a subtle spicy aromatic note with a gentle piquant aftertaste. This is a perfect salad to make in autumn using new season 'wet' walnuts.

Top and tail the beans and place in a steamer basket set over boiling water. Steam until only just tender – about 5 minutes. Tip onto a board and chop into 4cm/1$\frac{1}{2}$in pieces. Leave to cool.

Now make the dressing. Quarter and core the pear, saving one quarter to add to the salad. Peel and roughly chop the rest. Put in a blender or small food processor with the lemon juice, olive oil, crushed green peppercorns and a sprinkle of sea salt. Process for 30 seconds until smooth, then pour into a small jug.

To make the salad, quarter and core the pear but do not peel. Cut crossways into thin slices, including the quarter pear left from the dressing. Sprinkle with a little lemon juice to prevent browning.

Put the pear slices and beans in a bowl and toss with about 5 tablespoons of the dressing – enough to coat. Season with a pinch of crumbled sea salt flakes.

Arrange the greenery in a serving dish or on individual plates. Add the pear mixture and strew the nuts and cheese over the top. Spoon over some more dressing.

cook's notes
- If you don't have a steamer basket, cook the beans in boiling water but make sure they are properly drained and dried. Don't plunge them in cold water after cooking, as some writers tell you to do.
- You'll need smooth-fleshed eating pears such as Comice, Packham's Triumph or Red Bartlett, rather than grainy ones.
- Choose a crumbly blue cheese rather than a soft creamy one. Dorset Blue Vinny, Bleu d'Auvergne or Maytag Blue would be excellent.

variation
- Cobnuts are a delicious alternative to walnuts. Make sure they are fresh and moist.

peppered smoked mackerel, fennel and beetroot

uncooked beetroot 2 small, peeled and coarsely grated

black peppercorns 3/4 tsp, cracked

fennel seeds 3/4 tsp, crushed

sea salt flakes to taste

extra-virgin olive oil

lemon juice

fennel bulbs 2 small, with fronds

baby spinach 2 good handfuls

frisée (curly endive) 2 good handfuls

peppered mackerel fillets 3, skinned and broken into chunks

Serves 4 as a starter or light meal

A tasty combination of pungent, salty, lemony and sweet – peppery smoked mackerel, crunchy fresh-tasting fennel and sweet grated beetroot. I've spiked the beetroot with fennel seeds and cracked black pepper to tame its slightly overpowering flavour.

Toss the grated beetroot with the peppercorns, fennel seeds, some crumbled sea salt flakes, a tablespoon of olive oil and a squeeze of lemon juice. Leave this to develop its flavours while you prepare the rest of the salad.

Trim the fennel bulbs, leaving most of the root attached and reserving the feathery fronds. (Use the tough outer parts for soup or stock.) Slice the bulbs from top to bottom into quarters, then cut each quarter vertically into the thinnest possible slivers. Toss in a bowl with sea salt flakes, a good squeeze of lemon juice and a splash of olive oil. Chop up some fennel fronds to make two teaspoons and add these too.

Divide the spinach and frisée between the serving plates. Carefully place a small mound of beetroot in the middle – don't move the beetroot once you've positioned it, otherwise the salad will be swimming in red juice. Top with a mound of fennel then scatter chunks of mackerel over the top.

variation

- For deliciously crisp mackerel grill it before skinning and serve warm. This gets rid of some of the oiliness and makes the fish crisper. Get the grill good and hot, then put the mackerel, skin-side up, on a rack. Grill for 6 minutes, turning once. Break into chunks leaving the skin on – it will be nicely blistered.

soups

These recipes show you some of the ways in which pepper is used to good effect in soups – either to link and round off flavours, to add warmth, colour and aroma, to balance sweetness or to perk up blandness. Whatever its role, and however much or little is used, pepper makes itself felt and you would certainly notice if it was not there.

Taking a cook's look at soups around the world, it becomes obvious that pepper is a key ingredient, and with good reason. It provides gentle background warmth to that all-time comforter, Jewish chicken soup. It makes itself quietly felt in the British classics Scotch broth and cock-a-leekie, brightening the flavour of seemingly modest ingredients such as root vegetables, cabbage and pearl barley. Pepper works its magic on tomato-based soups such as gazpacho or Provençal fish soup, and it peps up chowders and creamy white bean soups.

With a slick of fruity olive oil, which is in itself peppery, coarsely ground pepper adds the finishing touch to robust Italian ribollita and Portuguese caldo verde. It contributes vital pungency to the classic Chinese Hot and Sour Soup (page 107) and to Rainbow Pepper Chicken Noodle Soup (page 109) – an unbeatable hangover cure. Sizzled in oil with other spices, a few cracked peppercorns add fragrance and zest to South Indian Tomato Rasam (page 112) and to a deliciously sloppy split-pea dhal-like soup (page 114).

Pepper is there for health reasons too: it perks up the appetite and helps the body to digest food. A well-made, judiciously seasoned soup gives you a feeling of well-being which can lift fatigue, is still satisfying even though easy to digest, and is perfect for both solitary meals or feeding a crowd. If the quantities in the recipes seem too generous, just halve the ingredients or make the full amount and freeze what you don't need.

roasted root soup with sizzled ginger and black pepper crème fraîche

red onion 1 medium
swede 1/2, weighing about
  250g/9oz
sweet potatoes 2, weighing
  about 450g/1lb in total
potato 1 medium
extra-virgin olive oil 5 tbsp
tomato purée 2 tbsp
black peppercorns 2 tsp,
  freshly ground
ground ginger 1 tsp
garlic cloves 2 large, unpeeled
chicken or **vegetable stock**
  850ml/1 1/2 pints, preferably
  home-made
white wine vinegar 2 tsp
salt 1 tsp

to garnish
sizzled ginger threads (see
  cook's notes)
Black Pepper Crème Fraîche
  (page 188)
flat-leaf parsley stems
  discarded, leaves sliced to
  make 4 tbsp

Serves 6

Slow-roasting root vegetables really brings out their inherent sweetness and intense flavours. Crisply sizzled ginger balances the sweetness and a swirl of peppery cream draws it all together.

Preheat the oven to 190°C/375°F/Gas 5. Cut the onion, swede, sweet potatoes and potato into large, even-sized chunks – about the size you'd make roast potatoes.

Mix the olive oil and tomato purée in a large bowl until well blended. Stir in the pepper and ginger. Add the vegetable chunks and the garlic and toss until evenly coated. Tip into a large shallow roasting tray, including any oily residue from the bowl. Roast for about 20 minutes or until the garlic cloves feel soft.

Remove the garlic and put it to one side. Give the other vegetables a toss and then continue roasting for another 20–25 minutes or until they start to caramelise round the edges.

This is a good time to make the sizzled ginger threads (see cook's notes) and the Black Pepper Crème Fraîche. Chill the cream and keep the ginger threads warm in a low oven while you finish the soup.

Once the vegetables are nicely roasted, remove from the oven and let them cool for a few minutes.

Peel the garlic and put in a food processor along with the vegetables. Process in short bursts, scraping down the bowl now and again, until you have a rough-textured purée.

Scrape the purée into a saucepan and pour in the stock. Add the vinegar and salt, then bring to the boil. Reduce the heat and simmer gently for a minute or two, stirring.

Pour the soup into shallow bowls, swirl in a spoonful of pepper cream and top with sizzled ginger threads and the parsley.

cook's notes
- The vegetables will cook better in a shallow roasting tray rather than a high-sided one. Make sure it's big enough to allow space between the vegetables – if you crowd them they'll steam in their own moisture instead of crisply roasting.
- To make sizzled ginger threads, slice two 5cm/2in pieces of ginger root lengthways into very thin shreds. Heat 2 tablespoons of groundnut oil in a small frying pan until hazy. Throw in the ginger and sizzle, turning with tongs, for about 1 minute until crisp. Immediately remove from the pan and drain on paper towels.

leek, celery and cannellini bean soup with green peppercorns and pancetta

cannellini beans 200g, soaked for several hours (or a 400g/14oz can)

butter or **vegetable oil** 4 tbsp

fat leeks 4, white part only, sliced

celery stalks 5, quartered lengthways and diced

fresh bay leaf 1

thyme sprigs 2

chicken stock 1.5 litres/2³/₄ pints, preferably home-made

dried green peppercorns 2 tbsp, lightly crushed

salt to taste

pancetta 75g/2³/₄oz

double cream 3–4 tbsp

chives 3 tbsp, chopped

Serves 6

This is a good mix of flavours and textures. The sweetness of the leeks goes well with earthy beans and salty crisp pancetta. Celery gives a bit of crunch and greenness, and the green peppercorns leave a mild smoky aftertaste.

If using dried beans, drain the soaking water and put the beans in a saucepan with fresh water to cover. Bring to the boil, boil for 15 minutes, then simmer for about 30 minutes more until the beans are just tender but not disintegrating. Drain, reserving the liquid. (If using canned beans, drain and rinse thoroughly.)

Melt the butter in a large saucepan. Add the leeks, celery, bay leaf and thyme sprigs. Cover and sweat over medium-low heat for 15 minutes until slightly soft.

Pour in the stock, then add the crushed peppercorns and the cooked or canned beans. Season with a little salt to taste, bearing in mind the saltiness of the pancetta. Simmer, partly covered, for another 15 minutes.

Meanwhile, fry the pancetta in a non-stick pan until crisp. Drain on paper towels and keep warm.

Fish out the bay leaf and thyme from the soup. Purée about two-thirds of the mixture in a food processor, then pour this back into the pan and reheat gently, stirring. If the soup seems too thick, use some of the reserved bean water or a bit more stock to thin it down.

Ladle into shallow soup plates. Swirl in a little cream and sprinkle with the chives. Crumble the pancetta over the top.

hot and sour soup

dried mushrooms 4 medium

dried shrimps 1 tbsp

lean pork 75g/2^3/$_4$oz, sliced
　　into matchstick strips

chicken stock 1.5 litres/2^3/$_4$
　　pints, preferably home-made

raw tiger prawns 6 large,
　　shelled

firm tofu 100g/3^1/$_2$oz, sliced
　　into 1cm/^{1}/$_2$in cubes

canned bamboo shoots
　　50g/1^3/$_4$oz, shredded

frozen peas 50g/1^3/$_4$oz

spring onions 2, finely
　　chopped

sea salt 1 tsp

egg 1, beaten

toasted sesame oil 2 tsp

for the hot and sour mixture

water 4 tbsp

white wine vinegar 3 tbsp

light soy sauce 2 tbsp

cornflour 1 tbsp

white peppercorns 1 tsp,
　　freshly ground

Serves 6

This classic Chinese soup recipe was given to me by Chef But of the late Ken Lo's Memories of China restaurant in Belgravia, London. He uses plenty of ground white pepper rather than chillies to create the necessary bite.

Put the mushrooms and shrimps in separate bowls and cover with boiling water. Leave to soak for 15 minutes, then drain. Slice the mushrooms into thin shreds.

Mix the hot and sour ingredients to a paste.

Put the pork, mushrooms, shrimps and stock in a large saucepan. Bring to the boil, then reduce the heat and simmer for 10 minutes.

Add the prawns, tofu, bamboo shoots, peas, spring onions and sea salt. Simmer gently for a few more minutes until the prawns and peas are cooked through.

Stir in the hot and sour paste. When the soup thickens, pour in the beaten egg in a thin stream. Ladle into bowls and sprinkle with a few drops of toasted sesame oil.

cook's note

- If possible, try to buy tofu from an Asian grocery. It will be infinitely superior to the brands sold in supermarkets.

p e p p e r

rainbow pepper chicken noodle soup

red chilli 1 small, deseeded
and finely chopped
lemon grass inner leaves from
2 stalks, finely chopped
kaffir lime leaves 4, finely
shredded
fresh galangal or **ginger root**
2 tsp, finely chopped
chicken stock 1.5 litres/2^3/$_4$
pints, preferably home-made
white, **pink** and **green**
peppercorns ^{1}/$_2$ tsp each,
crushed
boneless skinless chicken
thighs or **breasts** 450g/1lb
in total, cut into 1cm/^{1}/$_2$in
cubes
medium rice noodles
200g/7oz
limes juice from 2
fish sauce 1–3 tsp
coriander stems discarded,
leaves sliced to make 5 tbsp
mint leaves sliced to make
4 tbsp

Serves 6

A deeply comforting and restorative soup: chicken and noodles simmered in lemon grass- and chilli-infused stock, seasoned with a rainbow mix of crushed white, pink and green peppercorns. Normally I'm not in favour of mixing pink peppercorns with proper pepper, but it seems to work here.

Put the chilli, lemon grass, lime leaves and galangal in a bowl and pour over enough hot water to just cover. Leave to steep for 15 minutes, then mash to a coarse paste.

Heat the stock in a large saucepan with the mashed spice paste and the peppercorns. Add the chicken, bring to the boil, then simmer over low heat for 20 minutes.

Meanwhile, cook the noodles according to the packet instructions. Drain, cut them into slightly shorter lengths with scissors, and add to the soup.

Stir in the lime juice, fish sauce, coriander and mint. Simmer for a few minutes to heat through.

mulligatawny soup with rhubarb and coconut

vegetable oil 4 tbsp
onion 1 large, finely chopped
celery 2 stalks, diced
red or **yellow lentils** 175g/6oz
red chillies 1–3, deseeded and
  finely chopped
fat garlic cloves 4, thinly sliced
ginger root a thick piece about
  4cm/1$\frac{1}{2}$in long, finely
  chopped
black peppercorns 1 tbsp,
  crushed
curry powder 1 tbsp
cumin seeds 2 tsp, freshly
  ground
salt 1 tsp
chicken stock 1 litre/1$\frac{3}{4}$ pints,
  preferably home-made
**boneless skinless chicken
  breast** 1 large, weighing
  about 200g/7oz
rhubarb 3 thick pink or red
  stalks, weighing about
  250g/9oz
butter 2 tbsp
lime juice 1 tbsp
coconut milk 400g/14oz can
cooked Basmati rice about
  350g/12oz

to garnish
coriander a good handful,
  stems discarded, leaves
  picked and sliced
toasted coconut flakes
red chilli a few slivers

Serves 6–8

Literally meaning 'pepper water' (*molaga tanni*), mulligatawny was made by patient Indian cooks for British colonials who craved the familiarity of soup, even though it was not part of Indian cuisine. The British brought the recipe back to England and proceeded to wreak havoc with what was a judiciously spiced broth. It developed a dreary reputation – pieces of apple and inappropriate British vegetables floating in a flour-thickened liquid flavoured with curry powder.

This version made with pink rhubarb, good broth and coconut milk should put mulligatawny back on the culinary map. Simultaneously tart and spicy, it has a touch of sweetness from the coconut, the fresh green astringency of coriander leaves and a lovely warming after-glow from the black pepper and chilli. Almost a meal in itself, this is a great soup for feeding a crowd.

Heat the oil in a large, heavy-based saucepan over medium-low heat. Add the onion and celery, and cook, covered, for about 5 minutes or until the onion is translucent.

Add the lentils, stirring until well coated with the oil. Stir in the chilli, garlic, ginger, peppercorns, curry powder, cumin and salt. Mix well, then cover and cook for about 10 minutes or until the vegetables are soft. Stir every now and again to stop the lentils from sticking.

Pour in the stock and bring to the boil, then reduce the heat and simmer for about 20 minutes, partly covered.

Meanwhile, chop the chicken into 1cm/$\frac{1}{2}$in cubes.

Tip about half the soup mixture into a blender and whizz to a purée. Pour the purée back into the pan. Add the chicken and bring to the boil, then reduce the heat and simmer for another 15 minutes or until the chicken is cooked through.

While the chicken is simmering, prepare the rhubarb. Slice the stalks lengthways, then crossways to make 2cm/$\frac{3}{4}$in cubes. Heat the butter in a medium-sized, heavy-based pan until foaming. Add the rhubarb and toss gently for 3–4 minutes over medium heat until it just starts to soften.

Tip the rhubarb into the soup. Add the lime juice, then simmer gently for about 10 minutes or until the rhubarb is soft. Stir in the coconut milk and simmer gently to heat through – take care not to let it boil.

To serve, divide the rice between shallow soup plates. Ladle the soup over the rice and sprinkle generously with shredded coriander leaves. For the finishing touch, add a few toasted coconut flakes and a sliver or two of red chilli.

cook's notes

- Mulligatawny is traditionally made with tart apples but rhubarb makes an interesting change. It is pleasantly sharp and also adds a nice pink tinge to the soup (brownness is to be avoided at all costs). You could also try it with gooseberries.
- A few chunks of cooked white crab meat make a delicious garnish as well as, or instead of, the coconut flakes. The sweetness contrasts beautifully with tart rhubarb.
- This is one of the few occasions when I'm prepared to use shop-bought curry powder. It seems appropriate for this type of Anglo-Indian cuisine.

pepper water

The original mulligatawny, or pepper water, was a thin pungent soup flavoured with a little fried onion. This recipe is from a 19th-century cookbook:

'Required: a pint and a half of cold water, the juice of a lemon, a dessertspoonful of salt, two cloves of garlic, an onion, a dozen peppercorns, a tablespoonful of curry powder, and a bit of onion fried in butter. Cost, about 4d. Add the lemon juice to the water, then pound the spices and onion in a mortar; put all in a saucepan, and bring to the boil, and simmer for a quarter of an hour, then put in the fried onion, and give another boil, and strain through muslin. This should be bottled and corked for use. A little tamarind may be used instead of lemon, or in addition. This is useful for flavouring purposes. To increase the pungency, use more peppercorns or reduce the water. A few chillies may be added.'

tomato rasam

tamarind pulp 75g/2³/₄oz
hot water 450ml/16fl oz
vine-ripened tomatoes
 8–10 large
fat garlic cloves 4
ginger root 2.5cm/1in chunk
 from thickest part of the root
red lentils 3 tbsp
coriander large handful, stems
 discarded, leaves sliced
green or **red chilli** 1, halved
 lengthways and deseeded
freshly ground black pepper
 ¹/₂ tsp
turmeric powder 1 tsp
salt to taste

to finish
butter or **sunflower oil** 1 tbsp
mustard seeds 1 tsp
cumin seeds ¹/₂ tsp
dried red chilli 1, deseeded
asafoetida powder pinch
 (optional)
curry leaves a few (optional)

Serves 4

Rasam (meaning 'essence') is the soup of Southwest India where the health-conscious swear by its medicinal properties. Quickly made – despite the list of ingredients – rasam is clean-tasting, warming and easily digestible. Traditionally served in small glasses, it clears the palate and complements richer dishes. For a no-fuss light meal, it's hard to beat rasam and a bowl of plainly boiled rice.

Tear the tamarind pulp into chunks and put in a bowl with the hot water. Leave to soak for 15 minutes, breaking up the pulp with a fork as it softens.

Meanwhile, peel the tomatoes and roughly chop the flesh. Peel and slice the garlic and ginger. Whizz the three together in a food processor for at least 1 minute or until well blended.

Strain the tamarind pulp through a fine sieve set over a saucepan, using the back of a wooden spoon to press out as much pulp as you can. Discard the fibres and seeds. Simmer the strained liquid over medium heat for 5 minutes.

Add the lentils and the blended tomato mixture to the pan, along with the coriander, chilli, pepper and turmeric. Bring to the boil, then reduce the heat a bit and simmer for 15 minutes, stirring now and again to prevent sticking. Season with salt and carefully fish out the pieces of chilli.

To finish, heat the butter in a small frying pan until foaming. Add the mustard seeds and sizzle for a few seconds. When they start to splutter, add the cumin seeds, dried chilli, asafoetida and curry leaves, if you're using these. Pour the contents of the pan over the soup, give it a swirl and serve right away.

cook's notes
- Tamarind pulp comes in sticky blocks. You'll find it in larger supermarkets and Asian grocers. Alternatively, use tamarind concentrate which can be spooned straight from the jar.
- Tomato peel is satisfyingly easy to remove. Cover tomatoes with boiling water, leave for 30 seconds, drain, then nick the surface and slip off the peel.
- Asafoetida is a strange-smelling yellow powder that adds an onion-like flavour to vegetable dishes. It comes in attractive small tins sold in Asian grocers.
- Curry leaves are definitely worth using if you enjoy Keralan cooking. The flavour is uniquely lemony, spicy and faintly bitter – not like curry at all. The dried leaves are easy to find but it's far better to use fresh if you can. They'll keep in the freezer for months, so be sure to buy plenty of sprigs.

split pea and red pepper soup with sizzled spices

vegetable oil 4 tbsp
mustard seeds 1 tsp
onion 1 small, finely chopped
tomato 1 medium, peeled and
chopped
green or **red chillies**
1–2, deseeded and finely
chopped
garlic cloves 2, finely chopped
turmeric powder $^1/_2$ tsp
paprika $^1/_2$ tsp
yellow split peas 200g/7oz,
soaked for several hours
vegetable or **chicken stock**
1 litre/1$^3/_4$ pints, preferably
home-made
red peppers 2 small, halved
and deseeded
salt 1 tsp
lemon juice 2 tbsp
coriander stems discarded,
leaves sliced to make 4 tbsp
black peppercorns $^1/_2$ tsp,
crushed
cloves 4, crushed
green cardamom seeds from
6 pods, crushed

Serves 4–6

This is a colourful mix of soupy yellow split peas and roasted sweet red pepper spiked with green chillies, lemon juice and fresh coriander. A tempering of sizzled cracked black peppercorns, cloves and green cardamom adds the finishing touch.

Heat 1 tablespoon of the oil in a large saucepan over medium-high heat. Add the mustard seeds then, once they begin to pop, reduce the heat to medium and stir in the onion, tomato and chillies. Cook, stirring, for another minute, then add the garlic, turmeric and paprika.

Drain the split peas and add to the pan. Pour in the stock, cover and bring to the boil, then simmer over low heat for about 50 minutes or until the peas are mushy.

While the peas are cooking, put the red peppers, cut-side down, in a pan under a very hot grill. Grill for 10–15 minutes or until the skin blisters and blackens. Leave to cool, then peel off the skin and chop the flesh into neat 1cm/$^1/_2$in squares.

Once the peas are soft, break them up a bit with a potato masher or the back of a wooden spoon. Stir in the red peppers, salt, lemon juice and coriander. Simmer for a few more minutes to warm through.

Heat the remaining oil in a small, heavy-based frying pan. When almost smoking, add the peppercorns, cloves and cardamom seeds. Sizzle for a few seconds until fragrant, then pour into the soup. Cover and leave to stand for a few minutes before serving.

fish

Fish and pepper are excellent culinary partners. Imagine grilled salmon or Dover sole without a dusting of freshly ground pepper; or smoked mackerel fillets without their coating of cracked black peppercorns. Pepper is there for a reason – it cuts through oiliness and gives blandness a welcome boost, and used with a light touch it augments the delicate sweetness of good fresh fish. It's there for texture too – a full-on pepper crust adds welcome crunch as well as piquancy.

I have focused mainly on quick, simple techniques – grilling, flash-frying or brief roasting at a high temperature, for example – which allow you to appreciate the inherent tenderness and clean flavour of fish, as well as pepper's intriguing spicy aroma.

A generous grinding of pepper perks up batters and coatings. I cannot resist a crisp mound of deep-fried whitebait seasoned with peppery flour. Mike Smylie, herring devotee and author of *Herring: A History of the Silver Darlings*, is partial to fried herring fillets coated in a zesty lime-pepper crust (page 128). I like to serve fried peppery breadcrumbs with prawns or grilled sardines (page 123).

A teaspoon or so of lightly crushed black peppercorns invariably goes into fish stock and *court-bouillon*, the wine- or vinegar-based liquid used as a base for fish soups and sauces and for poaching whole fish. Here, pepper provides a necessary touch of pungency that balances acidity and enhances the flavour of fish rather than masking it. Peppercorns are also used in pickled and soused fish, and in the sweet-salty cure for Swedish gravlax (page 129).

However you choose to cook your fish, it goes without saying that it should be the freshest of fresh, as should your peppercorns. It's well worth finding a reliable fishmonger and using the very best pepper you can lay your hands on. The difference is remarkable.

lemon pepper plaice with chilli

plaice 2, each weighing about
   400g/14oz
olive oil or **extra-virgin**
   sunflower oil for brushing
sea salt flakes 2 tsp
coarsely ground black pepper
red chilli a few very thin slivers
lemon juice from $1/2$ lemon
thick lemon wedges to serve

Serves 2

Chef Cassie Williamson serves this dish at her pub – the White Horse Inn at Litton Cheney in Dorset. Deceptively simple, but dependent on absolutely fresh fish and good quality peppercorns. Cassie's plaice are line-caught in Lyme Bay and delivered to her door practically still wriggling. The pungent bite of freshly ground pepper and hint of heat from the chilli is perfect with the sweet juiciness of the plaice.

Preheat the oven to 240°C/475°F/Gas 9. Put a large baking sheet in the oven to heat.

Scale, wash and gut the fish leaving the heads on. Place on a board and, using a very sharp knife, make parallel diagonal slashes about 2cm/$3/4$in apart all over the dark skin, cutting into the flesh a bit. Then slash in the opposite direction to form a diamond pattern.

Brush the fish with oil on both sides. Place on the baking sheet, dark-side up. Sprinkle with the sea salt flakes and a generous amount of coarsely ground black pepper. Bake for 15 minutes or until the diamonds start to shrink and the skin becomes crisp at the edges. The flesh should look opaquely white and juicy.

Sprinkle with a sliver of chilli and the lemon juice. Serve at once with thick lemon wedges.

cook's note
- The trick here is to sprinkle the fish with considerably more pepper than you think necessary. Believe me – it will not be too overpowering once it has joined forces with the fish juices and lemon.

five-pepper tuna steaks with salsa

mixed peppercorns (black, white, green, Sichuan) 1 tbsp
allspice berries $1/4$ tsp
tuna steaks 2 (2.5cm/1in thick), each weighing about 175g/6oz
lime juice a squeeze
olive oil 1 tbsp
sea salt flakes a pinch
coriander a small handful, stems discarded, leaves sliced

for the salsa
tomatoes 3, deseeded and diced
avocado $1/2$, diced
red onion $1/2$, diced
cucumber 7cm/$2^3/4$in, peeled, deseeded and diced
sea salt flakes a pinch
lime juice 1 tbsp
coriander a small handful, stems discarded, leaves sliced

Serves 2

This is so easy and quick – perfect for when you want to cook a special supper for someone but don't want to spend a lot of time in the kitchen. The cooling salsa counteracts the heat of the peppery crust.

Combine all the salsa ingredients in a small serving bowl and set aside.

Using a mortar and pestle, grind the peppercorns and allspice berries to a coarse powder.

Massage the tuna steaks with lime juice and then the olive oil. Press the crushed spices onto both sides of the fish to form a crust. Sprinkle with a pinch of sea salt flakes crumbled between your finger and thumb.

Heat a ridged stove-top grill pan, preferably non-stick, until very hot. Grill the tuna for 2 minutes on each side. Garnish with a sprinkling of coriander and serve at once with the salsa.

cook's notes
- Slice the salsa vegetables into very small even dice. I find a small serrated knife is the best tool for this. It cuts cleanly through tough tomato skin and soft avocado flesh without leaving ragged edges.
- You might want to serve this with some plainly boiled Thai fragrant rice. If you have any, add two or three shredded lime leaves to the rice while it's cooking. Otherwise a good squeeze of lime juice will do.
- Make sure your peppercorns are well within their 'sell-by' date. Freshness matters here.
- For convenience, I sometimes use Bart Spices Five Pepper Bristol Blend instead of mixed peppercorns and allspice.
- Don't worry if the tuna looks very rare when it leaves the pan – it will continue to cook as it sits on the plate.

See also
Grinding, Crushing, Cracking, page 83
Allspice, page 54

salt and pepper prawns

large shell-on raw prawns
16–20, heads and legs
removed
Sichuan pepper 1 tsp
sea salt 1 tsp
sunflower oil 2 tbsp
garlic clove 1 large, thinly
sliced

**Serves 4 as a shared dish or
starter**

There are several versions of this dish but this is one of the simplest. Easy to cook and great for keeping guests happy while you make the rest of the meal. Some recipes suggest dry-frying the peppercorns before crushing but I don't think it's really necessary.

Peel away most of the shell from the prawns but leave the last segment and the tail attached. (This not only looks pretty but makes the prawns easier to hold when you eat them with your fingers.) Remove the dark vein running down the back.

Combine the Sichuan pepper and sea salt, and pound to a coarse powder using a mortar and pestle or an electric coffee grinder.

Heat half the oil in a medium-sized, non-stick frying pan. Add the garlic slices and sizzle over medium-high heat for a minute or two. As soon as the garlic starts to turn pale golden, scoop it out of the pan with a slotted spoon. Drain on paper towels and set aside.

Add the rest of the oil to the pan. When it is shimmering hot, toss in the prawns and fry for 2–3 minutes, turning with tongs, until they are evenly pink and cooked through.

Tip the prawns into a warm serving bowl and sprinkle with the salt and pepper mixture and the garlic.

cook's notes
- As a fledgling cook, it took me a while to realise that raw prawns are grey and cooked prawns are pink – probably because raw prawns weren't often available in those days. You need grey for this recipe. If you use pink, you'll be cooking them twice and then they'll be tough.
- You might want to add some ginger for extra zest. Cut two thickish slices of fresh ginger from the fattest part of the root. Slice into matchsticks and sizzle with the garlic.

See also
Grinding, Crushing, Cracking, page 83

*salt and pepper prawns
(page 119)*

pan-fried black pepper prawns

extra-large raw prawns 15–20
black peppercorns 1 tbsp
coriander seeds 1 tbsp
extra-virgin olive oil 1 tbsp
sea salt $1/4$ tsp
groundnut or **sunflower oil**
   125ml/4fl oz
lime juice from $1/2$ lime

**Serves 4 as a shared dish or
starter**

Adapted from *One Spice, Two Spice* by Floyd Cardoz of the restaurant Tabla in New York. The sweetness of the prawns, the heat of freshly ground black peppercorns and the citrusy flavour of the coriander seeds make a great combination.

Remove the heads and legs from the prawns. Peel away the shell and remove the dark vein running down the back.

Grind the peppercorns and coriander seeds separately in an electric coffee grinder until medium-fine. Tip into a bowl and mix with the olive oil. Add the prawns, tossing so they are well coated with oil and spices. Cover the bowl and leave in the fridge to marinate for at least an hour, or up to 24 hours.

When ready to cook, crumble the sea salt over the prawns.

Heat the groundnut oil in a large, heavy-based pan over medium-high heat until the oil just begins to shimmer. Carefully add the prawns and fry for about 2 minutes on each side until pink and crisp.

Drain on paper towels, tip into a serving dish and drizzle with the lime juice.

cook's notes
- The prawns can be grilled instead of fried but first brush the grill rack with oil so they don't stick.
- If you don't have an electric coffee grinder, grind the spices using a mortar and pestle, then sieve to remove any fine dust.
- A simple tomato and cucumber salad and perhaps some plainly boiled rice would go well with this.

See also
Grinding, Crushing, Cracking, page 83

grilled sardines with preserved lemons, cumin and peppery breadcrumbs

sardines 8 large
preserved lemons 2, roughly chopped
cumin seeds 2 tsp, crushed
thyme sprigs 8 small
olive oil for brushing
sea salt flakes
freshly ground black pepper to taste
Peppery Herbed Breadcrumbs (page 233)
flat-leaf parsley chopped to make 2 tbsp
lemon wedges to serve

Serves 4 as a starter or light meal

There is a nice little after-glow of pepper from the breadcrumbs which cuts the richness of the sardines.

Rinse the sardines under cold running water, rubbing off the scales with your fingers. Using a sharp knife, remove the heads then make a slit down the belly and pull out the innards. Rinse again, making sure the cavities are clean. Blot dry with paper towels.

Mix the preserved lemons with the cumin seeds. Push some of this mixture into the cavity of each sardine along with a sprig of thyme. Brush with olive oil and sprinkle with crumbled sea salt flakes and freshly ground pepper.

Now for the tricky bit. Holding a sardine belly-side up to keep the filling in place, push a kebab skewer through the tail end and out the opposite side. Gently bend the fish enough to push the skewer through the head end and out the other side. Thread another sardine onto the skewer, bending it the opposite way to the first, so the head of one and the tail of the other overlap slightly. Thread the remaining three pairs of sardines onto skewers. Place on a rack in a grill pan, making sure the fish remain belly-side up. Set aside while you deal with the breadcrumbs.

Preheat the grill until good and hot. With the pan about 15cm/6in from the heat source, grill the sardines for 7 minutes without turning until cooked through.

Slide the sardines off the skewers into a warm serving dish. Pour over any pan juices. Strew with the peppery breadcrumbs and the parsley, and serve with nice fat lemon wedges.

cook's note
- Preserved lemons from the Middle East are usually pickled in a brine solution with nigella seeds and safflower petals. They have an intriguing musty flavour which I love. I drain the brine and cover the lemons with olive oil (extra-virgin is unnecessary here). After a week or so, the oil takes on a terrific flavour from the lemons, which will gradually deepen the longer you leave it. Try brushing the oil over poultry or fish before grilling or roasting, or use it to lubricate couscous and other grain salads.

grilled sardines with preserved lemons, cumin and peppery breadcrumbs (page 123)

keralan fish in a parcel

sea bream 4, each weighing
about 400g/14oz
limes juice of 2
sea salt flakes 1 tsp
shallots 3–4, finely chopped
green chilli $^1/_2$, finely chopped
ginger root 4cm/1$^1/_2$in piece,
finely chopped
black peppercorns 1$^1/_2$ tbsp,
crushed
cayenne pepper 1–2 tsp
turmeric powder 1$^1/_2$ tsp
curry leaves from 2 sprigs,
about 15 leaves
coconut oil 2 tbsp

to garnish
lime wedges
red onion thinly sliced into
rings

Serves 4

This dish is memorable for the heady, fiery fragrance which hits you as you open the steaming parcel. Let's face it, pepper, ginger and chilli are a potent mix, so this is probably not for the faint-hearted. Plain rice and cold beer are what's needed.

Clean and scale the fish, leaving the heads on. Using a sharp knife, make a couple of diagonal slashes on each side of the fish. Put them in a dish large enough to take them in a single layer.

Combine the lime juice and sea salt flakes and pour over the fish, rubbing it all over the skin and into the slits. Leave to marinate for 15 minutes while you prepare the spice paste.

Put the shallots, chilli, ginger, crushed peppercorns, cayenne, turmeric and curry leaves into a blender and whizz to a paste. Smear the paste all over the fish, rubbing it well in.

Brush four large pieces of thick kitchen foil with the coconut oil. Place a fish on each piece of foil, along with any spice paste left in the dish. Wrap up securely and leave for 10–15 minutes.

Preheat the oven to 240°C/475°F/Gas 9. Put a baking tray in the oven to heat.

Bake the fish for 10 minutes, then turn the parcels over and cook for another 5 minutes.

Open the parcels, inhale the spicy fragrance, then carefully tip the fish into a warm serving dish. Alternatively, put the parcels directly onto serving plates and let people open their own.

Serve scattered with lime wedges and red onion rings.

cook's notes
- Keralan cooks wrap the fish in thick banana leaves and grill it in a pan over a very hot fire. I have improvised by wrapping it in thick foil and baking in a very hot oven. The result is very similar.
- If you can't get sea bream, use any white-fleshed fish. Red or grey mullet, mackerel or bass would be fine.
- Curry leaves provide a typical Keralan flavour – uniquely lemony, spicy and slightly bitter but not at all like curry powder. Dried leaves are easy to buy but it's better to use fresh if you can. They'll keep in the freezer for months so it's worth buying a good bunch.
- Coconuts and their oil are widely used in Keralan cooking and give it a special flavour. Unlike most oils, coconut oil is solid at room temperature and difficult to remove from narrow-necked bottles. A few seconds in the microwave or a jug of hot water will melt it to a pouring consistency. You could use a vegetable oil as an alternative.

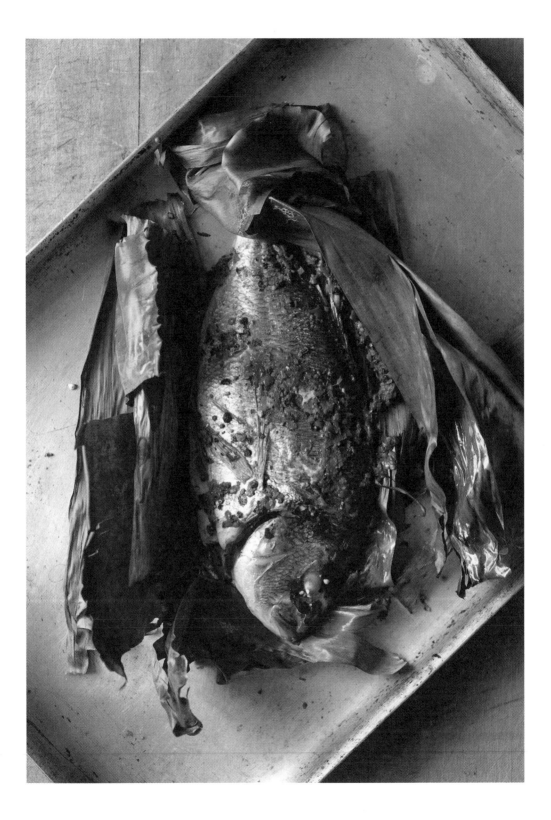

fried herring fillets with a lime pepper crust

limes 2
plain flour 1 tbsp
mixed peppercorns 1 heaped
   tsp, coarsely crushed
herring fillets 2, each weighing
   about 175–200g/6–7oz
olive oil 2 tbsp
sea salt flakes crushed

Serves 2

This is from *Herring: A History of the Silver Darlings* by Mike Smylie. Mike wants to see us eating more of this versatile fish, a wish I completely endorse. With a crisp coating of peppercorns and lime zest there's no excuse.

Finely grate the zest from the limes and add half to the flour. Mix with the peppercorns, spreading the mixture out on a flat plate.

Wipe the herring fillets dry and coat the flesh side with the peppercorn mixture. Press the fish well in to give a good coating, then dust with any remaining flour.

Heat the olive oil in a large frying pan until very hot. Fry the herring, flesh-side down, for 2–3 minutes or until golden underneath, then turn the fish over and fry on the other side for 2 minutes. Drain on crumpled paper towels.

Serve sprinkled with crushed sea salt flakes, the remaining lime zest, and the limes quartered to squeeze over.

gravlax

salmon (preferably organic)
 centre cut, about 1.3kg/3lb
coarse sea salt 4 tbsp
sugar 3 tbsp
white peppercorns 1 tbsp,
 crushed
black peppercorns 1 tbsp,
 crushed
large bunch of dill about
 75g/2³/₄oz, chopped

to serve
Dill Sauce (see cook's notes)
toast
lemon wedges

**Serves 6–8 as a starter or
light meal**

A Scandinavian speciality in which salmon fillets are cured in a mixture of salt, sugar, peppercorns and dill. White peppercorns are traditionally used, but I prefer equal quantities of white and black – white for bite and black for flavour.

Scale and wash the fish and cut off the fins. Using a very sharp knife, cut the fish in half lengthways along the backbone. Pull out the backbone and any small bones poking through the flesh.

Mix the sea salt, sugar and crushed peppercorns in a bowl.

Choose a glass or china dish just large enough to hold one of the pieces of fish. Scatter about one quarter of the dill over the bottom of the dish. Place a salmon fillet on top of the dill, skin-side down. Evenly sprinkle with half the salt mixture, massaging it well into the flesh – particularly the thicker areas. Cover with about three-quarters of the remaining dill, arranging it in an even layer. Sprinkle the rest of the salt mixture evenly over the dill. Place the second salmon fillet on top, skin-side up, with the thickest part on top of the thinnest part of the first fillet. Sprinkle the remaining dill on top.

Cover with a thick layer of kitchen foil. Weigh down evenly with a clean brick or a dish (slightly larger than the salmon) containing some heavy weights or food cans.

Leave in the fridge for at least 48 hours or up to 3 days, turning the fish over every 12 hours or so and basting between the layers with the juices that accumulate.

Drain the liquid and scrape off the dill and seasonings. Pat the salmon dry with paper towels.

To serve, place the two halves skin-side down on a serving board. Slice very thinly on the diagonal across the grain, detaching the skin from each slice. Serve with Dill Sauce (see cook's notes), toast and lemon wedges.

cook's notes
- It's a good idea to freeze the gravlax until an hour or two before you're ready to serve; it's far easier to slice.
- Ready-made gravlax is convenient to buy but it's fun to experiment with different cures and different fish. Try fennel fronds as an alternative to dill, and experiment with other oily fish such as mackerel or sea trout.
- To make the dill sauce, mix 4 tablespoons of Dijon mustard, 1 teaspoon of mustard powder, 3 tablespoons of caster sugar, 2 tablespoons of white wine vinegar and ¹/₂ teaspoon of salt. Gradually whisk in 150ml/¹/₄ pint of sunflower oil. Stir in 4 tablespoons of chopped dill.

hake cutlet au poivre

black and white peppercorns
  1 tbsp of each, coarsely
  crushed and sieved
hake cutlets 4, from a large
  fish
salt
flour about 3 tbsp
olive oil 2 tbsp
butter 50g/1³/₄oz
cognac 2 tbsp
strong chicken or **veal stock**
  4 tbsp
chopped parsley 1 tbsp

to serve
lemon wedges
watercress sprigs
new potatoes plainly boiled

Serves 4

This is from Simon Hopkinson's superb book *Second Helpings of Roast Chicken*. The heat of the peppercorns is tamed by the rich sauce so it does not overwhelm the delicate flavour of the fish.

Get a heavy-bottomed frying pan good and hot. Sprinkle the pepper over one surface only of the cutlets and press well in. Season with salt and dip carefully into the flour on both sides.

Add the oil to the pan and allow to become hazy. Gently lower each cutlet into the oil, pepper-side down, and leave to become crusty – about 4–5 minutes.

Now turn the fish over with a spatula or tongs and cook for a further 5–7 minutes. Once turned, add the butter and allow to froth. Turn the heat down and baste the fish with this buttery lotion as it finishes cooking. Remove the hake and put on a warmed serving dish.

Turn the heat up once more under the pan and, when frothing, pour in the cognac and set alight with a match. Once the flames have subsided, add the stock and stir together. Bring up to the boil and reduce slightly, whisking together until syrupy; you may need to add a further sliver of butter here.

Add the chopped parsley, swirl in, and pour over the hake. Serve with the lemon wedges and sprightly clumps of watercress. Good with plainly boiled new potatoes.

cook's notes
• Very fresh hake is a must for this. The flesh, though soft, should feel resilient when prodded. The skin should shine and the body look sleek and smell fresh.
• Ask your fishmonger to scale and trim the fish before cutting the cutlets. This recipe also works well with halibut, turbot or monkfish.
• Simon suggests that you may need to turn the heat down slightly while the first side of the fish is cooking, but he advises not to move the fish too early as it may stick.
• Check to see if the cutlets are cooked through by wiggling the central bone with your finger: the bone should start to come away from the flesh quite easily.

See also
Grinding, Crushing, Cracking, page 83

poultry

Whenever I prepare poultry the pepper mill is always at the ready. For simple roast chicken a light touch is usually sufficient – just season the cavity and rub the skin with freshly ground pepper and a little salt. For a more assertive flavour and moist buttery flesh, try massaging peppercorns and softened butter between the skin and flesh of the bird before roasting (page 142). Flat shapes like duck breasts or spatchcocked birds are superb anointed with a thick coating of cracked pepper *alla diavola* (page 139). The combination of crunchy piquant skin and succulent flesh is irresistible.

Pepper is the predominant spice in South-Indian curries, as Das Sreedharan's fiery Tellicherry Chicken Curry (page 133) shows. Pepper is used here in two ways: as a flavouring added during the early stages of cooking, and as a piquant condiment freshly stirred in just before serving. The result is an all-enveloping spicy heat reinforced by ginger and green chilli. As Das advises: 'Make sure you know your capacity to contain the power of pepper and use the spice accordingly'.

Asian cooks often opt for white pepper with poultry, preferring the purity of appearance. Vivek Singh of London's Cinnamon Club explains: 'White pepper is used as standard in most tandoori marinades as its neutral colour does not affect the appearance and it still supplies some heat'. Chinese Chef But follows the same principles in his zesty Stir-Fried Chicken with White Pepper (page 137).

Regardless of bird, pepper and poultry bring out the best in each other. The pungent bite stands up to the gamey flavours of pigeon or pheasant and cuts through the fattiness of duck and goose, making them more digestible. A few grindings of black pepper perk up white-fleshed chicken or turkey, coaxing out savoury flavours and providing welcome colour and crunch. The mild flesh, in turn, provides a culinary backdrop against which complex peppery flavours can be fully appreciated.

tandoori-style chicken with green spices, white pepper and mustard

**boneless skinless chicken
  thighs** (preferably corn-fed) 4

for the marinade
Garlic Paste (see cook's notes)
  1 tsp
Ginger Paste (see cook's notes)
  1 tsp
white peppercorns 1 tsp,
  finely ground
salt 1 tsp
lemon juice of 1

for the green spice mix
coriander (roots, stalks and
  leaves) 50g/1³/₄oz
mint leaves 25g/1oz
mustard leaves 50g/1³/₄oz
green chillies 3, chopped
vegetable oil 1¹/₂ tbsp
English mustard ¹/₂ tsp
wholegrain mustard 1 tbsp
salt ¹/₂ tsp
turmeric powder ¹/₈ tsp
Garam Masala (page 226)
  ¹/₂ tsp
Greek yogurt 1¹/₂ tbsp

Serves 4 as a main meal

This magnificently flavoured dish is adapted from *The Cinnamon Club Cookbook*. It demonstrates author Vivek Singh's belief that, in the context of Indian cooking in the west, spicing should be used to enhance the quality of ingredients, rather than overwhelming them. Vivek has been sparing with his use of pepper and has followed the tradition of using white pepper in tandoori-style dishes, so as not to affect the colour of the marinade.

Put the chicken thighs in a bowl, add all the marinade ingredients and mix well. Set aside for 30 minutes.

Put all the spice mix ingredients, except the yogurt, in a food processor or blender and mix to a smooth paste. Check the seasoning; it should taste quite pungent as its strength decreases during cooking. Rub the paste onto the chicken, add the yogurt and mix well. Leave to marinate for another 30 minutes.

Meanwhile, preheat the oven to 200°C/400°F/Gas 6. Place the chicken on a baking tray and bake for 20–25 minutes, turning once. If the meat starts to dry out, pour over some of the marinade.

cook's notes
- Because of the way they are processed, white peppercorns often have an oddly 'barnyardy' fragrance. Try to find Sarawak or single estate Keralan white peppercorns; they have a much cleaner aroma.
- Mustard leaves are sold in Asian food shops and they are also easy to grow. If you can't find any, Vivek suggests using double the amount of English mustard instead.
- To make Garlic Paste, chop up about 24 large garlic cloves and process to a paste with 5 tablespoons of water in a food processor or blender. This makes about 6 tablespoons and will keep for 1 week in the fridge or, if you substitute oil for water, up to 2 weeks.
- To make Ginger Paste, chop up 175g/6oz ginger root and process to a paste with 5 tablespoons of water in a food processor or blender. This makes about 6 tablespoons and will keep for 1 week in the fridge.

See also
Tasting Pepper, page 76
Grinding, Crushing, Cracking, page 83

tellicherry chicken curry

garlic cloves 3, roughly
  chopped
ginger root 2.5cm/1in chunk,
  thinly sliced
groundnut oil 4 tbsp
onions 2 medium, finely sliced
curry leaves 10
green chilli 1, halved
  lengthways and deseeded
black peppercorns
  4–5, cracked
coriander seeds 1 tsp,
  crushed
turmeric powder $1/2$ tsp
salt to taste
**boneless skinless chicken
  thighs** 6, cubed
water 225ml/8fl oz
Garam Masala (page 226) 1 tsp
freshly ground black pepper
  $1/2$ tsp

Serves 4 as a main course

This recipe comes from Das Sreedharan, owner of the Rasa chain of Keralan restaurants in London. Tellicherry, or Thallasserry as the town is now called, is well known for meat delicacies, thanks to the resident Muslim community. This is one of the most popular curries, seen both in local restaurants and at home. Black pepper is used in two ways here – as a background flavour in the early stages of cooking and as a condiment in the final tempering. It is a wonderful dish and very easy to make.

Using a mortar and pestle, pound the garlic and ginger to a smooth paste.

Heat the oil in a large frying pan over a medium heat. Add the onions, curry leaves, chilli and cracked peppercorns. Cook for about 15 minutes, stirring often, until the onions are golden.

Reduce the heat to medium-low, then add the garlic-ginger paste. Cook for 5 minutes, stirring now and then. Stir in the coriander seeds, turmeric and a little salt, and cook for another 5 minutes.

Add the chicken to the pan, give it a stir, then add the water and garam masala, mixing well. Cover and cook gently for 5 minutes or until the chicken is cooked through. Stir in the freshly ground pepper just before serving.

tellicherry chicken curry
(page 133)

pepper-crusted chicken in spicy soured cream

chicken quarters (preferably organic) 4, skin removed
soured cream 300ml/$^1/_2$ pint
lemon juice 2 tbsp
black peppercorns 2 tsp, freshly ground
cumin seeds 2 tsp, crushed
paprika 1 tsp
salt 1 tsp
garlic clove 1 large, crushed
fresh breadcrumbs 200g/7oz
black peppercorns 1 tbsp, crushed
olive oil 7 tbsp
flat-leaf parsley chopped to make 2 tbsp

Serves 4 as a main meal

You get a double hit of pepper here – in the marinade and in the breadcrumb coating. That said, the heat is not overwhelming, more of a gentle background spiciness that draws the other flavours together. I like this dish for its contrasting textures – crisp golden crumbs on top, and soft creaminess below.

Cut the chicken quarters in half and prick all over with a fork. In a bowl, combine the soured cream, lemon juice, ground black pepper, cumin, paprika, salt and garlic. Add the chicken and mix well. Cover and leave in the fridge for at least 6 hours.

Preheat the oven to 180°C/350°F/Gas 4. Combine the breadcrumbs and crushed peppercorns and spread out on a tray.

Remove the chicken from the marinade and roll the pieces in the breadcrumbs until thickly coated. Place in a shallow baking dish and pour the olive oil evenly over the chicken.

Bake for 1 hour, basting the topping with the juices from time to time. Sprinkle with the parsley just before serving.

cook's note
• If possible, use breadcrumbs from a good-quality artisan loaf, preferably organic. They'll have more flavour and a crisper texture than crumbs made with standard sliced white bread.

stir-fried chicken with white pepper

boneless skinless chicken breasts or **thighs** 3 medium
egg whites 2, lightly beaten
salt a pinch
cornflour 1$\frac{1}{2}$ tbsp
groundnut oil 4 tbsp
garlic cloves 2, finely chopped
ginger root a small chunk, finely chopped
spring onions 2, chopped, white and green parts separated
white peppercorns 1 tsp, crushed
rice wine or **dry sherry** 1 tbsp
light soy sauce 1 tbsp
oyster sauce 1 tbsp
sugar $\frac{1}{2}$ tsp
cashew nuts 5 tbsp
water 100ml/3$\frac{1}{2}$fl oz

Serves 2 as a light meal

This easy dish was adapted from a recipe given to me by Chef But at the Memories of China restaurant in London. The Chinese consider specks of black pepper unsightly, so white pepper is used here. It gives a nice clean hit of pungency without the more floral notes that you get from black pepper.

Cut the chicken into evenly-sized small pieces. Put in a shallow dish, add the egg whites and a pinch of salt, and mix well with a fork. Gradually sprinkle in all but 1 teaspoon of the cornflour. Stir well to get rid of any lumps. In a separate dish, mix the remaining teaspoon of cornflour with a little water to form a paste.

Heat a wok over high heat. Add the oil and when it's almost smoking, add the chicken and stir-fry for 5 minutes or until cooked through. Remove from the pan with a wok scoop or slotted spoon and drain on paper towels.

Reduce the heat a little, then add the garlic (take care that it doesn't burn), ginger, white spring onion and crushed white peppercorns. Stir for a few seconds, then tip the chicken pieces back into the wok and mix well.

Stir in the rice wine, soy sauce, oyster sauce, sugar, cashew nuts and water. Mix well, then stir in the cornflour paste to thicken the sauce. Cook for a few more seconds, sprinkle with chopped green onion and serve.

cook's note
- Because of the egg white coating, the chicken pieces will fuse together when you add them to the hot oil. Use tongs to lift and separate them into individual nuggets.

lemon devilled quails

quails 4, spatchcocked (see
   cook's notes)
black peppercorns $1/2$ tbsp,
   cracked, plus more for
   serving
white peppercorns $1/2$ tbsp,
   cracked, plus more for
   serving
lemon juice and finely grated
   zest of 1 lemon
extra-virgin olive oil 2 tbsp
sea salt flakes to taste

to serve
lemon wedges
watercress sprigs

Serves 2–4 as a main meal

In Rome, this is made with chicken and is called *alla diavola* because of the devilish amount of crushed peppercorns used. It is certainly peppery but it is also fragrant, particularly if you use top-notch peppercorns such as black Tellicherry and white Sarawak or Wynad. Definitely a dish for eating with your fingers.

Put the spatchcocked quails in a dish and rub the cracked peppercorns and lemon zest all over them. Pour over the lemon juice and olive oil and marinate for 1–2 hours in the fridge, turning and basting now and again.

When ready to cook, place the birds breast-side up on a board and arrange the legs so that the drumsticks and thighs are bent and turning inwards, nestling close to the rib cage. Insert a metal skewer (long enough to take two birds) through the drumstick, thigh and rib cage on one side, then out through the opposite thigh and drumstick. Insert a second skewer through the wing, breast and opposite wing. Thread another bird onto this pair of skewers, then repeat with the remaining birds using two more skewers.

Preheat the grill until very hot. Place the quails, skin-side up, in a grill pan without a rack and sprinkle with crumbled sea salt flakes. Position the pan approximately 15cm/6in from the heat source and grill for 10 minutes until the skin is golden brown. Baste with marinade and turn the birds over. Grill for another 10 minutes, then turn once more and grill for another 5 minutes or until the juices run clear when you pierce the thigh.

Remove the skewers and cut the quails in half lengthways. Arrange on warm plates, pour over any pan juices and sprinkle with more cracked peppercorns if you like. Serve with thick wedges of lemon and some peppery sprigs of watercress.

cook's notes
- The quail should be at room temperature when you grill them. Take them out of the fridge at least 30 minutes before you're ready to cook
- To spatchcock quails, or any poultry, put the birds on a board breast-side facing downwards. Snip off the wing tips and any feathery lumps at the ends of the legs. Remove the backbone and parson's nose by cutting along the entire length of the bird very close to both sides of the backbone. Open out the birds and turn them breast-side up. Press down sharply with your palm to break and flatten the breastbone. Rinse under running water and pat dry with paper towels.

seared pigeon breasts with balsamic vinegar, rocket and parmesan

pigeons 4
extra-virgin olive oil for brushing
sea salt flakes to taste
unsalted butter for frying
chicken or **pigeon stock** (see
    cook's notes) 4–5 tbsp
aged balsamic vinegar 1–2 tsp
freshly ground black pepper
    to taste

for the marinade
good red wine 100ml/3$^{1}/_{2}$fl oz
extra-virgin olive oil 2 tbsp
sage leaves 3–4, shredded
fresh bay leaves 2, shredded
garlic clove 1, crushed
white peppercorns 1 tsp,
    crushed
black peppercorns 1 tsp,
    crushed

to serve
rocket 4 small handfuls
radish sprouts 2 small
    handfuls (optional)
Parmesan shavings a few

**Serves 4 as a light meal or
starter**

An impressive and robustly-flavoured dish which is relatively quick and simple to cook once the marinade and stock are out of the way. Black and white peppercorns add gentle pungency, balanced by the mellow sweetness of aged balsamic vinegar.

Remove the breasts from the pigeons cutting the meat as close to the bone as possible. Put in a bowl with the marinade ingredients. Cover and leave in the fridge for at least 1 hour or up to 2 days. Discard the carcasses or use them to make stock (see cook's notes).

Reserving the marinade, pat the breasts dry with paper towels, scraping off any solids. Brush both sides with olive oil and sprinkle with crumbled sea salt flakes. Strain the marinade and set aside.

Heat a generous knob of butter in a heavy-based pan over medium-high heat. (Use a pan big enough to hold all the breasts without crowding them.) When the butter starts to sizzle, add the breasts and cook for 1 minute. Turn them over and cook for another minute.

Immediately take the breasts out of the pan. Put on a plate in a low oven with the door slightly ajar. Leave to rest for 10 minutes; the breasts will continue to cook, so don't worry if they look very rare to begin with.

Meanwhile, heat another knob of butter in the same pan. Once it's sizzling nicely, add 3–4 tablespoons of the reserved marinade, the same amount of stock, a teaspoon of balsamic vinegar and any juices from the breasts. Stir with a wooden spoon, scraping up any sediment, and simmer for a few minutes until slightly reduced. Add more salt, pepper or vinegar if necessary.

Arrange some rocket and radish sprouts, if you are using them, on plates. Place the pigeon breasts on top and spoon over the sauce. Scatter with Parmesan shavings and serve.

cook's notes
- Use aged or traditional balsamic vinegar. It's thick and syrupy with a fantastic mellow flavour. Cheap balsamic simply won't do.
- Radish sprouts are worth the search. Their glorious purple colour and peppery flavour really make the dish special.
- For a richly flavoured pigeon stock: chop the carcasses into smaller pieces. Melt 1$^{1}/_{2}$ tablespoons of butter in a saucepan and brown the carcasses. Cut a small onion, a celery stalk and a small carrot into chunks and add to the pan. Cover and simmer for a few minutes, then add a crushed garlic clove and a fresh bay leaf. Stir in 1 teaspoon of mixed allspice berries, black, white, green and pink peppercorns. Pour in 400ml/14fl oz of chicken stock and 300ml/$^{1}/_{2}$ pint of good red wine. Bring to the boil, then simmer gently for 1 hour. Strain and allow to cool. Strain again, through a sieve lined with damp muslin, to get rid of any sediment.

roast guinea fowl with orange and green peppercorn butter

guinea fowl 1, weighing about
1.3kg/3lb
unsalted butter 100g/3^1/$_2$oz,
softened
dried green peppercorns
1 tbsp, lightly crushed
orange finely grated zest and
juice of ^{1}/$_2$
garlic clove 1 large, crushed
sea salt flakes to taste
plain flour for sprinkling
chicken stock 450ml/16fl oz,
preferably home-made

Serves 2–3 as a main course

A tasty and emollient mix of softened butter, green peppercorns, garlic and orange zest are tucked between the skin and breast of the bird before roasting. Result: irresistibly golden crisp skin and moist fragrant flesh.

Preheat the oven to 180°C/350°F/Gas 4. Loosen the skin over the legs, thighs and breast of the guinea fowl by working your fingers underneath and detaching the membrane separating the skin from the flesh. Try not to tear the skin.

Mash together the butter, green peppercorns, orange zest, garlic and sea salt flakes. Insert some of the flavoured butter under the loosened skin, pushing it in as far as possible and smoothing it to the shape of the bird. Smear the rest of the butter over the skin.

Place on a rack in a roasting tin and roast for 40 minutes. Reduce the oven temperature to 170°C/325°F/Gas 3 and roast for another 40 minutes or until the juices run clear when you pierce the thickest part of the thigh.

Leave to rest for 10 minutes, then tip the juices from the cavity into the tin. Move the bird to a warm serving dish and keep hot while you make the gravy.

Pour off most of the fat from the tin and sprinkle the juices with flour. Stir over medium heat using a wooden spoon to scrape up the sticky residue from the bottom of the tin. Stir in the orange juice, then gradually add the stock, stirring constantly. Check the seasoning and add more salt, pepper or orange juice if necessary. Strain into a jug before serving.

cook's notes
- This dish can be made with a small organic or corn-fed chicken instead of guinea fowl.
- As an alternative to orange zest, try using 2 teaspoons of Orange and Pepper Powder (page 235). You might want to cut down on the green peppercorns if you do so.
- If you don't have dried green peppercorns, use drained and rinsed brine-cured peppercorns instead.

meat

I cannot think of any instances in meat cookery where pepper would be unwelcome, whether it be a light dusting or big-time seasoning. Pepper holds its own with substantial meaty flavours, while the meat itself disseminates pungency, resulting in dishes with magnificent depth of flavour. The classic *Steak au poivre* (page 151) springs immediately to mind – the texture of the meat as you bite into it, the full-bodied juices and meaty aroma, the fire and crunch of cracked peppercorns. There can be few gustatory experiences so powerful.

Black is my peppercorn of choice with red meat such as beef, lamb or venison; full-bodied flavours need the aroma as well as pungency. For that reason, I particularly like black pepper with liver. The Italian *fegato alla veneziana* – peppery calves liver and meltingly soft, fried onions is a mouth-watering combination as is food writer Rosemary Barron's Greek version with preserved lemon and parsley (page 156).

Black pepper is also good with roast pork, rubbed into the crevices of the scored skin along with sea salt flakes and crushed fennel seeds; the resulting crackling may cause unseemly squabbles.

The mild, sweetish flavour of pork lends itself to the lemony piquancy of green peppercorns. These are an essential component in pork-based Thai curries, though cooks in that part of the world use juicy sprigs of fresh green peppercorns rather than brine-cured or freeze-dried berries. The latter are better cooked more slowly so that the husks have time to soften – try them with braised rabbit (page 154).

As we saw in the chapter on poultry, pepper is a major player in the meat curries of south-west India. In Lamb Pepper Fry (page 152) pepper goes into the marinade, the sauce and the final tempering, each addition contributing another layer of complex piquant flavour.

A few turns of the pepper mill gives immediate fragrance and zest to grilled or pan-fried meat. However, added early on to a stew or braise, pepper imparts warm spiciness to the cooking liquid. This in turn penetrates other ingredients, slowly building an all-enveloping heat which pervades the whole dish and lingers on the tongue. The process of long leisurely simmering rounds out any searing harshness, so what may seem like an inordinate amount of pepper is actually not too excessive. That said, the process of testing these recipes undoubtedly raised my enjoyment and tolerance of peppery heat. Always taste as you go along, adding less rather than more to begin with, until you are sure of your capacity for this versatile spice.

lemon pepper pork burgers

minced pork 500g/1lb 2oz
onion 1/2 small, grated
garlic clove 1, very finely
chopped
lemon finely grated zest and
juice of 1
freshly ground black pepper
1 tsp
cumin seeds 1 tsp, crushed
sea salt 1 tsp
egg 1, beaten
olive oil 1 tbsp, plus extra for
frying
lemon wedges to serve

**Serves 4 as a light meal or
part of a** *meze*

There is just enough pepper here to make itself felt but you could add more if you like.

Put the pork, onion, garlic and lemon zest and juice in a bowl and mix well with a fork. Season with the pepper, cumin and sea salt, then stir in the beaten egg and the tablespoon of olive oil. Mix thoroughly again.

Divide the mixture into 12 balls, rolling them in the palm of your hand until firm. Flatten into patties about 2cm/³⁄₄in thick. Arrange in a single layer on a plate, cover with cling film and leave in the fridge for at least an hour, or overnight if necessary.

Heat about 5 tablespoons of oil in a large, heavy-based frying pan. When the oil starts to look hazy, slip the burgers into the pan, in batches if necessary – don't crowd the pan. Fry over medium-high heat for 4–5 minutes on each side or until golden brown and cooked through. Drain on paper towels and move to a warm serving dish. Serve with plenty of lemon wedges.

cook's notes
- The burgers can be served hot but they're also good at room temperature with plenty of crisp salad, tomato wedges, olives and slivers of red onion.
- Creamy tahini sauce or yogurt, mint and cucumber dip are excellent accompaniments.

membrillo- and pepper-glazed belly pork

pork belly 1.5kg/3lb 5oz in one
   piece
extra-virgin olive oil 2 tbsp,
   plus extra for rubbing in
black peppercorns $\frac{1}{2}$ tbsp,
   freshly ground
fennel seeds 1 tsp, crushed
sea salt flakes 2 tsp
membrillo (quince paste)
   125g/4$\frac{1}{2}$oz
lemon juice 2 tbsp

Serves 4 as a main meal

Made from the fragrant quince, membrillo is delicious with pork,
its unmistakable sweetness blending perfectly with fennel and
black pepper. This is bone-sucking stuff, definitely for eating with
your fingers.

Preheat the oven to 220°C/425°F/Gas 7. Using a sharp knife
(a Stanley knife is perfect), score the pork skin through the fat,
but not the flesh, making diagonal slashes about 2cm/$\frac{3}{4}$in apart.
Then cut the meat into eight strips, measuring about 13 x 5cm/
5 x 2in.
   Massage a lavish amount of olive oil into the pork skin, then
sprinkle with the pepper, fennel seeds and sea salt flakes, rubbing
well into the slashes. Arrange skin-side up on a rack in a shallow
roasting tin, and roast for 20 minutes.
   While the meat's sizzling away, put the membrillo, lemon juice
and the 2 tablespoons of olive oil into a small saucepan. Stir over
low heat until melted, then let it bubble gently for a minute or
two until slightly syrupy.
   Take the meat out of the oven and reduce the temperature
to 180°C/350°F/Gas 4. Brush the membrillo glaze over the meat,
making sure it gets into all the crevices. Put the meat back in
the oven and roast for 30–35 minutes, basting with the glaze
every 10 minutes or so.
   By now the skin should be starting to crackle. Increase the
temperature to 220°C/425°F/Gas 7, or as high as your oven will
go. Brush once more with the glaze, then give the meat a final
blast for 5–10 minutes to encourage the crackling to crackle
uniformly.
   Once the meat is golden and stickily crisp, leave to rest in a
warm place for 15 minutes. Drizzle with any remaining glaze
before serving.

cook's notes
- I often have trouble getting pork skin to crackle uniformly.
  Increasing the oven temperature at the end certainly helps, but
  it's also a good idea to keep turning the roasting tin every so
  often, in case your oven doesn't cook evenly. I've found this
  useful even with fan ovens.
- Be vigilant during the last stages of cooking; the glaze can
  suddenly burn and reduce the crackling to cinders.
- I love to serve this with Peppered Greens (page 158) and
  roasted sweet potatoes.

*membrillo- and pepper-glazed
belly pork (page 145)*

peppered beef with balsamic vinegar, molasses and garlic

shin of beef 1.3kg/3lb, cut into 4cm/1$\frac{1}{2}$in chunks
sea salt 1$\frac{1}{2}$ tsp
olive oil 3 tbsp
red wine 400ml/14fl oz
beef stock 300ml/$\frac{1}{2}$ pint, preferably home-made
tomato purée 3 tbsp
pickling onions 450g/1lb, peeled
garlic cloves 6, peeled and left whole
black peppercorns 2 tsp, cracked
fresh bay leaves 4
thyme, dried oregano or **winter savory** (or a mixture) 2 tbsp
short pasta shapes such as rigatoni or maccheroni, to serve

for the marinade
blackstrap molasses or **strong honey** 3 tbsp
balsamic vinegar 4 tbsp
black peppercorns 2 tbsp, cracked
garlic cloves 3, crushed

Serves 4–6 as a main meal

A glorious lip-smacking stew with rich, chestnut-brown, glossy gravy – perfect for winter weekends. It is hot and peppery but also slightly sweet, and balanced by a welcome touch of sharpness from the vinegar and red wine.

Stir the marinade ingredients together in a shallow bowl. Add the meat, making sure it's evenly coated. Cover with cling film and leave to marinate in the fridge for 2–24 hours – the longer the better. Give it a stir every so often.

Tip the meat and marinade into a sieve set over a bowl. Reserve the liquid and season the meat with the sea salt. Preheat the oven to 150°C/300°F/Gas 2.

Heat the olive oil in a large, heavy-based frying pan over medium-high heat. Add the meat and fry for 5–7 minutes, turning with tongs until browned and the juices are starting to evaporate. Transfer the meat to a large ovenproof casserole – a 4 litre/7 pint one should be big enough.

Pour the wine and the reserved marinade into the frying pan. Bring to the boil, scraping up any sediment with a wooden spoon, and boil for 2–3 minutes. Add the beef stock and tomato purée. Cook for another minute, then pour this over the meat.

Add the onions, garlic, peppercorns, bay leaves and your chosen herbs to the pot. Bring to the boil, then cover with a well-fitting lid, place the casserole in the oven and leave to simmer gently for 2 hours or until the meat is very tender. Have a look after 1$\frac{1}{2}$ hours and check that there's enough liquid. The juices should be thickened and slightly reduced but not drying out. If necessary, top up with a splash of stock or water.

Serve with rigatoni or maccheroni which you have anointed with plenty of butter and chopped flat-leaf parsley.

cook's note
• Peeling pickling onions can be fiddly. The easiest way is to trim the roots then drop the onions in a large pan of boiling water. Bring back to the boil, blanch for 2 minutes, then drain. When cool enough to handle, remove the outer layer of skin.

steak au poivre (pepper steak)

sirloin steak (preferably organic)
  2 (2.5cm/1in thick), each
  weighing about 225g/8oz
olive oil 1 tbsp, plus extra for
  frying
black peppercorns 1 tbsp,
  cracked and sieved
white peppercorns 1 tbsp,
  cracked and sieved
sea salt flakes to taste

Serves 2

An all-time classic in which pepper plays a key part. I have used an equal amount of white and black peppercorns – white for bite and black for flavour – but you could experiment with halving the white and adding green or pink, or use black on their own. Sieving after cracking is essential for ridding the crunchy coating of peppery dust.

Put the steaks in a shallow dish in which they will fit in a single layer. Pour over the tablespoon of olive oil and rub this all over the meat. Coat on both sides with the peppercorns, pressing them firmly into the meat. Cover and leave at room temperature for at least an hour, turning the steaks once.

When you're ready to cook, brush a heavy-based frying pan with a film of oil and place over very high heat. Crumble some sea salt flakes over the steaks and quickly slip them into the pan. Sear them on each side for about 1 minute, then reduce the heat slightly and carry on cooking for another 1–2 minutes depending on how you like your steaks.

cook's note
• Trim away excess fat if you prefer. However, a 1cm/$\frac{1}{2}$in margin left along the outer edge can be temptingly appetising. If you decide to leave the fat in place, cut through it (and the membrane separating the fat from the meat) at 3cm/1$\frac{1}{4}$in intervals to prevent the steaks from buckling during cooking.

variation
• For a retro experience, cook the steaks as above, using green peppercorns instead of black and white, and adding a generous knob of butter after the steaks have sizzled on each side. Allow the butter to foam and brown slightly, then remove the steaks to a warm plate. Remove excess fat from the pan then deglaze over high heat with a generous splash of cognac. Set light to the cognac then swirl in the best part of a small pot of cream and any juices from the steaks. Bring to the boil, bubble down until thickened, then pour over the steaks.

Those of a certain age might remember the Peter Evans Eating Houses in London where the treat of the week would invariably include prawn cocktail, *steak au poivre* with cream sauce, followed by Black Forest gâteau.

See also
Grinding, Crushing, Cracking, page 83

lamb pepper fry

boneless lamb 1kg/2lb 4oz, cut into 3cm/1¼in cubes

coconut or **vegetable oil** 5 tbsp

mustard seeds 2 tsp

garlic cloves 4 large, thinly sliced

ginger root 2.5cm/1in chunk, sliced into matchsticks

green chillies 1–2, halved lengthways and deseeded

curry leaves 15, plus extra to garnish

cinnamon stick 7cm/2¾in, broken into small pieces

cardamom pods 2 tbsp, crushed, husks discarded

cloves 8–10

onions 2, sliced

chopped tomatoes 400g/14oz can

dried coconut ribbons 50g/1¾oz, plus extra to garnish

salt to taste

Garam Masala (page 226) 2 tsp

black peppercorns 1 tbsp, crushed

fennel seeds 2 tsp, crushed

plainly boiled white rice to serve

for the spice paste

garlic cloves 4 large

ginger root 2.5cm/1in chunk

turmeric powder 1 tbsp

chilli powder 1 tsp

coriander seeds 1 tbsp, crushed

black peppercorns 1 tbsp, crushed

curry leaves 8–10

salt 1 tsp

Serves 4–6 as a main meal

The chef at the Shalimar Spice Garden in Kerala gave me this recipe for a rich, spicy lamb curry. Curry leaves, coconut and black pepper provide the characteristic Keralan flavours. It improves with reheating so can be made well before you plan to serve it.

First make the spice paste. Cut the garlic and ginger into chunks small enough to fit in a garlic press. Squeeze the juice into a small bowl, mixing in the residue left in the press. Stir in the other spices and the salt.

Put the lamb in a bowl, add the spice paste and turn the meat so it is evenly coated with the paste. Cover with cling film and leave for at least 1 hour or overnight in the fridge.

Put the lamb and the paste in a heavy-based saucepan. Add about 850ml/1½ pints of water, enough to barely cover the meat. Bring slowly to the boil, removing any scum, then cover and simmer gently for about 1 hour or until the lamb is tender.

Tip the contents of the pan into a sieve set over a bowl. Pour the liquid back into the pan and simmer briskly until reduced to about 400ml/14fl oz. Remove from the heat and reserve.

Heat the coconut oil in a large, high-sided sauté pan over medium-high heat. Add the mustard seeds and when they crackle, stir in the garlic, ginger, chillies and curry leaves. Stir for a few seconds then add the cinnamon, cardamom and cloves. Sizzle for a few more seconds, taking care not to let the spices burn.

Next, add the onions, reduce the heat a little and fry for 7–8 minutes or until golden brown. Stir in the tomatoes and cook for 3–4 minutes. Once thickened, add the cooked lamb, most of the reserved lamb stock, the coconut ribbons and salt to taste. Cook, uncovered, for about 20 minutes, adding the rest of the lamb stock, if necessary. The juices should be thick and cling to the meat, but they shouldn't be dry.

Just before you're ready to serve, sprinkle with the garam masala, peppercorns and fennel seeds. Stir briefly, then scatter over a few more curry leaves and coconut ribbons. Serve with plainly boiled white rice.

cook's notes
- If you can't find coconut oil, use 3 tablespoons of vegetable oil and 2 tablespoons of creamed coconut (from a block).
- The uniquely lemony, spicy and faintly bitter flavour of curry leaves is essential for this dish. The dried leaves are easy to find in the shops but it's far better to use fresh if you can. They'll keep in the freezer for months, so be sure to buy plenty of sprigs.
- In India, people are happy to leave whole spices on the side of the plate. However, you may want to fish them out before serving.

rabo encendido (tail on fire)

cannellini beans 400g/14oz,
soaked for several hours
vegetable oil 8 tbsp
onions 3 medium, roughly
chopped
carrots 3 medium, thickly
sliced
celery stalks 6, roughly
chopped
garlic cloves 4 large, thinly
sliced
tomato purée 2 tbsp
oxtail 2.25kg/5lb, cut into
5cm/2in pieces
Spiced Flour (page 226)
meat stock 1.2 litres/2 pints,
preferably home-made
robust red wine 425ml/³/₄ pint
thyme 2–3 sprigs
rosemary 2–3 sprigs
fresh bay leaves 4
sea salt to taste
freshly ground black pepper
to taste
flat-leaf parsley to garnish

Serves 6–8

This is loosely based on a Cuban spicy stew usually served on special occasions. Meaty chunks of oxtail are dredged with a piquant seasoning of flour, black pepper, dry mustard, thyme, allspice and paprika, then stewed at a leisurely pace until the meat is falling off the bone. Creamy cannellini beans, though not authentic, mellow the fiery juices.

Drain the beans, tip into a large saucepan and cover with fresh water. Bring to the boil, boil for 15 minutes, then reduce the heat a little and cook for 30 minutes to 1 hour until tender but not breaking up. (The exact cooking time will depend on the age of your beans.) Drain and set aside.

Preheat the oven to 150°C/300°F/Gas 2. Heat 2 tablespoons of the oil in a large, wide casserole over medium heat. Add the onions, carrots and celery, and gently fry with the lid on for about 10 minutes or until beginning to soften. Stir in the garlic and tomato purée and cook for a few minutes more.

While the vegetables are cooking, put the oxtail in a large polythene bag with the spiced flour and shake until evenly coated. Shake off any residue.

Next, heat the rest of the oil in a large, high-sided sauté pan over medium-high heat. Add the oxtail and fry, in batches if necessary, until browned on both sides. Remove the pieces from the pan as they brown and set aside on a plate.

Once the vegetables are cooked, add the oxtail pieces to the casserole, in a single layer if possible.

Pour about 150ml/¼ pint of the stock into the oxtail pan and stir over medium heat, scraping up all the sticky residue from the bottom of the pan. Pour this over the meat and vegetables.

Add the remaining stock and the wine to the casserole. Stir in the beans and herbs and season with salt and freshly ground black pepper. Put the lid on and bring slowly to the boil. Once bubbling away, place the casserole in the oven and cook for 2½ hours or until the meat is very tender. Check after 1½ hours and add more stock or water, if necessary. The sauce should be quite thick but not dry. Check the seasoning and add more salt and pepper if necessary. Garnish with parsley just before serving.

cook's note
• I have sometimes made this with drained and rinsed canned beans, adding them for the last hour of cooking, but they do taste sludgy compared with freshly cooked dried beans.

braised rabbit with green peppercorns and puy lentils

olive oil 6 tbsp
pancetta cubes 140g/5oz
onion 1 large, finely chopped
celery stalks 4, halved
  lengthways, then sliced
  crossways into 1.5cm/⅝in
  pieces
rabbits 2, each weighing about
  1 kg/2lb 4oz, jointed
garlic cloves 3 large, thinly
  sliced
fresh bay leaf 1
rosemary sprigs 2
dried green peppercorns
  2 tsp, crushed
sea salt 1 tsp
Puy lentils 350g/12oz
chicken or **game stock**
  1.5 litres/2¾ pints,
  preferably home-made
flat-leaf parsley leaves
  chopped to make 6 tbsp,
  stems discarded
lemon finely grated zest of 1

Serves 6 as a main meal

You can cook this with chicken if you are not fond of rabbit. The thickened juices are infused with the warm fresh bite of green peppercorns, balanced by the earthiness of Puy lentils. I've used enough peppercorns to give the dish noticeable zest but it is not overpowering. If you would like more heat, increase the amount to 1 tablespoon.

Heat 2 tablespoons of the olive oil in a large, heavy-based casserole. Add the pancetta cubes and fry over medium-high heat until beginning to crisp at the edges.

Add the onion and celery and shunt around the pan until translucent. Reduce the heat to low, cover the pan and leave the vegetables to relinquish their juices (or sweat, as many writers say) for 10 minutes, without letting them brown.

While the vegetables are softening, heat the rest of the oil in a large, high-sided sauté pan over medium-high heat. Add the rabbit joints, in batches if necessary – it's important not to overcrowd the pan. Fry for 8–10 minutes, turning, until browned. Set the joints aside on a large plate. (Don't wash the pan yet.)

Give the vegetables a stir, then add the garlic, bay leaf, rosemary, peppercorns and sea salt. Cook for a minute, then add the lentils and rabbit joints, along with any juices that have accumulated on the plate.

Pour a splash of stock into the pan you used for frying the rabbit. Stir over medium heat using a wooden spoon to scrape up all the tasty sediment. Pour this into the casserole along with the remaining stock. Cover, bring to the boil, then simmer very gently for 1¼ hours or maybe a little longer. The rabbit should be tender, the lentils plump and the juices thickened.

Combine the parsley and lemon zest. Stir all but 2 tablespoons into the casserole. Check the seasoning, adding more salt if necessary.

Transfer to a warm serving dish and sprinkle with the rest of the parsley and lemon zest mixture.

cook's notes
• Try to make sure the rabbits are young, especially if buying from a farmers' market. Old ones can be unbelievably tough and no amount of cooking will tenderise them.
• If the rabbits are wild they might taste slightly gamey. For a milder flavour, soak the joints in water and 3 tablespoons of vinegar for an hour or so before cooking.

peppery calves liver with preserved lemon and parsley

calves liver 350g/12oz in one
piece
lemon juice of 1
mustard powder $^1/_2$ tsp
extra-virgin olive oil 4 tbsp,
plus extra for brushing
preserved lemon finely
chopped to make 1 tbsp
flat-leaf parsley chopped to
make 2 tbsp
paprika $^1/_4$ tsp
sea salt flakes to taste
black peppercorns 1$^1/_2$ tbsp,
coarsely ground
meat stock or **water** 4–5 tbsp

Serves 2 as a light main meal

This recipe is adapted from Rosemary Barron's well-researched book *The Flavours of Greece*. In her recipe, Rosemary uses lamb's liver, which would be more authentic, but I prefer the more delicate flavour of calves liver. The liver is marinated in lemon juice, mustard and olive oil, then dusted with coarsely ground peppercorns before grilling.

Cut the liver into 5mm/$^1/_4$in slices and remove any membranes or tubes.

Whisk the lemon juice, mustard powder and olive oil in a bowl. Add the liver, stir to mix, then cover and leave to marinate for 30 minutes.

Meanwhile, mix together the preserved lemon, parsley, paprika and a pinch of sea salt flakes, and set aside.

Remove the liver from the marinade, reserving the liquid. Lightly brush with oil, then sprinkle with the pepper, pressing it into both sides and a little sea salt.

Brush a ridged stove-top grill pan with oil and place over high heat. Once the pan is good and hot, add the strips of liver. Cook for no more than 1 minute on each side. Quickly transfer the liver to a warm serving dish.

Add the reserved marinade and a few spoonfuls of stock or water to the pan. Bubble down over medium-high heat, scraping up any sediment. Spoon over the liver and scatter with the preserved lemon mixture.

cook's notes
- The secret is not to overcook the liver or it will become tough.
- In Greece this would probably be served with a colourful salad, but mashed potatoes and steamed greens are fine too.

vegetables

Whatever their flavour, most vegetables benefit from a judicious seasoning of pepper. A coarse grinding of black brightens the anaemic hue of cauliflower and adds texture and aroma to homely staples like mashed potato and swede. The assertive bite of white gives new meaning to the much-maligned cabbage; try Peppered Greens with Lemon and Coriander (page 158) if you're not convinced.

The recipes in this chapter focus mainly on vegetables that are either innately sweet and contrast with pepper's pungency, or those with strong savoury flavours that match it. Dense-fleshed vegetables such as pumpkins and carrots contain complex sugars that caramelise into a naturally sweet glaze when slowly roasted or braised. The resulting deep mellow flavours need pepper's contrasting piquant bite. Mushrooms cry out for it too, as do aubergines and earthy greens such as curly kale and *cavalo nero*.

It's interesting to experiment with different types of peppercorns. Hot and gingery grains of paradise work really well with baked sweet potatoes or in a creamy parsnip gratin (page 170). The numbing tang of Sichuan pepper is just about perfect in Fuchsia Dunlop's water spinach stir-fry (page 160), as are green peppercorns mashed with butter and lime zest and slathered over barbecued sweetcorn.

When and how much pepper to add depends on the vegetable and the way you're cooking it. Steamed or lightly boiled peas or beans need only a twist of the mill before serving but you can afford to be more profligate with grilled vegetables – asparagus, sweet peppers and tomatoes, for example. Stir-fries benefit from adding pepper during cooking – it mingles with the juices, infusing the dish with spicy heat. A hearty vegetable gratin or stew is better seasoned both during cooking and again when brought to the table. The double hit allows you to appreciate the full depth of pungency and aroma that good quality pepper provides.

peppered greens with lemon and coriander

spring greens 2 heads, weighing about 650g/1lb 7oz in total
unsalted butter a generous knob
lemon finely grated zest of 1
coriander stems discarded, leaves sliced to make 3–4 tbsp
sea salt flakes a large pinch
freshly ground white pepper

Serves 4 as a side dish

White pepper gives this dish a wonderful bite, balanced by the buttery juices and fresh flavours of lemon and coriander. When cut into ribbons and lightly steamed, the greens keep their colour and vitality.

Trim the base and tough stalks from the greens, including the part that runs down the middle of the leaf. Stack the leaves and slice crossways into broad ribbons.

Place in a steamer basket set over boiling water. Steam for 5–7 minutes or until tender but still slightly crisp.

Tip into a warmed serving bowl and stir in the butter, lemon zest and coriander. Crumble some sea salt flakes over the top, then season generously with freshly ground white pepper.

cook's notes
- White pepper plays a key role here, so try to use a good-quality variety such as Sarawak Creamy White or single estate Wynad. These have a clean bright flavour rather than the musty whiff of many unnamed varieties.
- An alternative to spring greens would be a couple of pointy pale green cabbages. Runner beans are good too. Whatever your choice of greens, make sure they are full of bounce.

See also
Tasting Pepper, page 76
Pepper Names, page 64

stir-fried water spinach with chillies and sichuan pepper

water spinach 300g/10¹/₂oz

Sichuan dried chillies a small
  handful

groundnut oil 3 tbsp

Sichuan pepper ¹/₂ tsp

salt ¹/₄–¹/₂ tsp

sesame oil 1 tsp

Serves 2 as a side dish

This is from Fuchsia Dunlop's award-winning book *Sichuan Cookery*. Pepper adds three dimensions here – colour, crunch and tingling heat.

Thoroughly wash the water spinach, discarding any wilted leaves and coarser stalks. Tear or cut into 10cm/4in sections. Snip the chillies in half or into 2cm/³/₄in sections, discarding the seeds as far as possible.

Heat the oil in a wok until hot but not smoking. Add the chillies and Sichuan pepper and stir-fry for 10–20 seconds until the oil smells spicy and the chillies are just beginning to turn a darker red – take care not to burn them.

Throw in all the spinach and stir-fry for about 3 minutes or until the leaves have wilted and the stems are tender and juicy, seasoning with salt to taste. Finally, remove from the heat and stir in the sesame oil.

cook's notes
- Water spinach is sold in Chinese stores but if you can't find it use ordinary spinach instead.
- If you can't get Sichuan dried chillies, Fuchsia recommends long mild Indian chillies (6–8cm/2¹/₂–3¹/₄in) rather than small Indian or Thai chillies. These would be deadly hot and unpalatable if used in Sichuanese quantities.

mushrooms, parmesan and sizzled sage on sourdough toast

olive oil 3 tbsp
unsalted butter 3 tbsp
sage leaves chopped to make 1 tbsp, plus 16–20 small whole leaves
mushrooms (see cook's note) 400g/14oz
lemon juice a squeeze
garlic clove 1 large, thinly sliced
flat-leaf parsley chopped to make 2 tbsp
freshly ground black pepper 1/4 tsp, plus extra to serve
freshly ground white pepper 1/4 tsp
sea salt flakes to taste
sourdough bread 4 slices
Parmesan cheese a few shavings

Serves 4 as a snack or light meal

Mushrooms, Parmesan and sage make a great trio. They have strong meaty flavours, and the pepper and sea salt bring it all together. This is one of my favourite weekend snacks.

Heat the olive oil and butter in a large frying pan over medium-high heat. Add half the chopped sage and sizzle for a few seconds. Add the mushrooms and fry for 3–4 minutes, stirring, until they start to soften and release their juices.

Add a squeeze of lemon juice, then the garlic and parsley. Season with the pepper and some crumbled sea salt flakes. Cook for another 5 minutes.

While the mushrooms are cooking, toast the bread on both sides. Put the toast on serving plates and pile the mushrooms on top.

Throw the whole sage leaves into the pan and sizzle for a few seconds in the remaining oil over high heat. Once they're crisp, scatter them over the mushrooms along with some Parmesan shavings. Season with more freshly ground black pepper.

cook's note
- Use small evenly-sized mushrooms such as organic crimini or chestnut mushrooms. Slice them in half if they are large.

black sticky carrots

large carrots (preferably organic) 2–3
groundnut oil 2 tbsp
unsalted butter a large knob
coarsely ground black pepper $1/4$–$1/2$ tsp
sugar $1/2$ tsp
sea salt flakes a generous pinch
soy sauce $1/2$ tsp
chicken or **vegetable stock** 2 tsp

Serves 2 as a side dish

This is surely the best way to cook carrots: fried in buttery juices until appetisingly caramelised and tender-crisp. The flavour is intensely sweet, savoury and peppery all at the same time.

Peel the carrots and slice into diagonal-cut ovals about 5mm/$1/4$in thick.

Heat the oil and the butter in a non-stick frying pan large enough to take the carrots in a single layer. When sizzling nicely, toss in the carrots and spread them out. Sprinkle with the pepper, sugar and some crumbled sea salt flakes.

Fry the carrots over medium-high heat for $2^{1}/_{2}$ minutes, then start to turn them using tongs. Keep turning them, one by one, removing them from the pan as they begin to blacken at the edges. Blot on paper towels and tip into a warm serving bowl.

Pour off most of the oil from the pan, then add another knob of butter. Swirl in the soy sauce and stock, scraping up any tasty sediment, then pour this over the carrots.

cook's notes
- If you don't have a large pan, fry the carrots in batches. It's important to cook them in a single layer.
- Be vigilant – you may need to reduce the heat a little towards the end of the cooking time.

balsamic- and pepper-glazed roast pumpkin

pumpkin or **winter squash**
 1kg/2lb 4oz
olive oil 4 tbsp
balsamic vinegar 1 tbsp
black peppercorns ¹/₂ tsp,
 crushed
white peppercorns ¹/₄ tsp,
 crushed
unsalted butter a large knob
thyme leaves a large pinch
sea salt flakes to taste

Serves 4 as a side dish

Sweet, peppery and slightly sharp, this is excellent with roast lamb or poultry. Look for green- and yellow-striped Delicata variety or the glowing orange Uchiki Kuri. Both have a fantastic sweet flavour which stands up well to the balsamic vinegar and pepper.

Preheat the oven to 200°C/400°F/Gas 6. Using a sturdy knife, slice the pumpkin into quarters, parallel with the ribs. Remove the peel and scoop out the seeds. Cut the flesh into eight big chunks about 8 x 6cm/3¹/₄ x 2¹/₂in.

In a large bowl, combine the olive oil, balsamic vinegar and peppercorns. Add the pumpkin chunks and turn until well coated with the oil mixture.

Arrange the chunks in a single layer in a shallow roasting tin, taking care not to overcrowd them. Dot with butter and sprinkle with thyme leaves and sea salt flakes.

Roast for 30–40 minutes, turning halfway through, until tender and beginning to brown at the edges. Sprinkle with more sea salt and black pepper if you like.

cook's notes
- You will need about 600g/1lb 5oz of prepared pumpkin once you have removed the skin and seeds.
- As an alternative, you could replace the balsamic vinegar with 2 tablespoons of concentrated apple juice. It is sharper and fruitier but just as delicious.

stir-fried butternut squash and shiitake mushrooms

butternut squash 1, weighing
  about 550g/1lb 4oz
olive oil 5 tbsp
coriander seeds 1/2 tsp,
  coarsely crushed
sea salt flakes to taste
black peppercorns 1 tsp,
  coarsely crushed
shiitake mushrooms
  200g/7oz, thinly sliced
chicken or **vegetable stock**
  4 tbsp
baby spinach 2 good handfuls,
  stalks removed
garlic croûtons to garnish

**Serves 4 as a starter or 2 as
a light meal**

A simple but filling autumnal dish of contrasting textures and temperatures – warm peppery squash and mushrooms on cool greens, with a crunchy topping.

Slice the squash crossways where the straight neck meets the bulbous end. Remove the peel and scoop out the seeds. Slice the rounded part lengthways into quarters, and then into crescents about 5mm/1/4in thick. Halve the neck-end lengthways, then slice each half into thin semi-circles.

Heat the olive oil with the coriander seeds in a large frying pan over medium-high heat. Fry the squash slices in a single layer, in batches, turning with tongs, for 5–7 minutes or until lightly browned and tender-crisp. Sprinkle with sea salt flakes and some of the crushed peppercorns. Using a slotted spoon, remove to a large sieve set over a bowl.

Add the mushrooms to the pan and fry for 5 minutes, adding some of the oil drained from the squash. Season with sea salt and the rest of the peppercorns. Return any drained oil to the pan. Stir in the stock and bubble down for a few seconds.

Arrange the spinach on plates. Pile the squash and mushrooms on top, then pour over the pan juices. Scatter over a few croûtons (make sure they are warm) before serving.

variation
• Replace the uncooked spinach with lightly steamed shredded kale, *cavalo nero* or Savoy cabbage. Serve with rice or lentils as a vegetarian main course.

spiced fried onion rings

cumin seeds 2 tsp
black peppercorns 1 tsp
white peppercorns 1 tsp
Sichuan pepper 1 tsp
sea salt flakes 1 tsp, plus
  extra for sprinkling
water 300ml/^{1}/$_2$ pint
self-raising flour 125g/4^1/$_2$oz,
  plus extra for dusting
onions 1 red and 1 white, each
  sliced horizontally into
  1cm/^{1}/$_2$in thick rings
groundnut oil for deep-frying
Black Pepper Crème Fraîche
  (page 188) to serve

Serves 4 as a snack

These are extremely addictive – thickly sliced red and white onions dipped in a tongue-tingling peppery batter and fried until golden and crisp.

Grind the cumin, peppercorns and sea salt together using a mortar and pestle, until you have a coarse powder.

Pour the water into a shallow dish. Gradually add the flour, shaking it through a sieve and beating with a fork. Stir in the ground spices and salt mixture.

Separate the onion slices into rings. Spread them out on a tray and lightly dust with flour, shaking off any excess.

Heat about 8cm/3^1/$_4$in of oil to 160–180°C/310–350°F in a large, heavy-based saucepan or electric deep-fat fryer. Line a tray with crumpled paper towels.

Once the oil is up to temperature, dip the onion rings in the batter and drop them into the oil a few at a time. Shunt them around using a slotted spoon or wire scoop. Fry for 2–3 minutes or until golden, then scoop them out of the pan and on to the paper towels to drain. Keep warm in a low oven while you cook the rest.

Tip into a warm serving bowl, sprinkle with more sea salt. Serve hot with Black Pepper Crème Fraîche or thick Greek yogurt for dipping.

cook's notes
- If the batter is too thin it won't cling to the onion rings. It should have the consistency of pouring cream and should coat a spoon. If necessary, adjust the density by adding more water or flour.
- Fry only a few onion rings at a time so that there is plenty of room for them to move around the pan.
- These are particularly good served with a selection of Indian pickles. Try the Fresh Green Peppercorn Pickle on page 193.

spiced fried onion rings
(page 167)

parsnips baked in paradise pepper cream

large parsnips 3, weighing about 750g/1lb 10oz in total

butter for greasing

double cream 425ml/³/₄ pint

chicken or **vegetable stock** 250ml/9fl oz

garlic cloves 2, crushed with the flat of a knife

grains of paradise ¹/₂ tsp, coarsely ground, plus extra for sprinkling

white peppercorns ¹/₄ tsp, coarsely ground

freshly grated nutmeg two large pinches, plus extra for sprinkling

sea salt to taste

Serves 6 as a side dish or 4 as a vegetarian main course

There is something fascinating about grains of paradise – not just the name, but also the spicy flavour with a hint of coconut, and the way the grains become creamy white when ground, though dark on the outside. Combined with white pepper and nutmeg, they lift parsnips out of the ordinary. If you can't buy grains of paradise, increase the amount of white pepper accordingly.

Preheat the oven to 180°C/350°F/Gas 4. Slice the parsnips thinly and place in a steamer basket set over boiling water. Steam for 3–4 minutes or until barely tender. Butter a large, ovenproof gratin dish and arrange the parsnips in it.

Heat the cream and stock in a saucepan with the garlic. Season with the grains of paradise, white pepper, a couple of pinches of freshly grated nutmeg and sea salt to taste.

Pour the hot cream mixture over the parsnips. Cover the dish with foil and bake for 30 minutes. Remove the foil and bake for another 20 minutes or until golden on top. Sprinkle with a little more nutmeg and grains of paradise before serving.

See also
Grains of Paradise, page 42
Grinding, Crushing, Cracking, page 83

hot and sour courgettes

courgettes 2 large, thinly
    sliced
salt 1 tsp
light sesame oil 1 tbsp
dark sesame oil 1 tbsp
red chilli 1, deseeded and
    sliced into strips
white peppercorns 1 tsp,
    freshly ground
ginger root 2 slices, chopped
garlic clove 1, crushed
rice vinegar 1 tbsp
soy sauce 1 tbsp
sugar 2 tsp
spring onion 1, finely chopped

Serves 4 as a side dish

Simple but good, this recipe is from Chef But at the late Kenneth Lo's Memories of China restaurant in London. The Chinese consider black specks of pepper unsightly, so white pepper is used here. It has a mild bite which combines well with chilli to make a seasoned oil with just a hint of heat.

Put the courgette slices in a large colander and sprinkle with the salt. Cover with a plate and set a weight on top. Leave to drain for 15 minutes. Rinse off the salt and pat the slices dry with paper towels.

Heat the oils in a wok over high heat. When very hot but not smoking, add the chilli and pepper. Sizzle for about 30 seconds, then remove the chilli with a slotted spoon.

Add the ginger and garlic, cook for another 30 seconds, then add the courgette slices. Toss them around, then add the rice vinegar, soy sauce and sugar. Stir-fry for 2 minutes, then add the spring onion just before serving.

cook's note
- Salt draws out moisture from the courgettes and helps them remain crisp when fried. It is extremely important to dry the slices very thoroughly.

pulses, pasta and rice

When we cook meat or fish, or indeed any moist or fatty ingredient, we usually add pepper and salt at the start of cooking. The juices or fat that flow from the food help to disperse the seasoning throughout the dish. However, this isn't the case with dry or dense foods such as pasta, pulses and grains such as rice; they need to soften and absorb moisture before they can take other flavours on board. So there is little point in adding pepper early on, although salt is added to cooking water for rice and pasta.

With foods like these, pepper comes into its own in the final stages of cooking or just before serving. Then you get to appreciate the aroma and piquancy as it mingles with and enhances the mild and deeply comforting flavour of plainly boiled Basmati rice, say, or deliciously silky egg pasta or earthy pulses. The one exception perhaps is polenta – I add crushed black peppercorns during the prolonged stirring that transforms the gritty grains to a smooth mush. The grains rapidly absorb moisture right from the start so the aroma and bite of pepper has a chance to permeate.

With such uncompromisingly plain ingredients, every flavour counts. Chickpeas with Feta and Preserved Lemons (page 174) needs good quality artisan cheese, sea salt and peppercorns to make it special. Deceptively simple dishes such as Black Pepper Rice (page 181) and the classic Roman pasta *Cacio e Pepe* (page 178) need the very best peppercorns you can find – try Tellicherry, single estate Wynad or organic Malaysian Rimbàs. Everyday kitchen pepper simply does not do them justice.

chickpeas with feta and preserved lemons

chickpeas 250g/9oz, soaked
for several hours
preserved lemon 1, finely
chopped
sea salt flakes 1 tsp
black peppercorns 2 tsp,
cracked
extra-virgin olive oil 3 tbsp
red onion 1/2 small, thinly
sliced into crescents
garlic cloves 2, crushed
lemon juice of 1/2
cumin seeds 1 1/2 tsp
dried red chilli flakes a pinch
oregano, thyme or **summer
savory** chopped to make
1 tsp
flat-leaf parsley stems
removed, leaves chopped to
make 5 tbsp
feta cheese 75g/2³/₄oz,
crumbled

**Serves 4–6 as a side dish or
light meal**

This is one of those dishes where pepper and salt are barely
noticeable but leave them out and you'll taste the difference.
They draw all the other elements together – earthy chickpeas,
fragrant herbs, salty cheese and the mysterious, faintly musty
flavour of Moroccan preserved lemons. This dish is delicious on
its own or as part of a *meze*; it also goes beautifully with grilled
lamb or chicken.

Drain the chickpeas and put in a saucepan with plenty of fresh
water to cover – don't add any salt. Bring to the boil and cook
for 30–40 minutes or until tender but not breaking up.

Drain, tip into a bowl and while still warm, add the preserved
lemon, sea salt flakes, black pepper, olive oil, onion, garlic,
lemon juice, cumin, chilli flakes and oregano.

Leave to cool, then stir in the parsley and scatter with the
feta. Check the seasoning, adding more salt, black pepper or
lemon juice. Serve at room temperature.

cook's notes
- If you have preserved lemons in oil, use the oil from the jar
  instead of olive oil. It has a beautiful lemony flavour.
- This will keep for several days in the fridge but it needs to come
  to room temperature before serving.

variations
- Add about eight sliced cherry tomatoes as well as, or instead of,
  the feta.
- Try it with sliced ribbons of Swiss chard or baby spinach instead
  of the parsley.

pock-marked mother chen's beancurd (ma po dou fu)

beancurd (tofu) 1 block
  weighing about 500g/1lb 2oz
salt to taste
baby leeks or **large spring
  onions** 4
groundnut oil 100ml/3½fl oz
minced beef (preferably
  organic) 150g/5½oz
Sichuan chilli bean paste
  2½ tbsp
black fermented beans 1 tbsp
Sichuan chillies ground to
  make 2 tsp
stock preferably Sichuan (see
  cook's note) 250ml/9fl oz
sugar 1 tsp
light soy sauce 2 tsp
potato flour 3 tbsp, mixed with
  4 tbsp water
Sichuan pepper ½ tsp, dry-
  fried until fragrant then
  ground

**Serves 2–3 as a main course
with rice and a vegetable dish**

This recipe is from Fuchsia Dunlop, consultant to London's Sichuan restaurant Bar Shu and author of the award-winning *Sichuan Cookery*. Spicy, aromatic and oily, this is one of the most famous Sichuan dishes and epitomizes Sichuan's culinary culture.

The dish is named after the smallpox-scarred wife of a Qing Dynasty restaurateur who is said to have prepared it for the labourers passing her restaurant. As Fuchsia says 'The Sichuan pepper will make your lips tingle pleasantly, and the tender beancurd will slip down your throat. It's rich and warming, a perfect winter dish'.

Cut the beancurd into 2cm/¾in cubes and leave to steep in very hot or gently simmering water which you have lightly salted.

Slice the leeks at a steep angle into thin 'horse-ear' slices.

Place a wok over a high flame, then add the oil and heat until smoking. Add the minced beef and stir-fry until it is crispy and a little brown, but not yet dry.

Turn the heat down to medium, add the chilli bean paste and stir-fry for about 30 seconds until the oil is a rich red colour. Add the black fermented beans and ground chillies, if using, and stir-fry for another 20–30 seconds until they are both fragrant and the chillies have added their colour to the oil.

Pour in the stock, stir well, and add the drained beancurd. Mix it in gently by pushing the back of your ladle, or wok scoop, gently from the edges to the centre of the wok. Do not stir or the beancurd may break up. Season with the sugar, soy sauce and salt to taste. Simmer for about 5 minutes until the beancurd has absorbed the flavours of the sauce.

Add the leeks and gently stir in. When they are just cooked, add the potato flour mixture in two or three stages, mixing well, until the sauce has thickened enough to cling glossily to the meat and beancurd. Don't add more than you need.

Finally, pour everything into a deep bowl, scatter with the ground Sichuan pepper and serve.

cook's note
• You can use a stock cube but, as Fuchsia points out, the flavour is inferior, and can be very salty. Sichuan cooks use an everyday stock – *xian tang* – made from pork bones and a raw chicken carcass. Duck bones are good too. To make the stock, smash the carcass and larger bones. Put the bones and meat in a large saucepan, cover with plenty of water, bring to a fast boil and skim. Add 40g/1½oz unpeeled ginger root, crushed, and a couple of spring onions. Reduce the heat and simmer gently for 2–3 hours. Strain and cool. Keep in the fridge for a few days or freeze.

black pepper polenta chips with mozzarella and parmesan

water 1 litre/1^3/$_4$ pints
salt ^{1}/$_2$ tsp
yellow polenta 200g/7oz
butter 75g/2^3/$_4$oz
mozzarella cheese 75g/2^3/$_4$oz,
   coarsely grated
Parmesan cheese 75g/2^3/$_4$oz,
   coarsely grated
black peppercorns 1 tsp,
   crushed and sieved, plus
   extra for serving
olive oil for frying
sea salt flakes to taste

Serves 4–6 as a snack or side dish

Often dismissed as bland mush, polenta is deeply comforting and is exactly what's needed to go with strongly flavoured dishes – rich meaty casseroles, chorizo, mushrooms, or garlicky tomato sauce, for example. Fried until crisp, it also makes fantastic chips. Like porridge, success depends on what you stir into it. Here, I have used salty cheese and plenty of black pepper to beef up the flavour.

Pour the water into a large, heavy-based saucepan, add the salt and bring to the boil. Stirring constantly with a long-handled wooden spoon, slowly add the polenta, trickling it through your fingers like sand.

Stir the polenta for 30–40 minutes until the mixture is very smooth and starts to come away from the sides of the pan. Then add the butter, cheeses and crushed peppercorns and stir until thoroughly mixed in.

Tip into an oiled shallow roasting tin measuring 20 x 30cm/ 8 x 12in, spreading the mixture into the corners and levelling the surface – a wet palette knife comes in handy. Once cool, slice the polenta into sticks, measuring about 6 x 1cm/2^1/$_2$ x ^{1}/$_2$in.

Heat some olive oil in a large, non-stick frying pan (enough to come about 8mm/^{3}/$_8$in up the sides of the pan). When the oil is hot but not yet smoking, fry the polenta chips in batches until crisp and golden, turning with tongs.

Drain on crumpled paper towels, tip into a warm dish and sprinkle with sea salt flakes and more black pepper.

cook's note
- The amount of water depends on how dense you ultimately want the polenta to be, and also the type of polenta – texture and absorption rate seems to vary depending on brand. I usually find that I need more water than the recommended amount, otherwise the polenta is too thick to stir. However, if you feel this mix is too sloppy (bearing in mind it will firm up once cool), just sprinkle in a bit more polenta before you add the other ingredients.

variation
- For a deliciously cheesy snack, slice the cooled polenta into eight rectangles. Arrange in a grill pan without a rack and sprinkle generously with coarsely grated cheese – about 200g/7oz mozzarella and 175g/6oz pecorino or Parmesan. Grill until melted and bubbling. Great with fresh tomato sauce, or even ketchup.

See also
Grinding, Crushing, Cracking, page 83

pasta with pecorino and black pepper (cacio e pepe)

spaghetti 225g/8oz
salt to taste
pecorino Romano cheese
50g/1³/₄oz, finely grated, plus
extra to serve
black peppercorns 2 tsp,
crushed and sieved, plus
extra to serve

**Serves 2 as a main course,
4 as a starter**

Cacio e Pepe is one of the best ways of cooking pasta and enjoying the pungency and crunch of black pepper mixed with melted pecorino cheese. The dish originated in the Romano Lazio region of Italy where the cheese is made with milk from the sheep that graze the hills. As with most deceptively simple dishes, the trick is to use good quality ingredients: durum wheat pasta (dried rather than fresh) and top-notch peppercorns.

Bring a large saucepan of water to the boil. Add the pasta and some salt, then bring back to the boil and cook until *al dente*.

Warm a roomy serving bowl either in a low oven or with hot water. When the pasta is nearly ready, decant about 100ml/3¹/₂fl oz of the starchy cooking water into the bowl. Add the cheese and stir until it melts.

Drain the pasta, reserving the water and without shaking off excess water – you want to keep the pasta as wet as possible. Tip it into the bowl, add the black pepper and toss several times so that the liquid and cheese amalgamate with the pasta to form a creamy coating. Add some of the reserved cooking water, if necessary.

Serve on warm plates with extra black pepper and grated cheese.

cook's notes
- Pecorino Romano is a hard, salty cheese. If you find it too strong, use Parmesan cheese instead, or a mixture of the two.
- Grate the cheese finely so that it melts easily without clumping.

black pepper rice

Basmati rice 400g/14oz
vegetable oil 8 tbsp
onion $1/2$ small, finely chopped
green chillies 2, split
   lengthways and deseeded
curry leaves 10
mustard seeds 1 tsp
cumin seeds 1 tsp
black peppercorns $1/2$ tsp,
   cracked
salt 1 tsp
water 600ml/1 pint, plus extra
   for soaking the rice

Serves 4 as a side dish

This recipe was given to me by Das Sreedharan, native of Kerala in Southwest India and owner of the London-based Rasa chain of restaurants. Das is passionate about pepper and its inextricable link to Keralan history, economics and culture. Growing and exporting pepper is a vital source of income, but it is also used as a medicine and, as Das says, Keralan people love to use it in cooking.

This is a simple, clean-tasting dish of fragrant Basmati rice and crispy fried onions spiked with green chilli, curry leaves and cracked black pepper.

Wash the rice in several changes of water until the water runs clear. Tip into a bowl, then cover with more water to a depth of 2.5cm/1in. Leave to soak for 30 minutes, then drain.

Heat 5 tablespoons of the oil in a wok or frying pan. When the oil is hot, add the onion and fry over medium heat for 5–6 minutes, stirring frequently until golden brown. Remove from the pan and drain on paper towels.

Heat the remaining oil in a large, heavy-based saucepan over medium-high heat. Add the chillies, curry leaves, mustard, cumin and pepper. Stir-fry for 10 seconds, then add the rice and salt, stirring gently.

Pour the 600ml/1 pint of water into the saucepan and bring to the boil. Cover tightly, reduce the heat right down and cook for 25 minutes. Remove the lid, fluff up the rice with a fork and sprinkle with the fried onions before serving.

See also
Grinding, Crushing, Cracking, page 83

moors and christians
(black beans and rice)

black beans 200g/7oz, soaked
  for several hours
onion $^{1}/_{2}$ small
garlic cloves 2, peeled and left
  whole
fresh bay leaf 1
oregano or **thyme** 1–2 sprigs
tomato purée 2 tsp
red wine vinegar 1 tsp
sugar $^{1}/_{2}$ tsp
freshly ground black pepper
  $^{1}/_{2}$ tsp
salt to taste
long-grain white rice
  300g/10$^{1}/_{2}$oz

for the sofrito
vegetable oil 1 tbsp
salt pork or **smoked pancetta**
  25g/1oz, diced
belly pork 50g/1$^{3}/_{4}$oz, diced
onion 1 small, chopped
garlic clove 1 large, finely
  chopped
green pepper $^{1}/_{2}$, deseeded
  and diced
red or **green chillies** $^{1}/_{2}$–1,
  deseeded and diced
dried oregano $^{1}/_{2}$ tsp
cumin seeds $^{1}/_{2}$ tsp, crushed

to garnish
spring onions 3, green parts
  included, chopped
**extra-virgin olive oil or Olio
  Santo** (page 237)
black peppercorns $^{1}/_{2}$ tsp,
  crushed and sieved

Serves 4 as a main course

Based on Cuba's national dish, a hearty mix of crisp nuggets of pork, black beans, green pepper and chillies on a bed of snowy white rice. Pepper is used in a relatively small amount here, but this is yet another dish where it makes a real difference. A few cracked peppercorns and a slick of fruity olive oil on the beans imparts an unmistakable bright warm flavour.

Despite the many ingredients, this is not difficult to make. The bean mixture improves with reheating so can be made a day ahead.

Drain the beans and put in a saucepan with the onion, garlic, bay leaf and oregano sprigs. Add plenty of water to cover, then bring to the boil and boil rapidly for 10 minutes. Reduce the heat slightly, then simmer briskly for 30–40 minutes or until the beans are tender but not disintegrating. Add more water if necessary.

While the beans are simmering away, you can get on with cooking the sofrito. Heat the oil in a large frying pan over medium-high heat. Add the two kinds of pork and sizzle until the fat starts to flow. Add the remaining ingredients and cook gently over medium heat for about 10 minutes or until soft.

Drain the beans, reserving the liquid. Fish out the herbs and onion, mash the beans a little, then add them to the sofrito. Stir in the tomato purée, vinegar, sugar and freshly ground black pepper. Season with salt to taste, bearing in mind the saltiness of the pork.

Add about 300ml/$^{1}/_{2}$ pint of the bean cooking water to the mashed bean mixture. Cook, partially-covered, for 20–30 minutes, stirring occasionally until soft and thickened.

Meanwhile, put the rice in a pan and cover with water to the depth of your thumb nail. Add $^{1}/_{2}$ teaspoon of salt, cover tightly and bring to the boil. Reduce the heat to very low and cook for 10–15 minutes or until all the water is absorbed. Tip into a warm shallow serving dish and fluff with a fork.

Check the bean mixture and add more oregano, vinegar, cumin and salt and pepper if you think it needs it. Pile the beans on top of the rice and strew with chopped spring onions. Dribble with extra-virgin olive oil, then some crushed and sieved peppercorns.

cook's notes
- The bean cooking time will depend on the age of your beans. Old beans take longer.
- Some Puerto Rican cooks add cubed pumpkin when cooking the beans. If you want to try this, use about 200g/7oz and add after the beans have boiled for 10 minutes. Leave out the $^{1}/_{2}$ teaspoon of sugar when mixing the beans with the sofrito.

drinks, dips and relishes

This chapter is a miscellany of peppery bits and bobs, both savoury and sweet. Black pepper is surprisingly good in drinks. It adds a contrasting touch of heat to chilled fruit juice that is actually very refreshing. Try freshly squeezed lime juice with best Tellicherry pepper (page 184). Diluted with sparkling mineral water and plenty of ice cubes, there is nothing more thirst-quenching on a blistering hot day.

Quinces were in season when I was testing the recipes and I became completely besotted with their fragrance and the way they turn a deep rosy pink when cooked. Working on a quince jelly (page 189) gave me the opportunity to experiment with pink peppercorns, which, until then, I had not found a use for. Their slightly resinous flavour and mild heat were perfect with the quinces and, of course, they looked stunning suspended in the translucent jelly.

Sprigs of fresh green peppercorns found in a Thai shop were another treat. The plump bright green berries turn black in a matter of days so I had to use them quickly. Fortunately I remembered a power-packed fresh pickle that I had enjoyed at Das Sreedharan's pepper restaurant, Rasa Machiram, in London. With Das's help, I came up with my own version (page 193) which I enjoyed for the weeks to come.

I also wanted to find a way of using gingery and pungent long pepper – the medieval cook's pepper of choice before black pepper came on the scene. The hard catkin-like cones are difficult to incorporate into most dishes and don't fit into a conventional pepper mill. However, I managed to shatter a few with a hefty pestle, and the spicy fragments ultimately found their way into a richly flavoured chicken pâté (page 195) that has since become a family favourite.

Pepper blends well with soft cheeses, yogurt and cream. For a tasty nibble with drinks, try rolling balls of goat cheese in coarsely crushed peppercorns – a mixture of black, white and green looks and tastes good. Mix freshly milled black or green peppercorns with ricotta or yogurt 'cheese' (page 194) and you have an instant peppery spread for crackers or a filling for home-made ravioli. For a sweet but piquant sauce, simmer thick cream with a little black pepper, sugar and lemon zest. Sieved, chilled and spooned over strawberries or a fruit tart, the combination of flavours is out of this world.

lime and pepper refresher (nimbu pani)

limes 4–5
sugar 1–2 tbsp
salt a pinch
freshly ground black pepper
(preferably Tellicherry) to taste
ice cubes
chilled water or **soda water**
300ml/¹/₂ pint

Serves 2

This rehydrating drink is served all over India. Zesty and clean-tasting, it really hit the spot while I was on my travels researching this book. I am convinced the pepper protected me from stomach bugs.

Squeeze the limes extracting as much juice as possible – you need about 200ml/7fl oz. Strain into a jug.

Mix in the sugar, salt and plenty of freshly ground black pepper – about 5 turns of the mill. Add ice cubes, then top up with chilled water, either still or sparkling. Taste and add more sugar, salt or pepper, if necessary.

pomegranate and pepper juice

pomegranates 4
lemon juice a squeeze
sugar 3 tbsp or to taste
long pepper or **black**
peppercorns 1 tsp, cracked
and sieved
water 200ml/7fl oz
lemon slices to serve

Serves 2–3

This is a flamboyant and alcohol-free cocktail of freshly squeezed pomegranate juice spiked with crushed long pepper. Long pepper has a lovely tropical flavour – hot and gingery but also slightly sweet and floral. It's well worth trying to get hold of it, but you can use good quality black pepper if necessary. Strain the juice before serving if you prefer to keep the pepper a secret.

Slice the pomegranates in half horizontally. Squeeze the juice, using the citrus attachment on a juicer or food processor. You should end up with about 300ml/¹/₂ pint.

Pour the juice into a saucepan and add the lemon juice, sugar, cracked long pepper and water. Bring to the boil and boil for 3 minutes or until slightly syrupy. Pour into a jug and leave to cool.

Taste and add more lemon juice, sugar or pepper, or more water if you find it too syrupy. Dilute with plenty of ice cubes and serve with slices of lemon.

cook's note
• The juice becomes more syrupy if boiled for longer and can then be used as a sauce or a glaze for fruit flans. Sublime served hot over very cold ice cream.

See also
Long Pepper, page 34
Sources, page 248

bloody paradise

celery salt $^1/_4$ tsp or to taste
grains of paradise $^1/_2$ tsp,
coarsely ground, plus more
to garnish
tomato juice (best quality)
225ml/8fl oz
lime juice of 1
balsamic vinegar 1 tbsp
vodka (best quality) 3 tbsp
ice cubes
basil or mint leaves 1–2, to
garnish

Serves 1–2

Adapted from a recipe by Jean-Georges Vongerichten, this is a truly delicious cocktail, guaranteed to impress. Balsamic vinegar turns the tomato juice a deep garnet red – a dramatic contrast to the potent white grains of paradise.

Mix together the celery salt, grains of paradise, tomato juice, lime juice, balsamic vinegar and vodka, preferably in a cocktail shaker. Give the mixture a good shake.

Pour over a glass (or two) of ice cubes and grind more grains over the top. Garnish with a basil or mint leaf.

See also
Grains of Paradise, page 42
Sources, page 248

black pepper crème fraîche

crème fraîche 150ml/¼ pint
black peppercorns 1 tsp,
  crushed and sieved

Makes 150ml/¼ pint

Crème fraîche is simply mixed with coarsely crushed black peppercorns which have been sieved to remove unsightly dust. This is also good using brine-cured green peppercorns (drain them first), or exotic varieties such as grains of paradise or long pepper. Serve as a dip, a dressing or swirl into soups.

Mix the crème fraîche and crushed pepper together, then chill until needed.

See also
Grinding, Crushing, Cracking, page 83

sweet pepper cream

double cream 300ml/½ pint
black peppercorns 2 tsp,
  crushed and sieved
lemon 2 slivers of zest
sugar to taste

Makes 250ml/9fl oz

This is sweetly peppery with a refreshing hint of lemon. Serve chilled with fruit tarts or gâteau.

Put the cream, crushed pepper and lemon zest in a saucepan. Bring to the boil, then simmer briskly for 2–3 minutes or until slightly reduced. Leave to cool, then fish out the lemon zest. Stir in a little sugar to taste.

See also
Grinding, Crushing, Cracking, page 83

quince and pink pepper jelly

quinces 2.25kg/5lb
pink peppercorns 2 tbsp
lemon juice to taste
sugar 750g/1lb 10oz per
  1 litre/1$^3/_4$ pints of juice

**Makes about three 350g/
12oz jars**

This mildly peppery jelly tastes good and looks superb – pink peppercorns and slivers of quince suspended in sparkling rosy red jelly. It's delicious with cheese or cold meats, especially pork and ham.

The jelly is relatively simple to make since there is no need to peel or core the quinces. However, be sure to allow enough time for steeping and straining the juice.

Set aside one small quince or half a large one. Without peeling or coring them, slice the remaining quinces into quarters or eighths, depending on size. Chop each segment into two or three chunks.

Put the chopped fruit, pips, peel and all, into a large, stainless steel saucepan or preserving pan. Pour in enough water to just cover. Bring to the boil, then boil for 45–55 minutes until the fruit is soft. Remove from the heat, cover and leave in a cool place to steep for up to 24 hours.

Dampen a jelly bag, then suspend it over a large bowl. Tip the quinces and their liquid into the bag and leave to drip, undisturbed, for several hours or overnight.

Coarsely grate the reserved quince (see cook's notes), pressing hard on the grater to make long slivers rather than a mush.

Measure the quince juice and pour it into a large saucepan. Add the peppercorns, a good squeeze of lemon juice and enough sugar and grated quince for the amount of juice. Stir with a wooden spoon over low heat until the sugar has dissolved. Bring the juice to the boil, then boil rapidly, without stirring, until set (105°C/220°F on a sugar thermometer).

Skim off the froth with a large metal spoon and pour into warm sterilised jars. Seal and cover, then store in a cool place.

cook's notes
- If you don't have a jelly bag, you can improvise with a large sieve lined with six layers of damp muslin.
- You'll need about 100g/3$^1/_2$oz of grated quince per 1 litre/1$^3/_4$ pints of juice.
- To test for setting point without a thermometer, drip a teaspoon of juice onto a chilled saucer. Wait for a few minutes, then push with your finger. If the surface wrinkles, the jelly is ready.

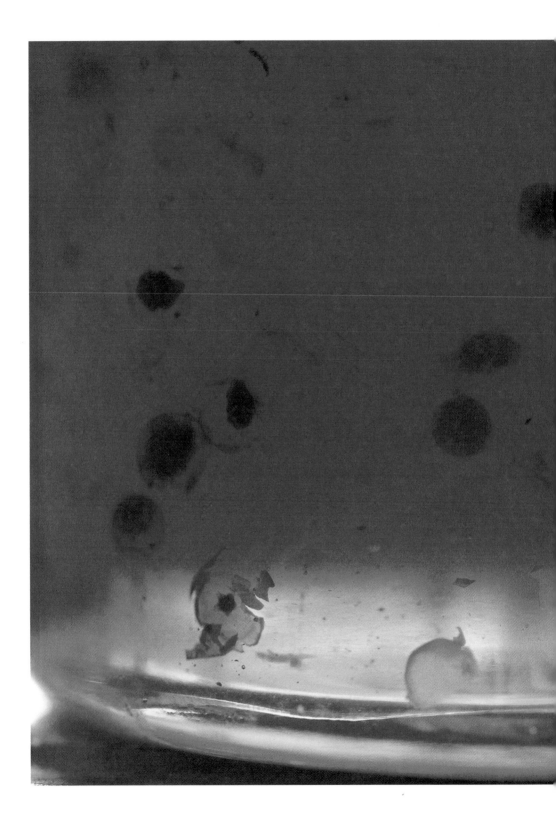

quince and pink pepper jelly
(page 189)

fresh green peppercorn pickle

fresh green peppercorns
250g/9oz
tamarind pulp 50g/1³/₄oz
hot water 150ml/¹/₄ pint
vegetable oil 3 tbsp
mustard seeds ¹/₂ tsp
curry leaves 10
Ginger Paste (page 132) 1 tbsp
Garlic Paste (page 132) 1 tbsp
jaggery or **dark muscovado**
sugar 50g/1³/₄oz
powdered fenugreek ¹/₄ tsp
asafoetida powder a pinch
salt to taste

Makes one 300g/10¹/₂oz jar

Served at Das Sreedharan's restaurant Rasa Machiram (the Indian word for pepper), this irresistibly hot-sweet-sour pickle is ambrosial with soft goat's cheese or ricotta on toasted ciabatta, or with plainly boiled rice or omelettes.

Fresh green peppercorns have a wonderfully clean bright flavour with plenty of kick. You can buy them in Asian grocers or specialist food halls.

Strip the pepper berries from the stem by gently pulling them through the tines of a fork. Rinse in several changes of cold water, then drain and dry on paper towels.

Stir the tamarind pulp into the hot water and leave to soften. Push through a sieve, pressing hard with the back of a wooden spoon.

Heat the oil in a large frying pan over medium heat. Add the mustard seeds and as they begin to pop, add the curry leaves and the ginger and garlic pastes. Cook briefly until beginning to colour – take care not to let it burn.

Add the peppercorns to the paste and cook for 10 minutes, stirring.

Reduce the heat and add the tamarind pulp and jaggery. Stir for a minute or two, then add the fenugreek, asafoetida and salt to taste. Simmer for about 10 minutes, stirring to prevent sticking, until thickened.

Remove from the heat, leave to cool, then store in a clean screw-top jar. The pickle will keep for about 2 weeks in the fridge.

cook's notes
- Tamarind pulp comes in sticky blocks. You'll find it in larger supermarkets and Asian grocers. Alternatively, use tamarind concentrate which can be spooned straight from the jar.
- Jaggery is made from sugar cane juice boiled until thick and fudge-like. It comes in cakes, cones or cylinders and is easy to find in Asian grocers. Dark muscovado sugar is a reasonable substitute but it doesn't quite have the same musky flavour.
- Asafoetida is made from a dried resinous gum and usually sold in powdered form in small tubes or tins. It has a dubious smell, which disappears once cooked. It is a very powerful seasoning and rounds out the flavour of any dish in which it is used.

See also
One Plant, Four Peppercorns, page 31

peppered yogurt cheese

plain yogurt preferably organic
1kg/2lb 4oz
sea salt flakes ¹/₂ tsp or more
to taste
black peppercorns 2 tsp,
cracked and sieved
green peppercorns 2 tsp,
crushed
white peppercorns (preferably
Sarawak or Wynad) 2 tsp,
cracked and sieved
Sichuan pepper 2 tsp, toasted

to serve
vegetable sticks (such as
carrots, celery, green peppers)
crackers, toast or **warm
flatbread**

Makes about 400g/14oz

This type of soft cheese is popular in the Middle East and India. Yogurt is tied up in muslin and left to strain for 6–36 hours – the shorter time making for a very soft mild cheese and the longer a denser cheese with a more pronounced flavour. Twelve hours is about right for this recipe. The end result is similar to cream cheese but lighter in texture and lower in fat.

Mixing different types of peppercorns with yogurt cheese is a pleasant way of experiencing their complex flavours without being overwhelmed by heat. Pepper also adds colour and crunch.

Dampen three large squares of muslin and use to line a colander, draping the corners over the sides. Spoon the yogurt into the centre of the muslin. Gather up the four corners and twist to squeeze the yogurt into a ball and remove excess liquid.

Tie tightly with string and fasten onto the handle of a wooden spoon. Rest the spoon on the rim of a deep bowl (or on two tall supports either side of the bowl). Make sure there is a reasonable gap underneath the ball for the liquid. Leave in a cool place to drip for 12 hours.

Season the cheese with sea salt to taste, then divide into four. Mix each portion with a different type of peppercorn. Leave to stand at room temperature for about 30 minutes so the flavours develop.

cook's notes
- Leave the yogurt to drip for longer so it is firm enough to shape into logs or balls. Roll in cracked peppercorns, either a single variety or a mixture.
- If you can find any fresh green peppercorns on the vine, use them instead of dried or brine-cured. They are deliciously fresh, moist and chewy and provide a nice glow of heat.

See also
One Plant Four Peppercorns, page 31
Sichuan Pepper, page 46
Grinding, Crushing, Cracking, page 83

chicken liver pâté

chicken livers 225g/8oz
unsalted butter 75g/2³/₄oz,
    plus extra for melting and
    covering
onion 1 medium, chopped
garlic clove 1 large, crushed
fresh bay leaf 1, shredded
thyme or **savory** leaves from
    1 sprig, chopped
dried oregano a pinch
sea salt flakes a large pinch
long pepper 1 tsp, coarsely
    ground
brandy 2 tsp (optional)

Serves 4–6 as a snack

I make this with deliciously gingery and pungent long pepper but you could use black pepper instead. Whatever your choice, pepper's piquant bite works wonders at cutting the richness.

Wash the livers and cut out any tubes or discoloured bits. Chop them into even-sized chunks.

Melt one-third of the butter in a frying pan and fry the onion over a medium heat until soft but not starting to brown. Stir in the garlic and gently fry for another 3 minutes.

Add the chopped chicken livers and cook, stirring, for 2 minutes. Sprinkle in the bay leaf, thyme and oregano. Season with sea salt flakes and the ground long pepper. Once the livers are cooked through, remove from the heat and allow to cool slightly.

Purée the liver mixture in a food processor with the remaining butter and the brandy, if you are using it.

Spoon the mixture into ramekins, or one larger bowl, pressing down well and smoothing the surface. Cover with a layer of melted butter, then chill or freeze.

See also
Long Pepper, page 34

peppered dried figs

semi-dried figs 24
black peppercorns 4 tbsp,
   cracked and sieved
fresh bay leaves 12–18

Makes 24

This is from Rosemary Barron's inspiring book *Flavours of Greece*. Semi-dried figs are rolled in cracked black peppercorns and layered with fresh bay leaves in a glass jar. The combination of pungent, crunchy black pepper and delectably sweet, sticky figs is excellent. Try them in savoury and sweet dishes – with Parma ham, as part of a *meze*, baked in crisp filo pastry (page 219) or served as a sweetmeat at the end of a festive meal.

Trim the fig stems if necessary. Gently roll each fig in the cracked pepper to coat.

Cover the bottom of a glass jar with a few of the bay leaves, then make alternate layers of figs and bay leaves, finishing with a layer of leaves.

Gently press down on the leaves with the palm of your hand to remove any air pockets. Cover the surface with cling film, then tightly seal the jar.

cook's notes
• I made this with organic semi-dried figs that were large and fleshy. The recipe doesn't work so well with figs that are completely dry.
• Rosemary recommends making this 3 days ahead for the richest flavour.
• The figs can be kept at room temperature for up to 1 month, but make sure the jar is airtight to prevent mould growing.

See also
Grinding, Crushing, Cracking, page 83

desserts and sweetmeats

Using pepper to flavour sweet dishes was commonplace in Roman and medieval kitchens but has not been part of the modern cook's repertoire until recently. As American food writer Michele Jordan comments, the practice re-emerged in the late '90s when chillies started showing up in desserts. Chefs then went on to discover the range of flavours of the peppercorn, which they realised could enhance rather than dominate a sweet dish.

This chapter was one of the most challenging. It took repeated testing to discover exactly how much pepper was needed to flavour different types of dessert. I found that chilled or frozen desserts can take more pepper than most, since low temperatures dull the pungency. However, once the chill wears off there is a slow after-burn so you still need to add pepper with care.

The wine-like flavour of good dark chocolate blends especially well with black pepper – a couple of tablespoons went into delectable chocolate truffles (page 205), some of which were dusted with even more pepper. Needless to say, the tasting team polished these off and had to mix up another batch – just to be sure.

Pepper works special magic on meringues; it adds just the right amount of peppery bite to tame the sweetness. Crushed pink and green peppercorns look and taste sublime in crisp grissini-shaped batons (page 206) served with cool creamy desserts or wobbly jellies.

I love pepper with fruit, especially sprinkled over chilled slices of mango or papaya, or mixed with sugar and stirred into a bowl of gleaming pomegranate seeds. And it's hard to beat the intense tropical flavours of pineapple studded with long pepper and fried until the sticky juices caramelise (page 209).

The development chef at Raymond Blanc's two-Michelin-starred restaurant, Le Manoir aux Quat' Saisons, showed me how strawberries reveal untold layers of flavour warmed in a buttery sauce with sugar, lemon, a slug of kirsch and an aromatic sprinkling of black pepper. As ever, you need top quality peppercorns and strawberries that actually taste of strawberries.

strawberry and black pepper ice cream

strawberries 450g/1lb, plus
extra to decorate
caster sugar 150g/5^1/$_2$oz
lemon juice 1 tbsp
black peppercorns 1 tbsp,
crushed and sieved, plus a
few whole peppercorns to
decorate
ricotta cheese 125g/4^1/$_2$oz
double cream 2 tbsp

Makes about 850ml/1^1/$_2$ pints

This is so easy to make – no syrup or custard involved, just pure ricotta, a little double cream, lemon juice and sugar. There's a bit of heat from the pepper, but it's subtle and slow and takes a back seat to the creamy richness of the strawberries.

Rinse, hull and dry the strawberries (in that order), reserving a few unhulled berries for decoration. Put the hulled fruit in a food processor along with the sugar, lemon juice and crushed peppercorns. Whizz to a purée, scrape into a bowl with a spatula, then cover and chill for at least an hour.

Slacken the ricotta with the cream, mixing well, then stir it into the strawberry purée.

Freeze the mixture in an ice-cream machine following the manufacturer's instructions (see cook's notes if you don't have a machine). Spoon into plastic boxes and press cling-film over the surface before putting on the lid.

Put the ice cream in the fridge to soften 20–25 minutes before you want to serve it. Spoon into glass bowls and decorate with a strawberry and a single black peppercorn.

cook's notes
- Don't be tempted to use regular kitchen pepper for this. To enjoy the ice cream at its best, you need top-quality, organic or single estate peppercorns, preferably Tellicherry or Wynad.
- For an extra hit of flavour you could purée Flambéed Strawberries with Kirsch and Black Pepper (page 201) and use these instead, once they've cooled down.
- To freeze ice cream without a machine, pour the mixture into a shallow freezer-proof container, cover and freeze for about 2 hours or until beginning to harden round the edges. Tip into a bowl and beat until smooth to get rid of ice crystals. Repeat the process twice more if you have time, then freeze until completely firm.
- Eat the ice cream right away or, at the most, within a day or two of making. The fresh fruity flavour starts to fade after that.

See also
Grinding, Crushing, Cracking, page 83
Tasting Pepper, page 76

devilled chocolate ice cream.

unsweetened cocoa powder
4 tbsp
black peppercorns 2 tsp,
coarsely ground
white peppercorns 2 tsp,
coarsely ground
sugar 115g/4oz
milk 400ml/14fl oz
vanilla extract 1 tsp
double cream 300ml/$\frac{1}{2}$ pint,
chilled

Makes about 1 litre/1$\frac{3}{4}$ pints

Sensory euphoria as good as it gets – very rich, very cold chocolate ice cream followed by the slow build and lingering heat of black and white peppercorns. It's imperative to use the very best peppercorns, preferably organic. I recommend Tellicherry black and a single estate white such as Wynad.

Put the cocoa, black and white pepper, sugar and milk in a saucepan. Bring to the boil, then reduce the heat and simmer gently for 5 minutes, stirring all the time. Pour the mixture into a bowl, then place the bowl in cold water so that it cools quickly.

Stir the vanilla extract and chilled cream into the cold cocoa mixture. Freeze in an ice-cream machine following the manufacturer's instructions (see cook's notes if you don't have a machine). Spoon into plastic boxes, pressing cling-film over the surface before putting on the lid.

Soften the ice cream in the fridge 20–25 minutes before you want to serve it.

cook's notes
- It's important to keep stirring the milk and cocoa so that the powder is properly amalgamated with the liquid and any trace of dustiness is eradicated.
- To freeze ice cream without a machine, pour the mixture into a shallow freezer-proof container, cover and freeze for about 2 hours or until beginning to harden round the edges. Tip into a bowl and beat until smooth to get rid of any ice crystals. Repeat the process twice more if you have time, then freeze until completely firm.

See also
Tasting Pepper, page 76

flambéed strawberries with kirsch and black pepper

strawberries 350g/12oz, halved
caster sugar
unsalted butter 1 tsp
kirsch eau de vie a splash
lemon juice a squeeze
freshly ground black pepper to taste

Serves 2

Nurdin Topham, Raymond Blanc's development chef at his two-Michelin-starred restaurant Le Manoir aux Quat' Saisons, demonstrated this to me to show how layers of flavour amplify the basic fruit. A little sugar brings out the natural flavour of strawberries, butter adds richness, kirsch further intensifies the flavour, lemon juice balances sweetness, while black pepper adds a final layer of floral pungency. Keep tasting as you add each ingredient and you'll see for yourself. Nurdin says this is excellent with eggy fried bread!

Put the strawberries in a shallow dish and sprinkle with the merest dusting of sugar. Leave to macerate for 20–30 minutes.

Heat the butter and 1 teaspoon of sugar in a heavy-based frying pan over medium-high heat. Just before the sugar starts to caramelise and the mixture looks pale gold, stir in a splash of kirsch and then add the strawberries.

Briefly shunt everything around the pan until the strawberries are warmed through but not disintegrating. Finish with a squeeze of lemon juice and a few turns of the pepper mill.

cook's notes
- It should go without saying that the strawberries must be perfectly ripe.
- You'll need top quality peppercorns for this. It's simply not worth making with standard kitchen pepper of unknown provenance.
- If your strawberries need a quick rinse, do this before hulling otherwise they'll start to ship water and become soggy. Drain and dry thoroughly on paper towels.

spiced yogurt with pomegranates and pistachios

shelled pistachio nuts 3 tbsp
Peppered Yogurt Cheese
　　(page 194) or **light curd**
　　cheese 400g/14oz
rose water 2 tbsp
Spiced Sugar (page 233) 2 tbsp
small pomegranate 1

Serves 4

A simple but exquisite dessert: jewel-like pomegranate seeds and a sprinkling of green pistachio nuts adorn a sweetly perfumed and faintly spicy mound of strained yogurt or light curd cheese such as quark.

My recipe is based on a traditional dessert known as *shrikhand* in Western India and *sikarni* in Nepal. It's made with creamy yogurt drained for several hours through muslin (see the Peppered Yogurt Cheese, page 194) until thickened. The resulting creamy 'cheese' is flavoured with sugar, black pepper and sweet spices.

Cover the pistachio nuts with boiling water, leave for 5 minutes then slip off the skins. Chop the nuts coarsely and set aside.

Beat the yogurt cheese with the rose water and Spiced Sugar. Divide the mixture between four serving bowls and chill until ready to serve.

With a small sharp knife, score the pomegranate skin from top to bottom into four segments, taking care not to puncture the juicy seeds inside. Break the pomegranate in half, then into quarters. Bend the skin back to release the seeds and remove any bits of yellow membrane.

Sprinkle the seeds over the yogurt and top with a sprinkling of pistachios.

cook's note
- Spiced Sugar can be replaced with plain sugar. If you do so, compensate by adding some spices to the yogurt: freshly ground black pepper, a small pinch each of ground cinnamon and ground cloves, and a few crushed cardamom seeds.

peppered chocolate truffles

plain chocolate (70% cocoa
  solids) 275g/9^1/$_2$oz
double cream 250ml/9fl oz
unsalted butter 3 tbsp
black peppercorns 2 tbsp,
  coarsely ground

coating 1
unsweetened cocoa powder
  2 tbsp

coating 2
icing sugar 1 tbsp
unsweetened cocoa powder
  1 tbsp

coating 3
caster sugar 1 tbsp
grains of paradise 1 tbsp,
  coarsely ground

Makes about 30

Pepper and chocolate is a culinary partnership that works really well. The volatile oils and pungency of black pepper balance and harmonize with the intense flavours of dark chocolate. These truffles are to die for – smooth peppery chocolate ganache dusted with unsweetened cocoa, or a sweeter combination of icing sugar and cocoa, or, best of all, a sparkling frost of caster sugar and crushed grains of paradise.

Chop the chocolate into pea-sized pieces and put in a heatproof bowl. Heat the cream until just boiling, then pour it over the chocolate in a thin stream, beating with a balloon whisk as you pour. The chocolate should melt as you pour the hot cream over it. If it doesn't melt completely, put the bowl over a saucepan of gently steaming (but not simmering or boiling) water and stir until melted. Keep stirring until the ganache is smooth and glossy.

Beat in the butter while the ganache is still warm, then mix in the pepper. Leave to firm up at room temperature for about an hour but don't chill it at this stage.

Using a teaspoon, divide the ganache into walnut-sized portions and roll into balls between your palms. Line them up on a tray lined with baking parchment.

Make up the coatings on three separate plates. Roll ten truffles in each coating, giving each one a quick turn in your palm to brush off any surplus powder. Chill on the tray until ready to serve.

cook's note
- Take great care when melting the chocolate as it can easily 'seize' and become unworkable. Unfortunately there is no rescue for this. Some food writers instruct you to put the chocolate into a saucepan of hot cream, or melt the chocolate separately before stirring it into hot cream. I have tried both ways without success.

See also
Grains of Paradise, page 42

pepper meringue grissini

egg whites from 3 large eggs,
   at room temperature
salt a pinch
caster sugar 150g/5$^{1}/_{2}$oz
cornflour $^{3}/_{4}$ tsp
white wine vinegar $^{3}/_{4}$ tsp
pink peppercorns $^{1}/_{2}$ tbsp,
   lightly crushed
dried green peppercorns
   $^{1}/_{2}$ tbsp, lightly crushed
white peppercorns (preferably
   single estate) $^{1}/_{2}$ tbsp, lightly
   crushed

Makes 30–35

No one can resist a meringue, especially when it can be nibbled like a grissini and is prettily flecked with green, pink and white peppercorns. These are stunning with any kind of indulgent dessert but especially so with Flambéed Strawberries (page 201) or Devilled Chocolate Ice Cream (page 200).

Preheat the oven to 110°C/225°F/Gas $^{1}/_{4}$. Line two baking sheets with baking parchment. Have ready a piping bag fitted with a plain 1.5cm/$^{5}/_{8}$in nozzle.

Tip the egg whites into a large clean bowl and add a pinch of salt (this helps to keep the foam stable). Whisk with a circular motion that lifts the whites and incorporates air until you have a uniformly foamy mass with soft droopy peaks. Continue to whisk until the foam forms stiffer, pointy peaks, then start adding half the caster sugar, a spoonful at a time, whisking well after each addition. By now the foam should be smooth and shiny.

Using a large metal spoon, lightly and evenly fold in the rest of the sugar. Sprinkle with the cornflour, vinegar and crushed peppercorns, and fold all this in too.

Spoon the foam into the piping bag and pipe 10cm/4in lengths onto the lined baking sheets. Bake in the lower third of the oven for about 1 hour until crisp, transposing the baking sheets halfway through. Turn the oven off but leave the grissini in the oven with the door closed until completely cool. Store in a completely airtight box until ready to serve.

cook's note
• Take care not to over-whisk the egg whites at the stiff peak stage, otherwise you'll end up with brittle lumps of foam.

variation
• Instead of the peppercorns, use 2 tablespoons of Orange and Pepper Powder (page 235). The powder tints the meringue the most divine shade of pale apricot and has an irresistible sweet, salty, peppery, orange flavour. For the best of both worlds, divide the basic meringue in half after adding the cornflour and vinegar. Add 1 tablespoon of the orange powder to one portion, and half the quantity of crushed peppercorns to the other.

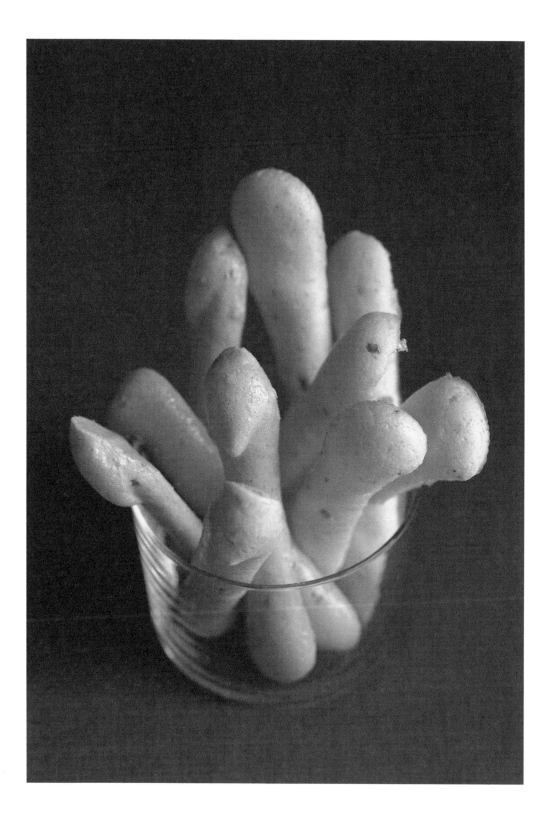

caramelised pineapple with long pepper and lime syrup

pineapple 1, weighing about
1.4kg/3lb 2oz
long pepper 6 cones, broken
into 2–3 pieces
unsalted butter 3 tbsp
lime wedges to decorate

for the syrup
sugar 150g/5$\frac{1}{2}$oz
water 100ml/3$\frac{1}{2}$fl oz
long pepper 3 cones, roughly
crushed
lime finely grated zest of $\frac{1}{2}$

Serves 4

Pineapple takes on a new dimension served warm and infused with the intense tropical flavours of long pepper and lime. Long pepper is both hot and slightly sweet, with complex floral and fruity notes. Though rarely used nowadays, it was once the pepper of choice and considered superior to black pepper. If you don't have long pepper, you could stud your pineapple with large Tellicherry black peppercorns but the flavour will be different.

First make the syrup. Put the sugar, water, long pepper and lime zest in a saucepan over gentle heat. Once the sugar has dissolved, increase the heat and boil hard for about 5 minutes until syrupy (the bubbles will look bigger and stickier at this stage). Remove from the heat and leave to cool.

Peel the pineapple, carefully removing the eyes. Slice the flesh horizontally into six thick rings and remove the core. Stud each ring with two or three pieces of long pepper, pressing them deeply into the flesh.

Arrange the pineapple in a single layer in a shallow dish. Strain the syrup and pour it over the rings. Cover and chill for several hours, basting occasionally.

Remove the pineapple from the dish, reserving the juices. Slice each ring in half to make two semi-circles.

Heat the butter in a large frying pan over medium-high heat until foaming. Slip in the pieces of pineapple, in batches if necessary, and fry for a few minutes, turning once, until beginning to brown at the edges. Pour in the reserved juices and boil hard until syrupy. Decant into your best white china bowls and decorate with a wedge of lime.

cook's notes
- It's worth trying to get hold of long pepper if you can; the little catkin-like cones are perfect for studding pineapple flesh. You should be able to find it in speciality food shops or by mail order from spice companies (see Sources, page 248).
- The pineapple can be left to marinate in the syrup for up to 2 days. The longer you leave it the more the long pepper flavour will penetrate.
- Remove the pepper cones if you think diners would find them disturbing. In India, people would simply leave whole spices to the side of the plate.

See also
Tasting Pepper, page 76
Long Pepper, page 34

ricotta tart with limoncello pepper syrup

butter (at room temperature)
2 tbsp, plus extra for greasing
flour for dusting
ricotta cheese 250g/9oz
Spiced Sugar (page 233)
90g/3$^{1}/_{4}$oz
eggs 2 large, yolks and whites
separated
lemon finely grated zest of 1
fine semolina 50g/1$^{3}/_{4}$oz
ground almonds 50g/1$^{3}/_{4}$oz
cream of tartar $^{1}/_{2}$ tsp
icing sugar for dusting the
cake

for the syrup
lemon 1
caster sugar 150g/5$^{1}/_{2}$oz
water 300ml/$^{1}/_{2}$ pint
black peppercorns $^{1}/_{2}$ tsp,
crushed and sieved
limoncello liqueur 3–5 tbsp

Serves 6

A quietly understated dessert brought to life by spiced sugar and the syrup – a zinging mix of peppery heat, intense lemony sweetness and a kick of alcohol.

I have called this a tart for want of a better word, but no pastry-making is involved.

First make the syrup: peel the lemon very thinly avoiding the bitter white pith. Slice the peel into very thin slivers and set aside. Put the sugar, water and crushed pepper in a saucepan over gentle heat. Once the sugar has dissolved, increase the heat and boil hard until syrupy (the bubbles will get bigger at this stage). Remove from the heat, add the slivers of lemon peel, then leave to cool and steep for an hour or two.

Preheat the oven to 190°C/375°F/Gas 5. Butter and flour a 20cm/8in fluted tart tin with a removable base.

Cream the ricotta and butter together, then beat in the spiced sugar. Stir in the egg yolks and lemon zest, mixing well, then add the semolina and ground almonds.

In a separate bowl, whisk the egg whites with the cream of tartar until stiff peaks form. Using a large metal spoon, fold about one-third into the ricotta mixture to slacken it, then gently fold in the rest.

Pour the mixture into the prepared tin and smooth the surface. Bake for 15–20 minutes or until golden and springy to touch. Let the tart cool a little in the tin, then carefully lift it on to a wire rack to cool completely. Dust with sifted icing sugar when ready to serve.

Strain the syrup, then add a good squeeze of lemon juice and limoncello to taste. Serve with the tart.

cook's note
- If you don't have any Spiced Sugar, use plain sugar mixed with some freshly ground black pepper, a pinch of ground cinnamon, a crushed clove and a few cardamom seeds.

cakes and biscuits

Cooks have used pepper in baking since ancient times, In 400BC the Greeks included pepper with nuts, seeds and honey wrapped in sweet pastry – my inspiration for Peppered Fig Parcels (page 219). Similar ingredients appear in the recipes in *Apicius*, the classical Roman cookbook:

'Pound pepper, pine nuts, honey, rue and *passum* (sweet raisin wine). Cook with milk and *tracta* (dough). Cook the thickened mixture with a little egg. Serve drenched in honey and sprinkled in pepper.' (*Apicius* 7.11.5 Grocock and Grainger)

The Crusaders brought back pepper and other exotics from the Orient, inspiring medieval cooks to enrich their baking. In Italy, the Sienese added a generous pinch of pepper to *panforte*, the dense dark sweetmeat which sustained many a medieval traveller.

In neighbouring Umbria, pepper is used in *Pan Pepato* (page 224), small chewy cakes made with rich dark chocolate, nuts and dried fruit – less dense than *panforte* but equally power-packed. I first came across *pan pepato* at a dinner in Spoleto hosted by the Chamber of Commerce. Served with fiery local *grappa* the cakes made a memorable end to the meal.

Cooks in Tudor times used pepper in gingerbread, made in those days with breadcrumbs rather than flour and richly coloured with natural dyes. Food historian Dawn Riggs quotes a 15th-century recipe from a Hampton Court Palace cookbook:

'Gyngerbrede... take goode hony and clarifie it on fere, take gratyd brede and strew it on y hony, and stere it well togyder, take it down and put erin gyngr, long pepir and safroun pouder, if thou wilt have it red coloure it with saunderys enow.'

A later recipe from a 17th-century cookbook specifies the same method but unusually includes popular spices from the medieval period – liquorice, aniseed and 'two ounces of graines'. Similarly inspired, I experimented with anise-flavoured liqueur and grains of paradise in a moist and colourful pumpkin cake (page 215). The grains provided a little bit of bite but with a rounded spiciness that doesn't overwhelm.

I discovered that white pepper in crisp buttery shortbread (page 218) also loses its assertive flavour; it becomes a mysterious spicy heat that slowly builds after the first bite or two. Black pepper and orange zest add a bright note to crunchy *Cantuccini* (page 220), perfect for dipping in a mean espresso or sweet *vin santo*. A good grinding of black pepper hit the spot in chocolate brownies, as did the pink peppercorns used somewhat frivolously in white chocolate blondies.

pink pepper blondies

white chocolate (preferably 30% cocoa solids) 200g/7oz
unsalted butter 150g/5$\frac{1}{2}$oz
plain flour 150g/5$\frac{1}{2}$oz
baking powder $\frac{1}{2}$ tsp
eggs 2
sugar 100g/3$\frac{1}{2}$oz
vanilla extract $\frac{1}{2}$ tsp
salt $\frac{1}{2}$ tsp
limes finely grated zest of 2
pink peppercorns 1$\frac{1}{2}$ tbsp

Makes 16–20

Prettily dotted with pink peppercorns, these are definitely for the girls. The resinous notes of pink pepper and the clean flavour of lime zest cuts through the sweet white chocolate.

Preheat the oven to 180°C/350°F/Gas 4. Grease and line a 20cm/ 8in square cake tin with baking parchment, allowing it to hang over the sides.

Chop the chocolate into pea-sized pieces. Put half of it in a heatproof bowl with the butter. Place the bowl over a pan of steaming, but not quite simmering, water, and stir until the chocolate and butter are melted and well mixed. Remove from the heat and leave to cool slightly.

Sift the flour and baking powder into a medium bowl.

In a separate bowl, whisk together the eggs, sugar, vanilla extract and salt for about 2 minutes until pale and fluffy.

Stir in the warm melted chocolate mixture, the lime zest and peppercorns. When well mixed, fold in the sifted flour and baking powder, and the rest of the chocolate.

Pour into the prepared tin and bake for 35–40 minutes or until the top is golden and springy and a skewer inserted in the middle comes out very slightly sticky.

Leave in the tin until completely cool. Lift from the tin using the overhanging baking parchment. Slice when ready to serve.

cook's note
- Compared with plain chocolate, white chocolate contains far fewer cocoa solids. It is basically cocoa butter with added sugar, milk and flavouring. Use the best quality you can find, 30% cocoa solids if possible. Swiss or French brands are usually better than British.

black pepper brownies

plain chocolate (at least 70% cocoa solids) 200g/7oz
unsalted butter 115g/4oz
unsweetened cocoa powder 3 tbsp
eggs 3 large
sugar 250g/9oz
vanilla extract 2 tsp
salt 1/2 tsp
black peppercorns 1 tbsp, freshly ground
plain flour 150g/5 1/2 oz

Makes about 20

These brownies are very dark, dense and immensely rich, best served in small portions. The subtle bite of black pepper helps balance the richness.

Preheat the oven to 180°C/350°F/Gas 4, moving the rack to just below the middle. Grease and line a 20cm/8in square baking tin with baking parchment, using enough to hang over the sides.

Break the chocolate into small pieces and put it in a heatproof bowl with the butter. Place the bowl over a pan of steaming, but not quite simmering, water, and stir until the chocolate and butter are melted and well mixed. Gradually sprinkle in the cocoa powder and whisk until smooth. Remove from the heat and leave to cool slightly.

Beat together the eggs, sugar, vanilla extract, salt and pepper until well mixed. Gradually beat in the still-warm chocolate mixture, then stir in the flour, mixing well.

Pour into the prepared tin and bake for 35–40 minutes until a skewer inserted in the middle comes out very slightly sticky – brownies are meant to be gooey in the middle.

Leave in the tin until completely cool. Lift from the tin using the overhanging baking parchment. Slice when ready to serve.

cook's notes
- For extra texture, stir in 100g/3 1/2 oz chopped walnuts when you add the chocolate mixture.
- No matter how tempted, it really is a good idea to wait until the brownies are completely cool before you slice them.
- Brownies will keep for 4–5 days if you wrap them in foil.

paradise cake

sultanas 50g/1³/₄oz
Galliano liqueur or **grappa**
100ml/3¹/₂fl oz
squash (see cook's notes)
600g/1lb 5oz, peeled,
deseeded and cubed
unsalted butter 150g/5¹/₂oz
salt a pinch
sugar 150g/5¹/₂oz
whole almonds 50g/1³/₄oz,
finely chopped
candied orange or **citron peel**
50g/1³/₄oz, finely chopped
lemon grated zest of 1
grains of paradise (see cook's
notes) 1 tbsp, coarsely ground
plain flour 85g/3oz
baking powder 1 heaped tsp
eggs 2, yolks and whites
separated
icing sugar for dusting

Serves 8–10

This is adapted from a recipe by Italian food writer Valentina Harris. It makes a great dessert for Thanksgiving for those who find the traditional pumpkin pie too sweet. I have spiced the cake with grains of paradise (*melagueta* pepper) which give it a beautifully warm and gingery flavour – just enough to make the tongue tingle, and perfect with the sweetness of the squash.

Put the sultanas and Galliano in a bowl and soak for at least 20 minutes until the sultanas are plump.

Preheat the oven to 180°C/350°F/Gas 4. Grease and line a 22–23cm/8¹/₂–9in shallow cake tin.

Put the cubed squash in a saucepan with the butter. Cover and cook over medium heat for about 15 minutes until soft. Add a pinch of salt, then tip the mixture into a bowl and beat until smooth.

Stir in the sugar, almonds, candied peel, lemon zest and grains of paradise. Add the sultanas and any remaining Galliano, mixing thoroughly.

Sift the flour and baking powder together, then gradually add to the squash mixture, beating well with each addition.

In a separate bowl, beat the egg yolks until pale and thick, then fold into the squash mixture. In another bowl, whisk the egg whites until stiff, then fold carefully into the squash mixture using a large metal spoon.

Spoon the mixture into the prepared tin and bake for 1–1¹/₄ hours or until a skewer inserted in the middle comes out clean. If the cake is browning too much, cover the top with a piece of foil. Turn out onto a wire rack to cool.

Dust with sifted icing sugar before serving.

cook's notes
- If you can't get grains of paradise, try a teaspoon each of ground ginger and black and white peppercorns instead.
- Use a dense-fleshed squash such as dark green Kaboucha or Sweet Mama, or bright orange Uchiki Kure. Butternut squash will do if you can't find other varieties but I think it lacks flavour.
- If pressed for time, use a 425g/15oz can of pumpkin purée instead of fresh squash, and ready-chopped mixed peel instead of whole chunks of orange or citron peel.

See also
Tasting Pepper, page 76
Grains of Paradise, page 42

paradise cake (page 215)

white pepper shortbread

white peppercorns preferably
   Sarawak or Wynad, 2 tsp
sugar 50g/1^3/$_4$oz
plain flour 125g/4^1/$_2$oz
rice flour 50g/1^3/$_4$oz
salt a pinch
unsalted butter at room
   temperature, 115g/4oz

Makes 12 slices

Those with a savoury tooth will appreciate the subtle bite of white pepper – more of a slow after-burn than out-and-out heat – which balances the somewhat cloying sweetness of shortbread. You'll smell the intriguing aroma of white pepper as you pound. It's quite different from black pepper.

Preheat the oven to 180°C/350°F/Gas 4. Using a roomy mortar and pestle, grind the peppercorns with a tablespoon of the sugar until you have a coarse powder. Mix this with the rest of the sugar.
   Sift the two flours and salt together into a bowl.
   In a separate bowl, cream the butter and peppery sugar together for a few minutes until pale, then gradually add the sifted flours.
   Work the dough with your hands until it clumps together. Mould into a flattened ball and place on a non-stick baking sheet.
   Use your fingers to press the dough into a 20cm/8in circle. Lightly level the surface with a rolling pin. Go round the edge, making indentations with the back of a fork and prick the surface all over.
   Bake for 20–25 minutes or until pale golden. Mark into 12 segments and leave to cool.

cook's note
• Shortbread is quite fragile when it comes out of the oven. It will firm up as it cools and is then easy to snap into segments.

See also
Pepper Names, page 64

peppered fig parcels

filo pastry three 35 x 46cm/14 x 18in sheets (defrosted, if frozen)
unsalted butter 75g/2³/₄oz
Peppered Dried Figs (page 196) or **semi-dried figs** (see cook's notes) 400g/14oz, roughly chopped
icing sugar for dusting

Makes 10 triangular parcels

An irresistible combination of sweet sticky figs, pungent pepper and crisp buttery filo pastry. The pepper flavour is not particularly strident here – sweetness helps tame it. For an extra hit serve with Sweet Pepper Cream (page 188).

Preheat the oven to 220°C/425°F/Gas 7. Line a baking sheet with baking parchment. Carefully unfold the sheets of filo pastry and cut each one into four 46cm/18in long strips. Cover with a clean, damp tea towel to keep them moist and pliable.

Melt the butter and brush a little over one of the filo strips. Place 2 tablespoons of the chopped peppered figs at one end of the strip. Fold one corner of pastry across the filling to form a triangle, then continue folding the strip to form a multi-layered triangular parcel. Repeat with the remaining filo strips and figs.

Arrange the parcels on the prepared baking sheet and brush with melted butter. Bake for 20 minutes or until golden brown and crisp. Let them cool on a wire rack. Dust with sifted icing sugar before serving.

cook's notes
- If you don't have Peppered Dried Figs, use semi-dried figs instead and mix with 2–3 tablespoons of cracked black peppercorns when you chop them.
- If your filo pastry sheets are a different size to the one specified, it's fine to trim and piece together as necessary.

cantuccini with black pepper and orange zest

eggs 2, plus 1 egg yolk
caster sugar 200g/7oz
finely grated orange zest 2 tsp
vanilla extract 1/2 tsp
plain flour 250g/9oz, plus extra
   for kneading
baking powder 1/2 tsp
aniseeds or **fennel seeds**
   1 tsp
black peppercorns 1 tsp,
   freshly ground
whole almonds 100g/3 1/2oz,
   with skins
vin santo to serve

Makes about 25

This is adapted from a recipe by my friend Rachel Demuth, owner of Demuths Restaurant and Vegetarian Cookery School in Bath. There is just enough pepper to make itself felt, and it combines beautifully with the sweet clean flavours of orange and aniseed.

Preheat the oven to 180°C/350°F/Gas 4. Line two baking trays with baking parchment.

In a large mixing bowl, whisk together the eggs, sugar, orange zest and vanilla extract. Sift in the flour and baking powder, then sprinkle over the aniseeds and black pepper. Now bring the dough together using a metal spoon, until it forms a sticky ball. Tip the dough out onto a well-floured work surface. Sprinkle over the whole almonds and knead them into the dough. If the dough is still too sticky, add a little more flour.

Divide the dough in half and roll out into log shapes about 4cm/1 1/2in wide and 24cm/9 1/2in long. Lay the rolls on the prepared baking trays and flatten slightly using the palm of your hand. Score the dough diagonally with a knife at 1.5cm/5/8in intervals.

Bake in the middle of the oven for 20 minutes or until pale golden and firm to touch. Remove from the oven and reduce the oven temperature to 150°C/300°F/Gas 2.

Cut through the score lines and lay the slices flat on the baking trays. Return to the oven for a further 15–20 minutes or until golden and no longer sticky.

Serve with a glass of sweet *vin santo* for dipping.

cook's notes
- If the cantuccini brown too quickly during the first baking, cover them with a loose piece of baking parchment.
- For completely hard, dry cantuccini, Rachel advises turning off the oven and leaving them to dry out until the oven is cold. If you prefer a chewy moist biscuit, don't let them dry out completely, just leave to cool a little and eat at once.

parmesan and green peppercorn wafers

Parmesan cheese
100g/3$^{1}/_{2}$oz, finely grated
dried green peppercorns
1 tsp, crushed

Makes 20–25

These are so simple and so quick to make – and so much tastier to serve with drinks than the ubiquitous black pepper crisps. The combination of pungent, slightly herbaceous, green peppercorns and strong-tasting Parmesan works really well.

Preheat the oven to 180°C/350°F/Gas 4. Line a baking tray with baking parchment.

Mix the Parmesan and peppercorns together in a bowl. Make little piles (about 2 teaspoons) on the prepared baking tray, leaving some space between to allow the mixture to spread.

Bake for 3–4 minutes or until bubbling and golden. Remove from the oven and leave for a minute until the wafers have solidified a little. Use a palette knife to ease them off the tray, then place on a wire rack. They'll become crisp once they've cooled down.

cook's notes
- To make these even more special, cool the wafers on a narrow rolling pin so that they set in a curved shape.
- The wafers will keep for a few days if you store them in an airtight box.

neapolitan taralli

unbleached plain flour
500g/1lb 2oz, warmed
salt 1 tsp
black peppercorns 1 tbsp,
freshly ground
dried easy-blend yeast
1 sachet or **fresh yeast**
15g/1/2oz or **dried active**
yeast 2 tsp
white wine 225ml/8fl oz,
warmed
olive oil 125ml/4fl oz, warmed,
plus extra for brushing
sea salt flakes

Makes 30–40

These crisp, salty biscuit rings are ideal with drinks or antipasti. A speciality of Southern Italy, they were at one time sold by street vendors. I first came across *taralli* in Naples where I bought them, still warm, from a neighbourhood bakery.

Taralli are seasoned with fennel seeds or black pepper, and sometimes studded with almonds. According to the venerable cookery teachers Margherita and Valeria Simili, who've been baking since they were barely old enough to stand, the traditional recipe specified at least 2 tablespoons of black pepper, about twice the amount I've used here.

Sift the flour, salt and black pepper into a large bowl. If using easy-blend yeast, add this to the flour as well. Keep warm in a very low oven with the door left ajar.

Crumble the fresh yeast or dried active yeast into the warm white wine and whisk to dissolve. Mix with the warm olive oil.

Make a well in the middle of the flour and pour in the wine and oil mixture. Stir with a fork, gradually drawing in the flour from around the edge of the well. Once you have a dough that holds together, turn it out onto a floured surface and knead for 10–15 minutes until silky smooth and springy.

Put the dough in a lightly oiled bowl, cover with a clean tea towel and leave in a warm place for about 1 hour until well risen.

Preheat the oven to 200°C/400°F/Gas 6. Pull off small pieces of dough and use the flat of your hand to roll into thin 'ropes' about the width of your little finger. Cut them into 6cm/2$\frac{1}{2}$in lengths. Bend the edges together to form a circle and place on a tray lined with a clean, lightly floured tea towel. Repeat until all the dough is used up.

Arrange the taralli on a baking sheet, brush with olive oil then sprinkle with sea salt flakes. Bake for 15 minutes then lower the temperature to 170°C/325°C/Gas 3 and bake for 5–10 minutes more until golden and crisp.

cook's note
- Some recipes specify dropping the taralli in boiling salted water for 2–3 minutes before baking. Having experimented with both methods, I found the texture of boiled taralli slightly less crisp than the baked.

pan pepato (peppered bread)

sultanas 100g/3$\frac{1}{2}$oz
walnuts 100g/3$\frac{1}{2}$oz
hazelnuts without skins
　100g/3$\frac{1}{2}$oz
almonds without skins
　100g/3$\frac{1}{2}$oz
candied citrus peel 85g/3oz
plain chocolate (70–85%
　cocoa solids) 100g/3$\frac{1}{2}$oz
clear honey 200g/7oz
unsalted butter 2 tbsp
sugar 5$\frac{1}{2}$ tbsp
unsweetened cocoa powder
　4 tbsp
black peppercorns 1 tbsp,
　freshly ground
ground cinnamon 1 tsp
freshly grated nutmeg $\frac{1}{2}$ tsp
ground cloves $\frac{1}{4}$ tsp
hot water 100ml/3$\frac{1}{2}$fl oz
plain flour 150–175g/5$\frac{1}{2}$–6oz

Makes 6

Dense, chewy and dark – a peppery chocolate and nut cake from Umbria, also eaten throughout central Italy. Pepper takes a back seat here but still adds a slight touch of pungency.

Soak the sultanas in plenty of warm water until they plump up – about 20 minutes. Roughly chop the nuts and candied peel. Break the chocolate into bite-sized pieces. Preheat the oven to 170°C/325°F/Gas 3.

Measure the honey into a heavy-based saucepan and warm over a low heat. Add the chocolate, butter and sugar and stir until melted. Stir in the cocoa, pepper, cinnamon, nutmeg and cloves.

Drain the sultanas and add to the pan along with the nuts and candied peel. By now the mixture will be getting very stiff so slacken it with the hot water. Sprinkle in the flour, a little at a time, stirring with each addition and using enough to bind the mixture. Keep stirring until you have a well-mixed dough.

Tip the dough onto a non-stick baking tray and press into a circle, using a wet palette knife. Slice the circle into six segments. When cool enough to handle, mould each segment into a ball, then flatten into cakes about 2.5cm/1in thick and 8cm/3$\frac{1}{4}$in wide.

Bake for 20–25 minutes or until firm. Remove from the oven and leave for 5 minutes, then put the cakes on a wire rack to cool completely.

cook's notes
- To remove the skin from hazelnuts and almonds, toast on a baking tray at 180°C/350°F/Gas 4 for about 5 minutes to dry the skins. Roll in a clean tea towel for 2 minutes using the palms of your hands. Unwrap the nuts and discard the skins.
- If possible, use whole chunks of Italian citron, orange and lemon peel. This has a much better flavour and colour than ready-chopped mixed peel.
- The easiest way to measure honey is to measure it directly into a saucepan placed on electronic scales (zero the scales first).

spice blends, seasonings and sauces

Along with indigenous crops and cooking methods, traditional spice blends give national cuisines their special character and flavour. Not so long ago these mixtures could be found only in far-flung markets, and intrepid cooks would bring back mysterious packages smelling of distant lands.

As a result of our desire for the authentic and the exotic, many of the blends can now be bought in the West, ready-ground and mixed. Though the quality and authenticity of ready-made spice blends is steadily improving, manufacturers still tend to standardise them to make them acceptable to a mass market. In doing so, the intriguing quirks and nuances of flavour found in blends made by a native cook are diluted or even lost. *Garam masala* and the ubiquitous curry powder are two prime examples.

Some ready-made blends are ground to a homogenous powder to prevent different textures from forming strata. As we know, black and green peppercorns lose their aroma within seconds once ground, and white peppercorns develop that unwelcome barnyard flavour, and uniformly powdered blends are therefore unlikely to taste as fresh as those containing whole spices. That said, companies do exist who create carefully mixed blends in which peppercorns and other volatile spices are left whole. It's a simple matter to crush these in a mortar and mix them with the rest of the blend.

I have included in this chapter a few of the classic blends so you can have the pleasure of making them yourself from scratch. I have gone into the subject more deeply on page 240 should you get the bit between your teeth and want to experiment further.

Also in this chapter are some peppery seasonings, both sweet and savoury, which take no time to make and can be kept in the fridge or store cupboard until needed. Spiced Flour (page 226) is a great for coating meat destined for a stew or braise – the thickened peppery juices will have your lips tingling. Another favourite is a deliciously sweet-salty-peppery mix of dried orange peel and pepper pulverised with icing sugar (page 235). It keeps forever and is superb sprinkled over anything from fish and vegetables to fruit salads and chilled desserts.

The chapter finishes with some ideas for dressings and sauces. I have not included obvious pepper classics like Cumberland Sauce or *Sauce Béarnaise* – these can be found in other cookbooks. Instead you'll find less well-known but equally delicious sauces from around the world in which pepper plays an important and fragrant part.

garam masala

coriander seeds $5\frac{1}{2}$ tbsp
cumin seeds 4 tbsp
green cardamom pods 10
cinnamon sticks 10, about
   2.5cm/1in long
cloves 1 tbsp
mace 5 blades
black cardamom pods 5
nutmeg $\frac{1}{4}$, freshly grated
black peppercorns $\frac{1}{2}$ tbsp
fresh bay leaves 2

Not to be confused with curry powder, this highly aromatic mixture is widely used in Indian meat dishes and occasionally with poultry and rice. For a mellow, background spiciness, fry it with other spices at the start of cooking; to appreciate fully its powerful fragrance sprinkle over the food as a final seasoning before serving.

Literally meaning 'hot' (garam) 'spices' (masala), the basic mix not surprisingly contains the spices that are thought to create heat in the body: black pepper, black cardamom, cinnamon and cloves. However, there are hundreds of variations depending on region, type of dish and the cook – every household has its own particular blend. Here is a good basic recipe adapted from *The Cinnamon Club Cookbook* by Iqbal Wahhab and Vivek Singh.

Preheat the oven to 110°C/225°F/Gas $\frac{1}{4}$. Put all the ingredients on a baking tray and place in the oven for 3–5 minutes; this intensifies the flavours. You could even dry the spices in a microwave for 20 seconds or so.

Grind everything to a powder in a clean electric coffee grinder, then sieve the mixture to remove any husks or large particles. Store in an airtight container in the fridge and use within 2 weeks.

cook's note
- If grating nutmeg seems too laborious, bash a whole nutmeg into chunks with a rolling pin and then grind a small piece with the other spices.

See also
Pepper and Health, page 70

spiced flour

black peppercorns 1 tbsp
fine sea salt 2 tsp
dried thyme or **oregano** $\frac{1}{2}$ tsp
dried red pepper flakes $\frac{1}{2}$ tsp
**allspice berries (Jamaica
   pepper)** $\frac{1}{4}$ tsp
mustard powder 1 tsp
paprika 2 tsp
plain flour 4 tbsp

This lively Latin-American blend is handy for adding a bit of zest to foods that are coated with flour before frying, or meat destined for a stew. The thickened juices will be wonderfully piquant.

Grind the peppercorns, sea salt, thyme, red pepper flakes and allspice to a powder in a clean electric coffee grinder or use a mortar and pestle. Mix with the mustard, paprika and flour. Store in an airtight container for 1–2 months.

aunty manjula's sarina pudi

vegetable oil 1 tbsp
asafoetida powder 1 tsp
black peppercorns, preferably
    Malabar, 2 tbsp
cumin seeds 2 tbsp
black mustard seeds 2 tbsp
fenugreek seeds 2 tbsp
coriander seeds 100g/3$^{1}/_{2}$oz
curry leaves 2 tbsp (about 40
    leaves)
dried red chillies 50g/1$^{3}/_{4}$oz
turmeric powder $^{1}/_{2}$ tsp
brown sugar $^{1}/_{2}$ tsp

This recipe comes from my Indian food writer friend Manisha Harkins. It is her aunt's special blend of roast and ground spices for seasoning *rasam* – a wonderfully restoring South Indian soup (page 112) also known as *saru*. The recipe was handed down from her mother. As Manisha says, count yourself lucky that her aunt shared her secret.

Heat 1 teaspoon of the oil in a heavy-based frying pan over medium-low heat. Add the asafoetida and peppercorns and stir for a few seconds until fragrant. Remove from the pan and set aside.

In the same pan, dry-fry the cumin seeds for a few seconds until slightly darkened, followed by the mustard and then the fenugreek seeds. Fry each spice separately as the cooking time and temperature vary. Be careful not to let them burn. Add them to the peppercorns and asafoetida.

Heat a second teaspoon of oil and dry-fry the coriander seeds and curry leaves, stirring all the time, until fragrant. Remove and add to the other spices.

Heat the final teaspoon of oil and fry the chillies until fragrant.

Combine all the spices, including the turmeric, and mix in the sugar. Grind to a fine powder in a clean electric coffee grinder, or use a mortar and pestle. Store in a tightly sealed container in the fridge for up to 2 months.

spiced pepper and salt

Sichuan pepper 1 tbsp
white peppercorns 1 tsp
cassia bark 5cm/2in piece,
 broken
star anise 2
sea salt flakes 5 tbsp
sugar 1 tsp

This is a pungent-salty-sweet mix of Sichuan pepper and white peppercorns, sea salt, fragrant sweet spices and a dash of sugar. It's great for seasoning seafood or roast chicken, or as a tasty dip for deep-fried foods, or sprinkled over toasted nuts.

Dry-fry both types of pepper, the cassia bark and star anise in a heavy-based pan over medium heat, shaking the pan, until the Sichuan pepper begins to smoke and smell fragrant.

Grind to a coarse powder with the sea salt flakes, using a clean electric coffee grinder or a hefty mortar and pestle. Stir in the sugar, then store in an airtight container for up to 2 months.

cook's note
• Cassia has a warm, woody, clove-like flavour similar to cinnamon, but it is much stronger, and slightly pungent and astringent. You'll find it in Asian grocers and good health food shops.

quatre épices (four-spices)

whole nutmeg 1
white peppercorns (preferably
   Sarawak or Wynad single
   estate) 3$\frac{1}{2}$ tbsp
cloves 1$\frac{1}{2}$ tsp
ground ginger 1$\frac{1}{2}$ tsp

French cooks are not known as spice enthusiasts, but this classic blend is the most popular in France where it is an ubiquitous seasoning in cured meats, salami, pâtés and terrines. White pepper is the key ingredient, although some blends include allspice berries (Jamaica pepper) instead of pepper, and cinnamon instead of ginger.

It is useful to have some made up at home; use it instead of pepper when you want a richer, more rounded flavour. Try it in wine-based meat stews or add a pinch to stuffings, mashed potatoes or savoury pies.

Bash the nutmeg into small chunks with a rolling pin. Put the pieces in a clean electric coffee grinder with the other spices and whizz to a fine powder. Store in an airtight container for up to 2 months.

tunisian five spices

whole nutmeg 2$\frac{1}{2}$
cinnamon stick about
   2cm/$\frac{3}{4}$in long
black peppercorns (preferably
   Tellicherry) 2 tsp
grains of paradise 1 tsp
cloves 2 tsp

Called *qalat daqqa* in Arabic, this blend combines the pungency of black pepper and grains of paradise with the warm, woody fragrance of cloves, nutmeg and cinnamon. It is only moderately hot and is a good seasoning for vegetables, couscous or slow-cooked tagines. It's also good as a rub for poultry or lamb.

Bash the nutmeg into small chunks using a rolling pin. Put in a clean electric coffee grinder with the other spices and grind to a powder. Store in an airtight container for up to 2 months.

chinese five-spice blend

Sichuan pepper $\frac{1}{2}$ tsp
star anise 2
cassia bark 5cm/2in piece
fennel seeds 1 tsp
cloves 6

The Chinese use five-spice sparingly in long-cooked stews and braises, as a rub for roasted meat and in marinades for grilled meat and poultry. It's well worth making your own since ready-made brands vary so much in flavour and quality.

The number five has special significance in Chinese culture and cooking. It's seen in the five basic flavours essential to Chinese food: sweet, sour, salty, bitter and hot, and in the elements of the cosmos which these particular spices are believed to represent: earth, fire, metal, water and wood.

That said, the blend is not always made from five spices – sometimes ginger, cardamom or other spices are added. Commercial blends often contain liquorice and dried tangerine peel. Sichuan pepper is the key ingredient, making it mildly hot and tingly on the tongue, but it is predominately aniseedy, slightly sweet and highly aromatic.

Preheat the oven to 110°C/225°F/Gas $\frac{1}{4}$. Put all the spices on a baking tray and place in the oven for 3–5 minutes to intensify the flavours. Grind everything to a powder in a clean electric coffee grinder, then sieve to remove any husks or large particles. Store in an airtight container for up to 2 months.

p e p p e r

spiced sugar

cloves 3
black peppercorns 2 tsp,
   cracked
green cardamom pods
   15, seeds removed, husks
   discarded
ground cinnamon ¹/₂ tsp
sugar 350g/12oz

This is good for adding mildly pungent spiciness to any number of sweet dishes. Mix with yogurt for an aromatic creamy dessert (page 202), use instead of plain sugar in cakes and biscuits, or sprinkle over pancakes or strawberries. I love it stirred into sparkling pomegranate seeds marinated in ruby port.

Using a mortar and pestle, grind the cloves, cracked peppercorns and cardamom seeds to a coarse powder. Add the cinnamon, then stir into the sugar. Store in a screw-top jar for up to 3 months.

peppery herbed breadcrumbs

coarse breadcrumbs
   75g/2³/₄oz preferably from a
   stale ciabatta or sourdough
   loaf
**mixed herbs such as thyme,
   oregano and rosemary**
   chopped to make 1 tbsp
black peppercorns ¹/₂–1 tsp,
   coarsely ground
sea salt flakes ¹/₂ tsp
olive oil 2 tbsp
unsalted butter a large knob
garlic clove 1, finely chopped

Crunchy, piquant breadcrumbs make a great topping for gratins and root vegetable bakes, and they give plainly cooked pasta an appetising texture – mix in the warm crumbs as you toss the pasta before serving. The crumbs are also good strewed over grilled tomatoes, fish or poultry. They will keep for a week in an airtight polythene bag in the fridge.

Tip the breadcrumbs onto a plate and mix with the herbs, black pepper and sea salt flakes. Heat the oil and butter in a large frying pan over a medium-high heat. When the butter is foaming, add the garlic and sizzle for a few seconds until barely coloured.

Add the breadcrumb mixture and fry for 3–4 minutes, tossing, until golden and crisp. Drain on paper towels.

west african pepper rub

black peppercorns 1 tbsp
white peppercorns 1 tbsp
cubebs 2 tsp
grains of paradise 2 tsp
allspice berries (Jamaica
   pepper) 2 tsp
dried chilli flakes 1 tsp
ground ginger 1 tsp

West African cooks use this all-purpose seasoning as a fiery rub for meat or chicken, and as a condiment for perking up root vegetables. They also cook it with onion, garlic, peppers and tomatoes to make a flavour base for soups, stews and sauces.

To me, the blend is a glorious celebration of all things peppery: it includes familiar black and white peppercorns as well as intriguing exotic pepper such as cubebs and grains of paradise, both indigenous to West Africa. Used sparingly, the hot, woody, gingery flavour will perk up almost any dish.

Grind the whole spices to a powder in a clean electric coffee grinder, then mix with the chilli flakes and ginger. Store in an airtight container for up to 2 months.

See also
Cubebs, page 38
Grains of Paradise, page 42

keralan curry powder

fresh curry leaves 20–30
dried red chillies 4–8, deseeded
cumin seeds 2 tbsp
coriander seeds 2 tbsp
mustard seeds 1 tbsp
fenugreek seeds 1/2 tbsp
urad dal or **toor dal** (split
   lentils) 1/2 tbsp
black peppercorns, preferably
   Malabar, 2 tsp
turmeric powder 2 tbsp

In India, curry blends vary depending on the region, the cook and the foods they are intended to season. The unique spicy lemony flavour of curry leaves is typical of this blend from Kerala in southwest India. It's perfect for seafood and chicken.

Combine the curry leaves, chillies, cumin, coriander, mustard fenugreek and dal in a heavy-based frying pan. Dry-fry over low heat, stirring all the time, until the spices darken slightly and start to smell fragrant – about 30–60 seconds – then immediately remove from the pan. Take great care not to let the fenugreek burn or it will become bitter.

Add the peppercorns to the roasted spices. Grind in batches in a clean electric coffee grinder, or use a mortar and pestle, until you have a uniformly fine powder. Add the turmeric, mixing well.

Store in a tightly sealed container for up to 6 weeks.

orange and pepper powder

oranges 4 medium
icing sugar for dusting
salt for sprinkling
black peppercorns 1 tsp,
    freshly ground

This sweet-pungent orange powder is sublime in meringues (page 206) and equally so sprinkled over grilled fish or poultry. It also puts orange peel to good use after you've juiced the fruit. As ever, use the best peppercorns you can buy – Tellicherry or a single estate variety such as Wynad.

Preheat the oven to 110°C/225°F/Gas $^1/_4$. Peel the outer layer of peel from the oranges, avoiding the bitter white pith. Bring a saucepan of water to the boil and add the orange peel. Bring back to the boil and boil for 1 minute to get rid of any bitterness.

Drain the peel under running water until cold then pat dry thoroughly with paper towels.

Spread out the strips of peel on a baking tray. Sprinkle with icing sugar, salt and the freshly ground pepper. Leave to dry in the oven for about 3 hours until crisp.

Pulse the peel in a food processor until you have a powder. Store in an airtight jar in the fridge for 3–4 weeks.

dukkah

shelled pistachio nuts 4 tbsp
hazelnuts 3 tbsp
sesame seeds 8 tbsp
coriander seeds 5 tbsp
cumin seeds 3 tbsp
black peppercorns 1–2 tsp,
    freshly ground
fine sea salt 1 tsp, or more to
    taste

This is an Egyptian blend of nuts, seeds and spices, traditionally eaten with pita bread dipped first in good fruity olive oil. Pepper adds its fragrant pungency and also rounds out the other flavours. The mixture should be loose and dry rather than a paste, so be careful not to over-process the nuts. They can become oily if ground too finely.

Preheat the oven to 200°C/400°F/Gas 6. Place the pistachios and hazelnuts on a baking sheet and roast for about 5 minutes or until brown and the skins are flaking off. Roll in a clean tea towel to remove all the skins. Roughly chop, then grind coarsely in a food processor.

Dry-fry the seeds separately in a heavy-based pan – just enough to darken them slightly but without burning. Once cool, grind to a coarse powder in a food processor.

Mix all the ingredients together and store in a tightly sealed container in the fridge for up to 2 weeks.

cambodian black pepper sauce

black peppercorns 2 tsp, finely ground
sea salt 2 tsp
limes juice of 2

In her article on pepper farming in Kep, the Cambodian pepper capital, American journalist Karen Coates writes, 'This is the pivotal condiment in Kep's seafood cuisine. It's the dip without which grilled fish, shrimp or crab simply wouldn't be.' It's certainly a palate-awakener – clean-tasting, tangy and pungent – and so simple to make.

Mix the black pepper and sea salt together, then stir in the lime juice. Stir again to dissolve the salt. Serve in individual saucers for dipping, or in a bowl in the middle of a seafood platter.

zhug

mild green or **red chillies**
4–5, deseeded and chopped
hot red chilli 1 small, deseeded and chopped
garlic cloves 4–6, crushed
coriander large handful, coarsely chopped
coriander seeds 2 tsp
cumin seeds 1 tsp
black peppercorns 10–15, crushed
green cardamom seeds from 6 pods
lemon juice 1 tbsp
salt to taste

Zhug is a fiery condiment popular in Israel where it was introduced by Yemenite Jews. Serve it with pita bread as a dip, or as a zesty sauce with grilled poultry or white fish. The recipe is not cast in stone – you can use flat leaf parsley instead of, or as well as, coriander, or use caraway seeds to replace the cumin. Peppercorns and chillies are a must, however.

Put all the ingredients in a food processor and blend briefly to a coarsely- textured paste. Thin with a little water, if necessary, to a salsa-like consistency. Store in a screw-top jar in the fridge for up to 2 weeks.

cook's note
- Supermarkets are getting better at stocking named varieties of chillies. When choosing, bear in mind that Anaheim, New Mexican and poblano are mildly hot, and the small smooth serrano and Thai chillies are lethal.

olio santo

black peppercorns $1/2$ tbsp, crushed
white peppercorns $1/2$ tbsp, crushed
fresh red chilli $1/2$, chopped
fresh bay leaf 1, broken in half
garlic cloves 2, finely chopped
green cardamom seeds from 2 large pods
salt $1/4$ tsp
extra-virgin olive oil (preferably single estate) 500ml/18fl oz bottle

Meaning 'holy oil' or 'oil of the saints', *olio santo* is a piquant seasoning of extra-virgin olive oil spiked with red chillies and other zesty seasonings. This particularly fragrant version comes from Clifford Wright's *Cucina Paradiso: The Heavenly Food of Sicily* and includes black and white peppercorns and cardamom.

I like to use it as a dip for bread, or to season plain foods such as grilled white fish or steamed vegetables. Shake the bottle before use making sure you include a few whole spices as you measure it out.

Mix together the crushed peppercorns, chilli, bay leaf, garlic, cardamom seeds and salt. Add this mixture to the bottle of olive oil. Cork or cap the bottle and leave for 20 days before using.

grilled tomato sauce

plum tomatoes 450g/1lb
garlic cloves 2 large, unpeeled
serrano chillies (or other
　mildly-hot green chillies)
　1–2, left whole
black peppercorns 1 tsp,
　crushed
sea salt flakes $\frac{1}{2}$ tsp
dried oregano $\frac{1}{4}$ tsp
unsalted butter 1 tsp

Makes 250ml/9fl oz

This is a good sauce for perking up starchy root vegetables, and it goes well with polenta (page 177) too. It doesn't contain that much pepper, but, together with sea salt and a swirl of butter, a small amount rounds out the other flavours.

Preheat the grill to high. Put the tomatoes, garlic and chillies in a grill pan without a rack and place under the hot grill. Turn frequently until the skins blister and start to blacken. The chillies will need about 5 minutes, the garlic 10 minutes and the tomatoes 15–20 minutes.

Peel the garlic and the chillies and remove the seeds from the chillies. Using a mortar and pestle, grind them to a paste with the crushed peppercorns and sea salt flakes.

Put the tomatoes in a food processor, including any blackened bits of skin, and pulse to a purée. Scrape the purée into a saucepan, add the oregano and bring to the boil. Reduce the heat a little, then leave to bubble away until reduced and thickened.

Stir in the garlic-chilli paste and simmer for another minute. Swirl in the butter and check the seasoning.

cherry sauce with pepper, honey and orange

cherries 600g/1lb 5oz, pitted
juniper berries 1 tsp
red wine 450ml/16fl oz
mild clear honey (such as acacia or orange blossom) 1$^1/_2$ tsp
freshly ground black pepper $^1/_4$–$^1/_2$ tsp
orange juice a squeeze
lemon juice a squeeze

Makes about 300ml/$^1/_2$ pint

This is my version of a recipe from Paul Kovi's fascinating gastro-history of Transylvanian cuisine. Cherries grow abundantly in that part of the world and pepper is a favourite spice. Here they are used together in a garnet-coloured sauce that is fruity, pungent and sweet. It's perfect with grilled duck breasts, roast pork or turkey, or, as served in Transylvania, spread on bread like jam.

Put the cherries and juniper berries in a saucepan with the red wine. Bring to the boil, then turn the heat down a little and cook for 20–25 minutes or until the cherries are soft. Remove from the heat and allow to cool a little. Whizz in a food processor or blender, then push the mixture through a sieve, pressing with the back of a wooden spoon.

Put the mixture back in the pan and add the honey, pepper and orange and lemon juices.

Bring to the boil, then let it bubble away for about 5 minutes, stirring, until thickened and slightly reduced. Taste and add more pepper, honey or citrus juice if needed. The sauce should be quite sharp and peppery but also sweet.

a spice blend glossary

Traditional spice blends are mysterious mixtures that give a national cuisine its characteristic flavour. They have exotic names and secret ingredients and the recipe for a particular mix will vary from region to region, village to village, and even family to family. What is constant in these mixes, though, are certain spices that appear time and again no matter the area of origin. Along with cloves, cinnamon and cumin, pepper is nearly always an ingredient, leaving an indelible footprint throughout the kitchens of the world.

Taking a whirlwind tour of classic spice blends, the most complex and intense are inevitably found in India, home of the pepper vine, and in the Middle East – hardly surprising given that the Arabs monopolised the pepper trade for thousands of years. North and East Africa also have some potent mixes, as does West Africa. Thanks to Greek, Roman and Arab influence, we find pepper in classic European blends, particularly in regions that have maintained their culinary traditions – southern Italy and Spain, for example.

Pepper has also found a place in Latin American spice blends, especially in Cuba, Puerto Rica and the Dominican Republic where the European influence was strong. In the United States pepper adds bite to Cajun and Creole seasonings, as well as to various rubs and pastes for the barbecue.

Across the Pacific in Malaysia and Indonesia, pepper is strangely absent from spice blends and the cuisines in general, even though the region is as ancient a pepper producer as India and is noted for the quality of its crops. Further north, though, in Thailand and in neighbouring Cambodia, pepper is used now and again in sauces and curry pastes. In China, white peppercorns and Sichuan pepper are part of a spiced pepper and salt blend (recipe page 229), and Sichuan pepper is a key ingredient in the classic five-spice blend (recipe page 231). Sansho pepper is one of seven spices in Japan's only blend, *shichimi togarishi* (Sichuan pepper and sansho, page 46).

In Australia, where chefs are experimenting with native bush foods, the leaves of mountain pepper (*Tasmannia lanceolata*) and lemon myrtle (*Backhausia citriodora*) are combined in a pungent native lemon pepper blend.

balancing flavours

A spice blend creates a unique and special flavour all of its own, quite different from the flavours of individual spices within it. Sometimes a predominant note might stand out – cinnamon or cloves are usually recognisable – but in general the spices work together like a well-rehearsed orchestra. In the words of Australian spice connoisseur Ian Hemphill, a well-constructed blend will bring together harmonious proportions of sweet, pungent, tangy, hot and 'amalgamating' or staple spices (turmeric, fennel and coriander, for example). Pepper is classified as hot and, as such, is usually added in the smallest proportion. However, as Ian rightly says, the hot group can make or break a dish. A judicious amount makes food appetising; a heavy hand simply gives spicy food a poor reputation.

making freshly ground blends

When making blends from scratch – and it's well worth doing so – it's useful to bear in mind that a blend needs time to settle. As Ian Hemphill advises, it will 'round out' and taste less harsh after about 24 hours, in the same way that a curry improves the next day.

Always use good quality whole spices that are well within their use-by date. It's best to grind small amounts as the flavour will deteriorate before too long. Leftover spice blends will keep for six to eight weeks if you store them in a small tightly sealed plastic bag or glass jar in the fridge or a cool place away from light.

Where I have specified quantities of spices as ratios, I suggest you use a standard level teaspoon measure (5ml) to represent 'one part'. If you want to make a larger quantity, then use two teaspoons (10ml) or a tablespoon (15ml) as one part.

india

Indian spice blends depend very much on regional and cultural differences, as does the cuisine. However, what is common to the depth of flavour and complexity of both the cooking and the spice combinations is the principle of six basic tastes: sweet, sour, salty, spicy, bitter and astringent. A well-balanced spice blend, or a meal, will contain all six.

curry powder
Of all the blends curry powder is probably the most well known in the West. Originating from Madras in southern India, it was dreamed up by Indian chefs for English curry addicts in the early 19th-century. Often standardised beyond recognition, ready-made mixes are viewed with suspicion by the purist but relied on by those who simply want to conveniently add a little more spice to their culinary life.

Curry powder can contain up to twenty different spices or as few as five or six. The mix varies depending on region, availability of ingredients and the type of food to be seasoned. A typical Madras-style mix contains coriander and turmeric as staple background spices; cumin, cloves and cardamom for depth of flavour; cinnamon for sweetness; and ginger, fenugreek, mustard seed, chilli and black pepper for the characteristic bite.

In Kerala, pepper is an indigenous crop and features more strongly as a predominant flavour. Typical flavours in a Keralan blend also include fresh curry leaves, coriander and cumin, with turmeric, mustard, fenugreek and chilli in the background (recipe page 234).

garam masala
Originating from the cooler climes of northern India, *garam masala* is made with spices that are believed to create heat in the body. The basic mix includes more or less equal quantities of black pepper, cloves and cinnamon, with a dash of black cardamom. Sweet spices such as mace and nutmeg may also be included, and some cooks add 'cooling' green cardamom and bay leaf.

The recipe on page 226 is a good basic mix from Vivek Singh, chef at London's highly acclaimed Cinnamon Club. Vivek also has a special version which includes dried rose petals, star anise and fennel seeds.

Garam masala is used mostly for seasoning meat, chicken and rice dishes; it is considered too potent for fish or vegetables. The mix is best when sprinkled over a dish towards the end of cooking – then you can appreciate the sensational aroma. It can also be added during the initial frying process although this will affect the taste of the dish in a different way.

rasam/saru powder
From southern India, this spice blend is used to season *rasam* and *saru*, delicious restorative soups served with piping hot rice. It is a pungent mix based on black pepper, cumin, mustard seeds and fenugreek, with coriander seeds providing a mild background spiciness. Lemony, astringent curry leaves give it the special flavour of the region. The recipe on page 228 was given to me by my food writer friend Manisha Harkins. Her family come from Karnataka in southern India and the blend is her aunt's special creation.

middle east

advieh
Meaning 'medicines' in Arabic, *advieh* is a traditional Iranian spice blend. As Margaret Shaida explains in *The Legendary Cuisine of Persia*, Iranian cooks will make up different blends depending on the delicacy or robustness

of the dish, or the food and mood of the occasion. The ingredients also depend on the region.

The spices used in the Persian Gulf are similar to those in an Indian *garam masala*, reflecting trade between the two countries. However, an Iranian recipe would never include chillies or ginger; black pepper is the sole provider of heat. A typical blend for hearty dishes contains 5 parts each cinnamon and coriander seeds, 3 parts ground turmeric, 2 parts cumin seed and 1 part each black peppercorns, cloves, caraway and cardamom seeds. Some cooks add dried lime powder for extra tartness.

Further north, nearer to the Caspian Sea, a blend for more delicate dishes includes 3 parts each coriander seed and ground cinnamon, 2 parts cardamom seed, 1 part each black peppercorns, cumin seed and freshly grated nutmeg.

baharat

Popular in Turkey and the Gulf states, *baharat* is an appetising well-rounded mix – sweet, sharp and distinctly pungent with warm peppery notes. It's the perfect seasoning for lamb – as somebody once commented 'it cuts the mutton'. Add it to lamb-based stews or tagines, or rub it over the meat as a dry marinade. Baharat is also good with rice or vegetables. I like it sprinkled over mashed roasted aubergine or hummus with a dribble of good olive oil.

A basic blend contains 6 parts each black peppercorns and mild paprika, 3 parts each cloves, coriander and cumin seeds, ½ part each green cardamom seeds and grated nutmeg, and a small piece of cassia or cinnamon bark. Proportions vary depending on region, and some cooks add a little ground ginger and chilli.

dukkah

This is an addictive Egyptian concoction of roasted nuts, sesame seeds, salt and aromatic spices which include cumin, coriander, cinnamon and a zesty kick of black pepper (recipe page 235). *Dukkah* is delicious with pita bread dipped first in fruity olive oil, or sprinkled over cream cheese, hard-boiled eggs

or as a crunchy coating for grilled meat or fish.

hawaj

Popular in the Yemen, this blend is excellent in soups and vegetable dishes, and as a dry rub for grilled meat. Consisting of black peppercorns, green cardamom, coriander and cumin seeds, the blend has an earthy rustic flavour with a strong hit of pepper.

khmeli suneli

East meets West in *khmeli suneli* (literally, 'a mixture of dried smells') from the Black Sea region of Georgia. The blend consists of dried green herbs with black pepper, cumin and sometimes other spices. Used in mutton stews and the sweet-sour-fruity sauces typical of the region, it is to Georgian cuisine what *garam masala* is to Indian.

zhug

This popular Yemeni spice paste is the Middle Eastern equivalent of pesto. There are red versions based on red peppers and garlic, and green versions with more fresh coriander and parsley. Spices generally include black peppercorns, green cardamom, coriander and cumin seeds, but there is no set formula. Some people include caraway instead of cumin, and others add cloves (recipe page 236).

Spread over warm pita bread, *zhug* makes a fiery appetiser. It's great as a marinade for mackerel or sardines – it cuts the oiliness – or you can use it as a sauce for grilled meat and chicken.

africa

The cuisines and spice blends of this vast continent have been influenced by a melting pot of cultures: Arabs, Greeks, Romans, French, Portuguese and Indians have all left their mark.

The foods of the four basic geographical regions – North, South, East and West Africa – each have their own distinctive flavours but starchy root vegetables, bread and grains are staples in most regions, as are the spicy condiments that bring such foods to life. Pepper takes pride of place in many of the blends, and copious amounts are used to spike the stews that accompany starch-based meals.

berbere
This is a classic Ethiopian and Eritrean blend, combining elements from Arabic and Indian cuisines. It is a complex mix – sweet, pungent and very peppery, containing long pepper and black pepper as well as chillies. Sweetness comes from allspice, nutmeg and cinnamon, while fenugreek, ginger, ajowan, cloves, cumin and coriander provide a basic pungency.

Berbere is the indispensable seasoning for Ethiopian stews called *wots*, the mainstay of the cuisine. It is also used as a coating for grilled fish or meat, and as a condiment for soups, rice, vegetables and fish.

la kama
Mellow, sweet and peppery, *la kama* is a simple Moroccan spice mix in which pepper rather than chilli provides the heat. The blend contains black pepper, ginger, cinnamon and nutmeg, and is typically used to flavour soups and stews. It is particularly good with chicken and lamb.

qalat daqqa
This heady Tunisian 'five-spice' mixture combines the sultry heat of grains of paradise and black peppercorns with the fragrance of nutmeg, cinnamon and cloves (recipe page 230). It's a great seasoning for lamb or vegetable stews, or for rubbing over fish or meat before grilling.

ras el hanout
This sensational blend from Morocco has to be the *ne plus ultra* of spice blends. Loosely translated, the name means 'head of the shop', and historically it was the spice merchant's signature creation, representing the very best he had to offer. Sometimes containing more than twenty ingredients, including several types of pepper, is a spectacular example of how the sum of the parts is often infinitely superior to individual components.

In her classic book *Traditional Moroccan Cooking* (published 1958), Madame Zette Guinaudeau-Franc evocatively describes *ras el hanout* as 'a synthesis of spices, rose-buds and cinnamon together with pimento and black pepper. The metallic glint of the cantharide (Spanish fly) is mingled with the grey stalks of ginger and more than two dozen spices are needed to complete the intoxicating aroma in which the nomad warrior has combined all the scents of the countries he has passed through'.

Madame Guinaudeau lists as ingredients Guinea pepper (grains of paradise) 'an aphrodisiac from the Ivory Coast', long pepper 'from India and Malaya', black pepper, cubeb pepper 'grey scented pepper from Malaya and Borneo', and monk's pepper 'an aphrodisiac from Morocco'. Other ingredients, too numerous to mention in full, include familiar spices such as cardamom, nutmeg and mace, as well as herbs, flowers and, alarmingly, Spanish fly (sales were banned in the 1990s) and dried belladonna berries ('very few are needed').

These days, exported blends are unlikely to include belladonna or Spanish fly, but nevertheless *ras el hanout* is a pungent and pervasive mixture, still believed to be an aphrodisiac. A small amount will perk up practically any dish with a curry-like pungency and floral fragrance. In Morocco it is used to season pastilla, a sumptuous pigeon and almond pie. It is particularly good in lamb or chicken tagines, or stirred into rice or couscous.

west african pepper blend
Stews made mostly from beans or root vegetables with only a little meat or fish form the basis of West African cooking. These dishes are seasoned with fiery sauces and dried spice blends, which usually contain a high proportion of pepper indigenous to the area.

A popular seasoning is an incendiary mix of black and white peppercorns, cubeb pepper, grains of paradise, allspice (Jamaica pepper), ginger and dried red chilli (recipe page 234). It is used as an essential flavour base for spicy soups and stews, a dry rub for meat and chicken before grilling, and a condiment for vegetables.

europe

In southern Europe, thanks to Arab and Greek influence, black pepper and other pungent spices are popular seasonings. However, they more often appear in traditional sauces and pastes, rather than in dry spice blends. In the north, there are surprisingly few indigenous blends in use today, considering that spices were once the mainstay of medieval European kitchens.

fish-curing spices
Scandinavian blends for preserving oily fish such as salmon include black and white peppercorns, salt, sugar and dill (recipe page 129).

italian spice mixture
Jill Norman mentions this sweetly pungent blend in her authoritative book *Herb and Spice: the Cook's Reference*. It is superb sprinkled on pork or poultry to be grilled, or rubbed into slow-roasted lamb or pork joints. It is made up of 3 parts black or white peppercorns, 2 parts freshly grated nutmeg, 1 part juniper berries and $\frac{1}{4}$ part cloves.

kitchen pepper
This traditional English blend is also mentioned in Jill Norman's book *Herb and Spice: the Cook's Reference*. She recommends it for seasoning stews and hearty winter soups, for bean dishes, spiced red cabbage and for sprinkling over root vegetables before roasting them. The blend contains 8 parts freshly grated nutmeg, 3 parts each black peppercorns, anise and coriander seeds, 2 parts each cloves and dried ginger.

pickling spice
A particularly English mixture, this is used for preserving vegetables and fruits in vinegar. Spices are used whole, rather than ground, to keep the liquid clear; they are often tied in a muslin bag and removed once the pickle is cooked. There is no fixed formula but the mix usually includes 3 parts allspice (Jamaica pepper), 2 parts each black peppercorns, cloves, dried ginger, mace and coriander seeds, and $1\frac{1}{2}$ parts mustard seeds. One or two dried red chillies are sometimes included.

quatre épices
The French are conservative with spice blends and this is one of the few that are popular. The mix is based on white peppercorns, nutmeg, ginger and cloves (recipe page 230). There is also a sweet version in which allspice berries (Jamaica pepper) are used instead of peppercorns, and cinnamon replaces ginger. The savoury version is a standard seasoning for French charcuterie, pâtés and other dense-textured meat products. *Quatre épices* is useful to have at home. It has a mellow well-rounded flavour and is sometimes a better option than white pepper on its own.

latin america and the caribbean

With its melting pot of cultures, many of the region's spice blends can be traced back to Indian, Sri Lankan, Asian, African or European origins. I have concentrated on dry spice blends, rather than sauces and pastes, as it is in these that pepper features most strongly.

adobo powder
This is an indispensable all-purpose seasoning in Cuban, Puerto Rican and Dominican kitchens. It is sold as a dry spice mix to which oil, citrus juice or vinegar are often added. The basic mix contains salt, white or black pepper, garlic powder, Mexican oregano, cumin and turmeric. It will perk up almost any dish – I particularly

like it rubbed over lamb or pork chops, or whole fish such as mackerel, bream or sea bass. It's also good stirred into rice or bean dishes.

colombo powder
Named after the capital of Sri Lanka, this is a relatively mild curry powder used in the French Caribbean islands of Martinique and Guadeloupe. It contains black peppercorns, mustard seed, fenugreek, cumin, coriander, turmeric and cloves. The flavour is deliciously warm and mellow with a hint of citrus – lovely with pork, chicken or fish, or stirred into mayonnaise or cream cheese.

jerk spices
Jerk is the archetypical Jamaican seasoning, and also refers to a particular way of cooking meat or fish over a wood fire – either in a portable oil drum or in a pit dug in the ground. The recipe is a matter of great secrecy and varies from village to village, and family to family. A basic mix is likely to contain 6 parts freshly ground black pepper, 5 parts salt, 4 parts garlic powder, 3 parts freshly grated nutmeg, 2 parts ground cinnamon and 1 part ground cloves. Once the spices are thoroughly mixed they are mashed with searing hot red chillies and plenty of chopped chives. .

recado spices
Originally a Mayan blend, recado spices are essential to the cuisine of the Mexican region of Yucatan. The blend comes in red, black or khaki, depending on the ingredients added to the basic mix. The most widely used is *recado rojo*, which contains brick red achiote seeds (annatto).

A basic blend is likely to contain black pepper, allspice (Jamaica pepper), Mexican oregano, cumin, cloves and cinnamon. The dry spices are moistened as needed with sour orange juice or vinegar, and garlic and salt added to make a tasty rub for fish, meat or poultry.

united states

Pepper found its way into the spice blends of the United States via the cuisines of Africa, the Caribbean and Europe. It is prevalent in the southeast – Louisiana, Mississippi and Alabama – where it is used in Creole and Cajun cooking. Elsewhere, pepper is used in various blends for the barbecue but tends to be somewhat overshadowed by chillies.

cajun spices
Cajun cooking is well known for its basic down-home earthiness – favourite dishes are dirty rice, gumbo and 'blackened' fish or meat. A typical blackening blend includes black and white pepper, cayenne, mustard seeds, paprika, cumin, Mexican oregano, thyme and salt. The flavour is rich, peppery and very hot.

old bay seasoning
This is an American classic originating from the east coast and used primarily for shrimp or crab dishes. The most famous commercial brand contains celery salt, mustard, red pepper, black pepper, bay leaves, cloves, allspice (Jamaica pepper), ginger, mace, cardamom, cinnamon and paprika. It is used for anything from steamed shrimp, crab cakes and prawn cocktails to fried chicken, potato salad and pizza toppings.

See also
Grinding, Crushing, Cracking, page 83
Spice Blends, Seasonings and Sauces, page 225
Sources, page 248

information

pepper grades

Once graded, peppercorns are given names that are commonplace in the trade but intriguing to an outsider. If you are interested in buying good quality peppercorns, it is worth becoming aware of the nuances of size, texture and colour as well as criteria for cleaning. The better the quality, the lower the content of pinheads, lights and 'extraneous matter' – a catch-all phrase for harmless bits and pieces like chaff.

sarawak creamy white
The best grade of white pepper, grown in selected areas of Sarawak, Borneo.
• Even-sized berries, minimum diameter 4mm, uniformly cream or ivory white. • Maximum moisture content 14.5%, pepper dust 0.01%.
• Free from lights, pinheads, dark berries, extraneous matter.

sarawak naturally clean black
• Processed at designated plants in Sarawak, Borneo. Dried mechanically to minimise bacterial contamination without resorting to chemicals or irradiation. • Maximum moisture content 10%, light berries 2%, extraneous matter 1%. • Free from salmonella, insects, excreta.

tellicherry garbled (TG)
• Even-sized, nearly globular, diameter 4.0-4.25mm. • Maximum moisture content 11%, light berries 3%, extraneous matter 0.5%.
• Free from mould, insects and other adulterants.

tellicherry garbled extra bold (TGEB)
• Even-sized, nearly globular, diameter 4.25mm. • Maximum moisture content 11%, light berries 3%, extraneous matter 0.5%.
• Free from mould, insects and other adulterants.

tellicherry garbled special extra bold (TGSEB)
The highest grade and largest black peppercorns. • Even-sized, nearly globular, diameter 4.75mm. • Maximum moisture content 11%, light berries 3%, extraneous matter 0.5%. • Free from mould, insects and other adulterants.

malabar garbled black pepper grade 1 (MG1)
Even-sized, nearly globular. • Maximum moisture content 11%, light berries 2%, extraneous matter 0.5%. • Free from mould, insects and other adulterants.

malabar ungarbled black pepper grade 1 (MUG1)
Maximum moisture content 12%, light berries 7%, mould 2%, extraneous matter (including pinheads) 2%. • Free from insects.

garbled light black pepper grade 1 (GL1)
Pepper in which 50% or more are lights (see Pepper Jargon, opposite) • Maximum extraneous matter 3%, pinheads 5%.
• Well-dried, free from insects.

ungarbled light black pepper grade 1 (UGL1)
Pepper in which 50% or more are lights (see Pepper Jargon, opposite). • Maximum extraneous matter 4%, pinheads 5%.
• Well-dried, free from insects.

pinheads grade 1 (PH1)
• Maximum extraneous matter 6%.
• Reasonably dry, free from insects.

non-specified black pepper grade X (NSGX)
• Pepper of different grades mixed in proportions specified by buyers. For export only.
• Extraneous matter (including pinheads) 4%.

pepper jargon

Like any specialist industry the pepper trade has its own idiosyncratic jargon. The following expressions are the ones I have come across most often.

bold A large peppercorn.

decorticated Black peppercorns from which the husk has been removed by mechanical abrasion. Decorticated berries resemble white pepper but don't have the characteristic pungency – they taste more like mediocre black peppercorns. They are used as a substitute for white pepper when white pepper is in short supply.

FAQ Fair to average quality.

garbled Cleaned peppercorns with stems, dust and most of the 'lights' removed.

lights Black peppercorns without a kernel and which float when stirred into an alcohol or methylated spirit solution.

pinheads Very small immature and/or broken black peppercorns usually reserved for oleoresin extraction or for grinding.

special The best grade for flavour.

ungarbled Peppercorns that include a variety of sizes.

pepper organisations

Pepper organisations are good news for the consumer and for producers. They regulate standards in pepper production, promote and develop the pepper industry and keep their finger on the pulse of international pepper trading. Some provide invaluable help for small farmers. The Spices Board of India, for example, provides marketing expertise, financial aid for processing equipment, and educational programmes for quality control and post-harvest hygiene.

American Spice Trade Association
The ASTA, founded in 1907, headquarters in Washington DC. The prefix ASTA is sometimes combined with pepper classifications, usually those from Indonesia and Malaysia. It means that the pepper meets the minimum standards laid down by ASTA for quality, cleanliness, packaging, essential oil, piperine and moisture levels, etc.

European Spice Association
The ESA, based in Bonn, established in 1985. Monitors and lobbies legislation, quality control and hygiene standards.

International Pepper Community
The IPC, an inter-governmental organisation of pepper-producing communities, established in 1972, based in Jakarta, Indonesia. The IPC has a remarkable website packed with information that outsiders can access for a limited period without payment.

Malaysian Pepper Board
The MPB, formerly the Pepper Marketing Board (PMB). Established in 1972 to regulate, promote and improve the marketing of Sarawak pepper. The Board has an underlying objective of improving the economic wellbeing of pepper farmers.

Spices Board of India
The SBI, established 1986, headquarters in Cochin, Kerala. The regulatory and promotion agency for all Indian spices. Helps with post-harvest improvement, supports export initiatives by upgrading quality and brand promotion, promotes organic production, processing and certification, supports and educates countless small producers in rural areas.

sources

Australia

Herbie's Spices
745 Darling Street
Rozelle
NSW 2039
Phone 02 9555 6035
www.herbies.com.au

Vic Cherikoff Food Services
167 Kingsgrove Road
Kingsgrove
NSW 2208
Phone 612 95549477
www.cherikoff.net

Canada

Francesco Sirene, Spicer
RR#2, Site 38, Comp BO
Peachland
BC V0H 1X0
www.silk.net

France

Goumanyat® et Son Royaume
3 Rue Charles-François Dupuis
Paris 75003
Phone 0144 789 674
www.goumanyat.com

Izraël Épicerie du Monde
30 Rue François-Miron
75004 Paris
Phone 0142 726 623

Le Comptoir des Poivres
10 Avenue Saint Promasse
Forcalquier 04300
Phone 0492 753 839
www.lecomptoirdespoivres.com

UK

Bart Spices
York Road, Bedminster
Bristol BS3 4AD
Phone 01179 977 3474
www.bartspices.com

Fiddes Payne
Unit 3A, Thorpe Park
Thorpe Way
Banbury
Oxfordshire OX16 4SP
Phone 01295 253888
www.fiddespayne.co.uk

Seasoned Pioneers
Unit 8 Stadium Court
Stadium Road
Plantation Business Park
Bromborough, Wirral
Cheshire CH62 3RP
Phone 0800 068 2348 *or*
0151 343 1122
www.seasonedpioneers.co.uk

Steenbergs Organic Pepper and Spice
6 Hallikeld Close
Barker Business Park
Melmerby, Ripon HG4 5GZ
Phone 01765 640088
www.steenbergs.co.uk

The Spice Shop
1 Blenheim Crescent
London W11 2EE
Phone 020 7221 4448
www.thespiceshop.co.uk

USA

Kalustyan's
123 Lexington Avenue
New York
NY 10016
Phone 800 352 3451
www.kalustyans.com

Penzeys Spices
12001 West Capitol Drive
Wauwatosa WI 53222
Phone 1-800 741 7787
www.penzeys.com

Portland Spice & Trading Company
34 Vannah Avenue
Portland
ME 04103
Phone 207 228 2048
www.portlandspice.com

The Spice House
1512 North Wells Street
Chicago
IL 60610
Phone 312 274 0378
www.thespicehouse.com

bibliography

Achaya, K.T. *Indian food: a historical companion.* Oxford University Press, New Delhi 1994

Accum, F. *A treatise on adulterations of food, and culinary poisons.* Abraham Small, Philadelphia 1820

Arctander, S. *Perfume and flavour materials of natural origin.* Elizabeth, N.J., USA 1960

Barron, R. *Flavours of Greece.* Grub Street, London 2000

Bell, G.A., Watson, A.J. (editors) *Tastes and aromas: the chemical senses in science and industry.* Blackwell Science, Oxford 1999

Buxton, M. *Medieval cooking today.* The Kylin Press, Buckinghamshire 1983

Cardoz, F. *One spice, two spice.* Absolute Press, Bath 2007

Cheney, D. *Tasting.* Dorling Kindersley, London, New York 2006

Cherikoff, V. *The bushfood handbook.* Cherikoff Pty Ltd, New South Wales, Australia 2000

Collingham, L. *Curry a biography.* Chatto & Windus, London 2005

Cook's Illustrated (editors) *The America's test kitchen cookbook.* Boston Common Press, Brookline, Massachusetts 2001

Culpeper, N. *Culpeper's complete herbal.* (Originally published in 1652) Foulsham, London reprint c.1940

Dalby, A. *Dangerous tastes: the story of spices.* British Museum Press, London 2000

Dalby, A. *Food in the ancient world from A to Z.* Routledge, London and New York 2003

David, E. *Spices, salt and aromatics in the English kitchen.* Penguin Books, London 1975

Davidson, A. *The Oxford companion to food.* Oxford University Press, Oxford 1999

DeWitt, D., Gerlach, N. *The spicy food lover's bible.* Stewart, Tabori & Chang, New York 2005

Dorje, R. *Food in Tibetan life.* Prospect Books, London 1987

Dunlop, F. *Sichuan cookery.* Penguin Books, London 2003

Faas, P. *Around the Roman table.* Macmillan, London 2003

Fernández-Armesto, F. *Food, a history.* Pan Books, London 2002

Fisher, C., Scott, T.R. *Food flavours: biology and chemistry.* The Royal Society of Chemistry, Cambridge 1997

Food and Agriculture Organization of the United Nations *Utilization of tropical foods: sugars, spices and stimulants.* FAO Food and Nutrition Paper 47/6, Rome 1989

Gozzini Giacosa, I. *A taste of ancient Rome.* The University of Chicago Press, 1992

Grocock, C., Grainger, S. *Apicius.* Prospect Books, Totnes, Devon, 2006

Guinaudeau-Franc, Z. *Traditional Moroccan cooking: recipes from Fez.* Serif, London 1994

Heath, H.B. *Source book of flavours.* AVI Publishing Company, New York 1981

Hemphill, I. *Spice notes: a cook's compendium of herbs and spices.* Macmillan, Sydney 2002

Heritage, L. *Cassell's universal cookery book.* Cassell, London 1901

Hicks, A. *Red peppercorns – what they really are.* Petit Propos Culinaires 10, Prospect Books, London 1982

Hopkinson, S. *Second helpings of roast chicken.* Ebury Press, London 2001

Hyman, P. and M. *Long pepper: a short history.* Petit Propos Culinaires 6, Prospect Books, London 1980

Jordan, M.A. *Salt & pepper.* Broadway Books, New York 1999

Kaneva-Johnson, M. *The melting pot: Balkan food and cookery.* Prospect Books, Totnes, Devon 1999

Kunz, G. and Kaminsky, P. *The elements of taste.* Little, Brown and Company, New York 2001

Mariani, J.F. *The encyclopedia of American food & drink.* Lebhar-Friedman Books, New York 1999

Mennell, S. *All manners of food.* Basil Blackwell, Oxford and New York 1987

Monroe, J. *Star of India: the spicy adventures of curry.* John Wiley, Chichester 2004

Narayan, S. *Monsoon diary: reveries and recipes from South India.* Bantam Books, London 2004

Norman, J. *Herb and spice: the cook's reference.* Dorling Kindersley, London 2002

Parry, J.W. *The spice handbook.* Chemical Publishing Co. Inc., New York 1945

Pliny the Elder *The natural history.* Bostock, J., Riley, H.T. (eds). Taylor and Francis, London 1855

Proceedings of the Oxford Symposium on Food and Cookery *Spicing up the palate: studies of flavourings – ancient and modern.* Prospect Books, Devon 1992

Pruthi, J.S. *Spices and condiments*. National Book Trust, New Delhi 1987

Purseglove, J.W. et al. *Spices: vols 1 and 2*. Longman, London 1981

Redgrove, S. *Spices and condiments*. Isaac Pitman Co., London 1933

Redon, O., Sabban, F., Serventi S. Translated by Edward Schneider *The medieval kitchen: recipes from France and Italy*. The University of Chicago Press, London and Chicago 1998

Ridley, H.N. *Spices*. Macmillan, New York 1912

Root, W. *Food*. Simon and Schuster, New York 1980

Root, W. *The food of Italy*. Vintage Books, New York 1992

Root, W., de Rochemont, R. *Eating in America*. The Ecco Press, New York 1981

Rosengarten, F., Jr. *The book of spices*. Livingston Publishing Company, Pennsylvania 1969

Roussel, B. and Verdeaux, F. *Natural Patrimony and Local Communities in Ethiopia*. University of Illinois at Urbana Campaign, Illinois 2003

Santolini, A. *La cucina delle regioni d'Italia: Napoli in bocca*. Opportunity Books, Rimini 2000

Schivelbusch, W. *Das Paradies, der Geschmack und die Vernunst*. Fischer, Frankfurt am Main 1995

Shaida, M. *The legendary cuisine of Persia*. Penguin Books, London 1994

Singh, B. *Mrs. Balbir Singh's Indian cookery*. Mills & Boon, London 1967

Singh, D. *Indian cookery*. Penguin, London 1973

Smylie. M. *Herring: a history of the silver darlings*. Tempus Publishing, Stroud 2004

Spencer, C. *British food: an extraordinary thousand years of history*. Grub Street, London 2004.

Sreedharan, D. *The new tastes of India*. Headline, London 2001

Toussaint-Samat, M. *A history of food*. Trans. Anthea Bell. Blackwell Publishers, Oxford 1994

Trager, J. *The food chronology*. Henry Holt &Co. Inc., New York 1995

Turner, J. *Spice: the history of a temptation*. Vintage Books, New York 2004

Uhl, S. R. *Handbook of spices, seasonings and flavourings*. Technomic Publishing Co. Inc., Lancaster USA 2000

Varier, P.S. *Indian medicinal plants: a compendium of 500 species, volume 4*. Orient Longman, 1995

Wahhab, I., Singh, V. *The Cinnamon Club cookbook*. Absolute Press, Bath 2003

Wheaton, Barbara Ketcham *Savoring the past: the French kitchen and table from 1300 to 1789*. Simon & Schuster, New York 1983

Wright, C.A. *Cucina Paradiso: The Heavenly Food of Sicily*. SImon & Schuster, New York 1992.

websites consulted

www.alchemy-works.com
www.astaspice.org
www.botanical.com
www.britannica.com
www.calicutpressclub.com
www.celtnet.org.uk
www.cherikoff.net
www.chow.com
www.economist.com
www.en.wikipedia.org
www.fao.org
www.fiery-foods.com
www.florilegium.org
www.foodhistorynews.com
www.globalprovince.com/spicelines
www.historicfood.com
www.indiaagronet.com
www.indianspices.com
www.ingredientsdumonde.centerall.com
www.ipcnet.org
www.medherb.com
www.pbm.com/~lindahl/food.html
www.pepperindia.com
www.peppertrade.com.br
www.peppertrail.com
www.perseus.tufts.edu
www.plantcultures.org.uk
www.plantnames.unimelb.edu.au
www.questhealthlibrary.com
www.reluctantgourmet.com
www.sarawakpepper.gov.my
http://sulcus.berkeley.edu
http://tastetests.cooksillustrated.com
www.theepicentre.com
www.theoldfoodie.blogspot.com
www.uni-graz.at/~katzer
www.unitproj1.library.ucla.edu
www.worldonaplate.org

index

a

Accum, Fredrick *23*
addictive effects of pepper *68–9*
adobo powder *244–5*
adulteration/contamination of pepper
   16, 23, 28
advieh *241–2*
Alaric, King *17*
Alleppey pepper *64*
alligator pepper *see* grains of paradise
allspice *20–1, 54–7*
American Spice Trade Association
   (ASTA) *247*
Americans, pepper and *22*
aphrodisiac, pepper as an *71, 72–3*
Apicius, Marcus Gavius *18*
Arab monopoly *14*
Ashanti pepper *39, 58–9*
Ayurvedic medicine *70*

b

baharat *242*
baies roses *see* pink peppercorns
balsamic vinegar
   Balsamic- and pepper-glazed roast
      pumpkin *164*
   Bloody paradise *187*
   Peppered beef with balsamic
      vinegar, molasses and garlic *148*
   Seared pigeon breasts with balsamic
      vinegar, rocket and parmesan
      140
beancurd, Pock-marked Mother Chen's
   (Ma po dou fu) *176*
Béarnaise sauce *81*
beef
   Peppered beef with balsamic
      vinegar, molasses and garlic *148*
   Steak au poivre (Pepper steak) *151*
Beeton, Isabella *23, 71, 73*
Benin pepper *39*
berbere *57, 243*
betel pepper *58*
biscuits
   Cantuccini with black pepper and
      orange zest *220*
   Neapolitan taralli *223*
   Parmesan and green peppercorn
      wafers *222*
   White pepper shortbread *218*
black peppercorns *29, 32, 77–8, 81*
   Black pepper brownies *214*
   Black pepper crème fraîche *188*
   Black pepper polenta chips with
      mozzarella and Parmesan *177*
   Black pepper rice *181*
   Cambodian black pepper sauce *236*
   Cantuccini with black pepper and

orange zest *220*
Devilled chocolate ice cream *200*
Dukkah *235*
Gravlax *129*
Hake cutlet au poivre *130*
Keralan curry powder *234*
Lamb pepper fry *152*
Lemon devilled quails *139*
Lemon pepper plaice *116*
Membrillo- and pepper-glazed belly
   pork *145*
Mulligatawny soup with rhubarb
   and coconut *110*
Neapolitan taralli *223*
Olio santo *237*
Orange and pepper powder *235*
Pan-fried black pepper prawns *122*
Pan pepato *224*
Pasta with pecorino and black
   pepper (cacio e pepe) *178*
Pepper-crusted chicken in spicy
   soured cream *136*
Peppered beef with balsamic
   vinegar, molasses and garlic *148*
Peppered chocolate truffles *205*
Peppered dried figs *196*
Peppered figs, air-dried ham and
   celery *97*
Peppered smoked mackerel, fennel
   and beetroot *102*
Peppered yogurt cheese *194*
Peppery calves liver with preserved
   lemon and parsley *156*
Peppery herbed breadcrumbs *233*
Rainbow pepper chicken noodle
   soup *109*
Ricotta tart with limoncello pepper
   syrup *210*
Spiced sugar *233*
Steak au poivre *151*
Strawberry and black pepper ice
   cream *198*
Sweet pepper cream *188*
West African pepper rub *234*
Zhug *236*
Brazilian black pepper *77*
breadcrumbs, Peppery herbed *233*
British East India Company *22*
brownies, Black pepper *214*
butternut squash, Stir-fried, and
   shiitake mushrooms *166*

c

Cacio e pepe *178*
cakes
   Black pepper brownies *214*
   Pan pepato (peppered bread) *224*
   Paradise cake *215*
   Peppered fig parcels *219*
   Pink pepper blondies *212*

Cajun spices *245*
capsaicin *68*
Carnes, Jonathan *22*
carrots, Black sticky *162*
carryover stocks *62*
celery
   Leek, celery and cannellini bean
      soup with green peppercorns and
      pancetta *106*
   Peppered figs, air-dried ham and
      celery *97*
Chaucer, Geoffrey: *Romance of the
   Rose* (trans.) *43*
cheese
   Black pepper polenta chips with
      mozzarella and Parmesan *177*
   Chickpeas with feta and preserved
      lemons *174*
   Mushrooms, Parmesan and sizzled
      sage on sourdough toast *161*
   Parmesan and green peppercorn
      wafers *222*
   Pasta with pecorino and black
      pepper (Cacio e pepe) *178*
   Pear, green beans, blue cheese and
      walnuts with green peppercorn
      dressing *100*
   Ricotta tart with limoncello pepper
      syrup *210*
   Seared pigeon breasts with balsamic
      vinegar, rocket and Parmesan
      140
Cherry sauce with pepper, honey and
   orange *239*
Chickpeas with feta and preserved
   lemons *174*
chicken
   Chicken liver, pancetta and
      mangetout *96*
   Chicken liver pâté *195*
   Mulligatawny soup with rhubarb
      and coconut *110–11*
   Numbing chicken noodle salad *94*
   Pepper-crusted chicken in spicy
      soured cream *136*
   Rainbow pepper chicken noodle
      soup *109*
   Stir-fried chicken with white pepper
      137
   Tandoori-style chicken with green
      spices, white pepper and mustard
      132
   Tellicherry chicken curry *133*
chillies
   Lemon pepper plaice with chilli *116*
   pepper and chillies *20*
   Stir-fried water spinach with chillies
      and Sichuan pepper *160*
Chinese traditional medicine *70*
chocolate
   Black pepper brownies *214*

Devilled chocolate ice cream *200*
Pan pepato (Peppered bread) *224*
Peppered chocolate truffles *205*
Christmas berry *see* pink peppercorns
Colombo powder *245*
Columbus, Christopher *17, 20–1, 55*
Constantine (Benedictine monk) *72*
contamination/adulteration of pepper
16, 23, 28
courgettes, Hot and sour *172*
cream, Sweet pepper *188*
crème fraîche, Black pepper *188*
cresson *58*
cubeb pepper *16, 38–41, 72, 79, 234*
Culpeper, Nicholas *70, 71*
currency, pepper as *15, 17*
curry powder *241*
curry powder, Keralan *234*

d

decorticated peppercorns *247*
De re coquinaria 18
desserts
Caramelised pineapple with long
pepper and lime syrup *209*
Devilled chocolate ice cream *200*
Flambéed strawberries with kirsch
and black pepper *201*
Pepper meringue grissini *206*
Peppered chocolate truffles *205*
Ricotta tart with limoncello pepper
syrup *210*
Spiced yogurt with pomegranates
and pistachios *202*
Strawberry and black pepper ice
cream *198*
Dill sauce *129*
Dioscorides *12, 20*
Diphilus of Siphnos *12*
dips and relishes
Black pepper crème fraîche *188*
Chicken liver pâté *195*
Fresh green peppercorn pickle *193*
Peppered dried figs *196*
Peppered yogurt cheese *194*
Quince and pink pepper jelly *189*
Sweet pepper cream *188*
Zhug *236, 242*
Drake, Sir Francis *17*
drinks
Bloody paradise *187*
Lime and pepper refresher (nimbu
pani) *184*
Pomegranate and pepper juice *184*
dry-frying peppercorns *49, 81*
Dukkah *235, 242*
dust *86*

e

Ecuador black pepper *77*
electric grinders *85*
English pepper *see* allspice
escabeche *56*
essential oil *31, 63, 69*
Ethelred 'the Unready,' King *17*
European Spice Association (ESA) *247*

f

fagara *47*
figs
Peppered dried figs *196*
Peppered fig parcels *219*
Peppered figs, air-dried ham and
celery *97*
fish (*see also* specific fish)
Five-pepper tuna steaks with salsa *118*
Fried herring fillets with a lime
pepper crust *128*
Gravlax *129*
Grilled sardines with preserved
lemons, cumin and peppery
breadcrumbs *123*
Hake cutlet au poivre *130*
Keralan fish in a parcel *126*
Lemon pepper plaice with chilli *116*
Pan-fried black pepper prawns *122*
Peppered smoked mackerel, fennel
and beetroot *102*
Salt and pepper prawns *119*
fish-curing spices *244*
Florida Holly *see* pink peppercorns
flour, Spiced *226*
flower pepper *see* Sichuan pepper
freeze-drying *32, 79*
Fried herring fillets with a lime pepper
crust *128*
fruit (*see also* specific fruit)
Caramelised pineapple with long
pepper and lime syrup *209*
Cherry sauce with pepper, honey
and orange *239*
Flambéed strawberries with kirsch
and black pepper *201*
Mulligatawny soup with rhubarb
and coconut *110*
Orange and pepper powder *235*
Pomegranate and pepper juice *184*
Strawberry and black pepper ice
cream *198*

g

Gama, Vasco da *14, 17*
Garam masala *226, 241*
Gerard, John *35, 43*
glossary *240*

grades of pepper *246*
Graham, Sylvester *73*
grains of paradise *16, 42–5, 59, 79, 91*
Bloody paradise *187*
Paradise cake *215*
Parsnips baked in paradise pepper
cream *170*
Peppered chocolate truffles *205*
Syrup of grains of paradise and
rosemary *45*
West African pepper rub *234*
grains of Selim *59*
Gravlax *129*
green peppercorns *31–2, 79, 81–2, 90*
Braised rabbit with green
peppercorns and Puy lentils *154*
Fresh green peppercorn pickle *193*
Leek, celery and cannellini bean
soup with green peppercorns and
pancetta *106*
Parmesan and green peppercorn
wafers *222*
Pear, green beans, blue cheese and
walnuts with green peppercorn
dressing *100*
Pepper meringue grissini *206*
Peppered yogurt cheese *194*
Rainbow pepper chicken noodle
soup *109*
Roast guinea fowl with orange and
green peppercorn butter *142*
greens, Peppered, with lemon and
coriander *158*
Grilled sardines with preserved
lemons, cumin and peppery
breadcrumbs *123*
Grilled tomato sauce *238*
grinding peppercorns *83–6*
Guild of Pepperers, London *16*
guinea fowl, Roast, with orange and
green peppercorn butter *142*
Guinea pepper *59*

h

Hake cutlet au poivre *130*
Hand of Glory *37*
hawaj *242*
health, pepper and *70*
herring fillets, Fried, with a lime
pepper crust *128*
Hippocrates *12, 70, 72*

i

Indonesian lemon pepper *see* Sichuan
pepper
International Pepper Community (IPC)
28, 247
Isidore of Seville, Saint *20*
Italian spice mixture *244*

j

jaggery *193*
Jamaica pepper *see* allspice
jargon *246*
jerk spices *56, 245*

k

Kama Sutra/Kamasutram *71, 72*
Karimunda pepper *26*
kava-kava *58*
Kerala, India *7, 12, 14, 17, 26–7, 28,
    29, 32, 33*
Keralan curry powder *234*
Keralan fish in a parcel *126*
khmeli suneli *242*
kinome *47*
kitchen pepper *244*
Kuching black pepper *29*

l

la kama *243*
lá lót *58*
Lamb pepper fry *152*
Lampong black pepper *64, 77*
Land of Cockayne, The (anon. poem) *39*
Leek, celery and cannellini bean soup
    with green peppercorns and
    pancetta *106*
lemon
    Lemon devilled quails *139*
    Lemon pepper plaice with chilli *116*
    Lemon pepper pork burgers *144*
    Peppered greens with lemon and
        coriander *158*
    Ricotta tart with limoncello pepper
        syrup *210*
    see also preserved lemons
lime
    Cambodian black pepper sauce *236*
    Caramelised pineapple with long
        pepper and lime syrup *209*
    Fried herring fillets with a lime
        pepper crust *128*
    Lime and pepper refresher (Nimbu
        pani) *184*
liver
    Chicken liver, pancetta and
        mangetout *96*
    Chicken liver pâté *195*
    Peppery calves liver with preserved
        lemon and parsley *156*
long pepper *15, 16, 20, 34–7, 70, 71,
    72, 79, 91*
    Caramelised pineapple with long
        pepper and lime syrup *209*
    Chicken liver pâté *195*
    Pomegranate and pepper juice *184*

m

Ma po dou fu (Pock-marked Mother
    Chen's beancurd) *176*
mackerel, Peppered smoked, fennel
    and beetroot *102*
Madagascan black pepper *77*
Magellan, Ferdinand *17*
Malabar black pepper *64, 77, 246*
Malaysian Pepper Board (MPB) *28, 247*
mali kruhki *73*
marsh pepper *59*
Mary Rose (ship) *17*
meat (*see also* specific meat)
    Braised rabbit with green
        peppercorns and puy lentils *154*
    Lamb pepper fry *152*
    Lemon pepper pork burgers *144*
    Membrillo- and pepper-glazed belly
        pork *145*
    Peppered beef with balsamic
        vinegar, molasses and garlic *148*
    Peppery calves liver with preserved
        lemon and parsley *156*
    Rabo encendido (tail on fire) *153*
    Steak au poivre (pepper steak) *151*
medicine and pepper *12, 36, 40, 44, 70–1*
medieval cuisine *16*
melegueta pepper *see* grains of
    paradise
Membrillo- and pepper-glazed belly
    pork *145*
Mexican pepperleaf *58*
moor pepper *59*
mortars and pestles *85*
mountain pepper *59*
Mulligatawny soup with rhubarb and
    coconut *110–11*
Muntok white pepper *64, 78*
mushrooms
    Mushrooms, Parmesan and sizzled
        sage on sourdough toast *161*
    Stir-fried butternut squash and
        shiitake mushrooms *166*
myrtle pepper *see* allspice
myths about pepper *20–1*

n

Neapolitan taralli *223*
negro pepper *59*
Nimbu pani *184*
Numbing chicken noodle salad *94*
nuts
    Dukkah *235, 242*
    Mulligatawny soup with rhubarb
        and coconut *110*
    Pan pepato (Peppered bread) *224*
    Pear, green beans, blue cheese and
        walnuts with green peppercorn

dressing *100*
Spiced yogurt with pomegranates
    and pistachios *202*

o

oil, pepper *63*
Old Bay seasoning *245*
oleoresin *63*
Olio santo *237*
onion rings, Spiced fried *167*
orange
    Cantuccini with black pepper and
        orange zest *220*
    Cherry sauce with pepper, honey
        and orange *239*
    Orange and pepper powder *235*
    Roast guinea fowl with orange and
        green peppercorn butter *142*
Orta, García de *20*
oxtail, Rabo encendido (tail on fire)
    153

p

Pan-fried black pepper prawns *122*
Pan pepato (Peppered bread) *224*
pancetta
    Chicken liver, pancetta and
        mangetout *96*
    Leek, celery and cannellini bean
        soup with green peppercorns and
        pancetta *106*
Panniyur pepper *26*
Parameswaran estate, Kerala, India *28*
Parsnips baked in paradise pepper
    cream *170*
pasta
    Pasta with pecorino and black
        pepper (cacio e pepe) *178*
pâté, Chicken liver *195*
Pazhoor plantation, Kerala, India *26–7*
Pear, green beans, blue cheese and
    walnuts with green peppercorn
    dressing *100*
Penja pepper *77–8*
pepper
    addictive effects *68–9*
    adulteration/contamination *16, 23, 28*
    as aphrodisiac *71, 72–3*
    cultivation *26–7, 29*
    as currency *15, 17*
    essential oil *31, 63, 69*
    food industry and *63*
    grades *246*
    harvesting/processing *27–8*
    measuring *91–2*
    and medicine *12, 36, 40, 44, 70–1*
    myths *20–1*
    names *64*
    oil *63*

oleoresin 63
pungency 68–9
quality control 28
storage 91
structure of peppercorns 31
tasting 76–80
terms 246–7
trade 62
vine 26
Pepper Exchange, The 62
pepper mills 83–5
Pepper water 111
peppercorn rents 15–16, 17
perfumes 63
pickle, Fresh green peppercorn 193
pickling spice 244
pigeon breasts, Seared, with balsamic
    vinegar, rocket and Parmesan 140
pimienta/pimento 20, 21, 55
pineapple, Caramelised, with long
    pepper and lime syrup 209
pink peppercorns 50–3, 79, 81
    Pepper meringue grissini 206
    Pink pepper blondies 212
    Quince and pink pepper jelly 189
    Rainbow pepper chicken noodle
        soup 109
piperine 31, 63, 68, 69, 71, 72, 80
pistachio nuts
    Dukkah 235
    Spiced yogurt with pomegranates
        and pistachios 202
plaice, Lemon pepper, with chilli 116
Plato 12
Pliny the Elder 12, 15, 20, 35
poivre rose/poivre de Bourbon see pink
    peppercorns
polenta chips, Black pepper, with
    mozzarella and Parmesan 177
Polo, Marco 16–17, 20, 22
pomegranates
    Pomegranate and pepper juice 184
    Spiced yogurt with pomegranates
        and pistachios 202
pork
    Hot and sour soup 107
    Lemon pepper pork burgers 144
    Membrillo- and pepper-glazed belly
        pork 145
    Moors and Christians (Black beans
        and rice) 182
poultry (see also specific poultry)
    Lemon devilled quails 139
    Pepper-crusted chicken in spicy
        soured cream 136
    Roast guinea fowl with orange and
        green peppercorn butter 142
    Seared pigeon breasts with balsamic
        vinegar, rocket and Parmesan 140
    Stir-fried chicken with white pepper
        137

Tandoori-style chicken with green
    spices, white pepper and mustard
    132
Tellicherry chicken curry 133
prawns
    Hot and sour soup 107
    Pan-fried black pepper prawns 122
    Salt and pepper prawns 119
preserved lemons 123
    Chickpeas with feta and preserved
        lemons 174
    Grilled sardines with preserved
        lemons, cumin and peppery
        breadcrumbs 123
    Peppery calves liver with preserved
        lemon and parsley 156
pulses
    Black beans and rice (Moors and
        Christians) 182
    Braised rabbit with green
        peppercorns and Puy lentils 154
    Chickpeas with feta and preserved
        lemons 174
    Pock-marked mother chen's
        beancurd (ma po dou fu) 176
    Split pea and red pepper soup with
        sizzled spices 114
pumpkin
    Balsamic- and pepper-glazed roast
        pumpkin 164
    Paradise cake 215
pungency 68–9

q

Qalat daqqa 44, 230, 243
quails, Lemon devilled 139
quality control 28
Quatre épices (four-spices) 230, 244
Quince and pink pepper jelly 189

r

rabbit, Braised, with green
    peppercorns and Puy lentils 154
Rameses II, Pharaoh 12
ras el hanout 41, 44, 243
rasam, Tomato 112
rasam spice blend 241
recado spices 245
red peppercorns 32–3, 79, 82
relishes (see dips and relishes)
rice
    Black pepper rice 181
    Moors and christians (black beans
        and rice) 182
    Ricotta tart with limoncello pepper
        syrup 210
Rimbàs black and white pepper 29, 78
roasting peppercorns 81
Romance of the Rose (Chaucer's

trans.) 43
Romans, ancient 14–15, 18–19, 35
rough-leaved pepper 58

s

sacred pepper 58
Salem, Massachusetts 22
salads
    Chicken liver, pancetta and
        mangetout 96
    Numbing chicken noodle salad 94
    Pear, green beans, blue cheese and
        walnuts with green peppercorn
        dressing 100
    Peppered figs, air-dried ham and
        celery 97
    Peppered smoked mackerel, fennel
        and beetroot 102
    Salsa 118
Sansho 46–9, 79
Santa Maria leaf 58
Sarawak black and white pepper 28,
    29, 64, 78, 90, 246
sardines, Grilled, with preserved
    lemons, cumin and peppery
    breadcrumbs 123
saru spice blend 241
sauces
    Cambodian black pepper sauce 236
    Cherry sauce with pepper, honey
        and orange 239
    Dill sauce 129
    Grilled tomato sauce 238
    Zhug 236
Scoville Units 68
Senegal pepper 59
shichimi togarashi 48–9
shortbread, White pepper 218
Sichuan (or Szechwan) pepper
    46–9, 59, 79, 81, 90–1
    Chinese five-spice blend 231
    Numbing chicken noodle salad 94
    Peppered yogurt cheese 194
    Pock-marked mother chen's
        beancurd (ma po dou fu) 176
    Salt and pepper prawns 119
    Spiced fried onion rings 167
    Spiced pepper and salt 229
    Stir-fried water spinach with chillies
        and Sichuan pepper 160
soups
    Hot and sour soup 107
    Leek, celery and cannellini bean
        soup with green peppercorns and
        pancetta 106
    Mulligatawny soup with rhubarb
        and coconut 110
    Rainbow pepper chicken noodle
        soup 109
    Roasted root soup with sizzled

ginger and black pepper crème fraîche *104*
Split pea and red pepper soup with sizzled spices *114*
Tomato rasam *112*
sources *248*
spice blends and seasonings
Aunty Manjula's sarina pudi *228*
Chinese five-spice blend *231*
Dukkah *235*
Garam masala *226*
Keralan curry powder *234*
Olio santo *237*
Orange and pepper powder *235*
Peppery herbed breadcrumbs *233*
Quatre épices (four-spices) *230*
Spiced flour *226*
Spiced pepper and salt *229*
Spiced sugar *233*
Tunisian five spices *230*
West African pepper rub *234*
Spices Board of India (SBI) *23, 28, 247*
spinach, water, Stir-fried, with chillies and Sichuan pepper *160*
Sri Lankan black pepper *78*
Steak au poivre (Pepper steak) *151*
storing pepper *91*
strawberries
Flambéed strawberries with kirsch and black pepper *201*
Strawberry and black pepper ice cream *198*
sugar, Spiced *233*
'Sultan's Paste' *72*
suppliers *see* sources
Sweet pepper cream *188*
Syrup of grains of paradise and rosemary *45*
Szechwan pepper *see* Sichuan pepper

t

Tandoori-style chicken with green spices, white pepper and mustard *132*
taralli, Neapolitan *223*
Tasmanian pepper *59*
tasting pepper *76–80*
Tellicherry chicken curry *133*
Tellicherry pepper *63, 64, 78, 90, 246*
terms *246–7*
Thai white pepper *78*
Theophrastus *12*
tomato rasam *112*
trade *12–15, 16–17, 62–3*
traditional Chinese medicine *70*
tsiperifery *39, 79*
tuna steaks, Five-pepper, with salsa *118*
Tunisian five spices (Qalat daqqa) *230, 243*

u

Unani medicine *70*

v

vegetables (*see also* specific vegetables)
Balsamic- and pepper-glazed roast pumpkin *164*
Black sticky carrots *162*
Hot and sour courgettes *172*
Mushrooms, Parmesan and sizzled sage on sourdough toast *161*
Parsnips baked in paradise pepper cream *170*
Peppered greens with lemon and coriander *158*
Spiced fried onion rings *167*
Stir-fried butternut squash and shiitake mushrooms *166*
Stir-fried water spinach with chillies and sichuan pepper *160*
Tomato rasam *112*
Vietnamese black pepper *78*

w

water pepper *59*
white peppercorns *20, 27–8, 32, 64, 70, 71, 78, 81, 90*
Devilled chocolate ice cream *200*
Gravlax *129*
Hake cutlet au poivre *130*
Hot and sour courgettes *172*
Hot and sour soup *107*
Lemon devilled quails *139*
Olio santo *237*
Pepper meringue grissini *206*
Peppered greens with lemon and coriander *158s*
Peppered yogurt cheese *194*
Quatre épices *230*
Rainbow pepper chicken noodle soup *109*
Spiced fried onion rings *167*
Spiced pepper and salt *229*
Steak au poivre *151*
Stir-fried chicken with white pepper *137*
Tandoori-style chicken with green spices, white pepper and mustard *132*
West African pepper rub *234*
White pepper shortbread *218*
white sauce *81*
Wynad black and white pepper *28, 78*

y

Yale, Elihu *22*
yerma *49*
yogurt
Peppered yogurt cheese *194*
Spiced yogurt with pomegranates and pistachios *202*

z

Zhug *236, 242*

acknowledgements

Writing this book often seemed like a solitary process, but I am inevitably bowled over by the number of people who directly or indirectly helped to make it happen. My sincerest thanks to the following friends and colleagues:

Meg Avent at Absolute Press for her enthusiasm for the book.
Chef But and his wife Su at the Memories of China restaurant for information on how the Chinese use pepper.
Amy 'Curly' Carter for stoically testing recipe after recipe.
Jon Croft at Absolute Press for his enthusiasm and speedy decision to publish the book.
Rachel Demuth for ongoing support and hospitality in Bath.
Fuchsia Dunlop for generously sharing her in-depth knowledge of Sichuan cookery.
Manisha Harkins and her aunt for contributing a family recipe and clarifying the difference between rasam, sambar and saru.
Trish Hilferty for preparing the food for photography and making it look so good.
Matt Inwood at Absolute Press for his good humour and patience, and for designing the book so beautifully.
Tom Jaine for publishing obscure books that contribute to an important body of knowledge.
Emi Kazuko for generously sharing her knowledge of Japanese cuisine.
Jason Lowe for inspiring photography.
Ottavia Mazzoni for help with researching taralli.
Michael and Joy Michaud for endless encouragement, and for enduring lengthy peppercorn-tasting sessions.
Rosemary Moon for travelling with me to India.
Steven Osbourne at Maldon Crystal Salt for supplying pepper samples and mills.
Sri and Roger Owen for information on Indonesian cuisine.
Biju Paul and family for their warm hospitality in Kerala.
Mr Ramalingum ('Ram') of the Spices Board in India for enjoyable field trips.
Jeff Riley of T&G Woodware for in-depth advice on pepper mills.
Edward Shaw of Bart Spices for endless encouragement, support and advice.
Anne Sheasby for meticulous recipe-editing.
Vivek Singh of The Cinnamon Club for insights on how chefs use pepper in modern Indian cuisine.
Das Sreedharan for recipes and lengthy lunches discussing pepper and what it means to him.
Steenbergs Organic Pepper and Spice for supplying pepper samples.
Mark Steene of Seasoned Pioneers for introducing my taste buds to obscure and wonderful varieties of pepper, and supplying samples.
Dr Thampi of the Spices Board in India for arranging visits to pepper plantations.
Cassie Williamson at The White Horse for feeding me when I was tired.

Absolute Press wish to thank the following copyright holders for permission to reprint recipes:

Hake Cutlet au Poivre from *Second Helpings of Roast Chicken* by Simon Hopkinson, Ebury.
Fried Herring Fillets with a Lime Pepper Crust from *Herring: the History of the Silver Darlings* by Mike Smylie, Tempus Publishing.
Peppery Calves Liver with Preserved Lemon and Parsley based on a recipe from *Flavours of Greece* by Rosemary Barron, Grub Street.
Stir-Fried Water Spinach with Chillies and Sichuan Pepper and Pock-Marked Mother Chen's Beancurd from *Sichuan Cookery* by Fuchsia Dunlop, Penguin.
Peppered Dried Figs from *Flavours of Greece* by Rosemary Barron, Grub Street.
Recipes for Kitchen Pepper and Italian Spice Mixture from *Herb & Spice: the Cook's Reference* by Jill Norman, Dorling Kindersley.
Tellicherry Chicken Curry and Black Pepper Rice from *The New Tastes of India* by Das Sreedharan, Headline.